The Complete Guide to Special Event Management

Business Insights, Financial Advice,
and Successful Strategies from
Ernst & Young, Advisors to the
Olympics, the Emmy Awards and the
PGA Tour

Dwight W. Catherwood
Richard L. Van Kirk

JOHN WILEY & SONS

New York • Chichester • Brisbane • Toronto • Singapore

This publication is designed to provide accurate and
authoritative information in regard to the subject
matter covered. It is sold with the understanding that
the publisher is not engaged in rendering legal, accounting,
or other professional services. If legal advice or other
expert assistance is required, the services of a competent
professional person should be sought. *From a Declaration
of Principles jointly adopted by a Committee of the
American Bar Association and a Committee of Publishers.*

Library of Congress Cataloging-in-Publication Data

The Complete guide to special event management : business insights
    financial advice, and successful strategies from Ernst & Young,
    consultants to the Olympics, the Emmy Awards, and the PGA tour /
    Ernst & Young.
       p.   cm. —
    Includes bibliographical references.
    ISBN 0-471-54908-8
      1. Meetings—Planning—Handbooks, manuals, etc. I. Ernst &
  Young. II. Series.
  AS6.C555 1992
  658.4'56—dc20   91-41832
                                             CIP

Printed and bound by Courier Companies, Inc.

10 9 8 7 6 5 4 3

A B O U T   T H E   A U T H O R S

Dwight W. Catherwood

Mr. Catherwood is an information technology consulting partner in the Los Angeles offices of Ernst & Young. He has more than 25 years of experience in information technology as a systems engineer, systems analyst, and project manager and over the last ten years he has been heavily involved in the field of sports technology. He was in charge of the Management and Operations of the Results System for the 1984 Los Angeles Olympic Games and served as a consultant to the 1988 Olympics in Seoul on Results and other games management systems. Mr. Catherwood also provided consulting services to the Barcelona Olympic Organizing Committee, and sports technology advisory services to the Asian Games, the Pan American Games, the All Africa Games and the U.S. Olympic Festival. He has been actively involved in sports sponsorship and marketing programs for Ernst & Young at the international and national level.

Richard L. Van Kirk

Mr. Van Kirk is the Manufacturing/High Technology coordinator for Management Consulting at Ernst & Young in the West Region. His 25 years of consulting experience with the firm have focused primarily on performance improvement programs for a variety of clients. He has led and participated in projects to reduce costs, streamline organizations and operations, plan and develop new information systems and introduce Total Quality into client organizations. He has presented numerous speeches to professional and service organizations on topics ranging from Special Events to Operations Improvement. He has also served as Vice President of Technology for the Los Angeles Olympic Organizing Committee. Mr. Van Kirk received a Bachelor of Science in Mechanical Engineering from California Institute of Technology and a Masters of Business Economics from the Claremont Graduate School.

PREFACE

The 1984 Olympic Games have been called a watershed in the management of special events. Before that, sponsors and organizers tended to see events of any size—from a community barbecue to a world-class sports competition—as a source of pride, not profit. Afterwards, people started realizing that these events could be financially sound as well.

I headed the 1984 Los Angeles Olympic Organizing Committee for many reasons. First and foremost, it was a pleasure working with a talented team of people—including the authors of this book—who, all together, made the Games such a success. In addition, I wanted the multitude of corporate sponsors, team representatives, and community spokespersons to find the experience as worthwhile as I did, and to justify our sponsors' efforts in dollars and cents.

There's no reason why even the largest event has to run in the red. The kinds of financial difficulties experienced by world-class sporting events in the past need not be the shape of the future.

We can all be proud of what we accomplished in Los Angeles in 1984, but our success wasn't magic. It was pride of our city and country, good solid planning and common business sense.

During the 1990s special events will become a more and more significant means for sponsors and organizers to reach their target markets. These events have visibility and high impact. They can be a powerful way to zero in on specific market segments. The days are over when you can simply run a newspaper ad or a TV commercial and hope you'll get a good return on your investment. Helping to plan an event can be one of the key experiences of a lifetime. You grow into them. You grow with them. You grow from them.

Participating in the preparations can, in fact, become the highlight of an entire career. I saw this often during the preparations for the Games of the XXIIIrd Olympiad. Some people on the team made decisions that had more impact than anything they had ever done before or would ever do again, in terms of their responsibility levels and involvement with the community.

This wasn't just a matter of inner satisfaction, either—though it certainly was that as well. In some instances it became an outer transformation. One accountant I know got involved in the Olympics, became the head of their ticketing operation, and later became a worldwide consultant to special events. A young graduate student worked on the Olympics and ultimately became a nationally known expert on major events. A secretary assumed responsibility for coordinating public relations for a major event and moved from secretarial work to public relations in community involvement.

In short, the personal and financial dimensions of planning special events aren't contradictory. You don't have to choose between personal satisfaction and financial payoff. Both are possible at the same time. You can succeed both at the finish line *and* the bottom line.

—Peter V. Ueberroth

INTRODUCTION

Today, special events range from the Olympics to a community-wide barbecue; from the Super Bowl and the NCAA Final Four basketball tournament to the "Treasures of Tutankhamun" exhibition; from world gymnastics championships and an international chili cookoff to a community fair and a children's cultural exhibit.

But special events are more than just well-known athletic competitions and cultural performances. They are also thousands of smaller special events that take place every year. They can bring a community together for purposes of fund raising, change a city's image, expand its trade, stimulate its economy, and help companies to market and introduce products.

Special events are opportunities, not only for the promoter/manager to bring a unique project to a community and profit from it, but for the community and local companies to benefit as sponsors of the event. In today's competitive business environment, companies need a marketing edge, a more economical way to reach customers—and event sponsorships offer this opportunity.

Staging a special event takes more than a dream or wish. It takes hundreds, sometimes thousands, of hours of preparation. Preparation is the key to any successful event. They do not just happen; they are well planned and coordinated.

But the best intentions and most thorough plans can go awry. That's why the best promoters/managers surround themselves with teams of the most skilled advisors that they can assemble (both outside and inside the organization) for financial, marketing, operational, and legal matters. All of these parties will be called upon during every stage to scrutinize, carefully evaluate, and deal with a vast array of matters, from the site location to the method of ticketing, to the final wrap-up.

Together with his/her advisors as part of a team, the promoter/manager must be a psychologist, prognosticator, and, most importantly, a business person who assures that the fiscal goals—along with the entertainment goals—of the event are achieved. For the person who has these talents—

and uses them effectively—the management and promotion of special events can offer significant rewards.

The team must be able to evaluate the market, be able to project conditions months or years in advance, and project the outcome of the project. They must be able to deal with the average ticket buyer as well as the celebrities participating in the event. They must know the importance of sponsorship, what will make the event attractive to different kinds of sponsors, and be able to explain these attractions to reluctant sponsors who are unclear about them. They must know how to develop promotional tie-ins and what makes news for electronic and print media.

This book has called upon the experiences of many promoters/managers and the advisors who helped make their special events possible. It also tells of the rise of a phenomenon called *cause-related marketing*, a concept that enables a firm to use sponsorship of an event, not only to become a good corporate citizen, but to further its sales and marketing efforts and justify its investment. A good example of this is Fuji Film, a relatively new name in the United States in the 1980s when it became an exclusive sponsor of the 1984 Summer Olympic Games. Fuji Film used its Olympic involvement to increase its distribution, enhance its image, and cut dramatically into their competitors' positions. Another example which we will look at later in this volume was the involvement of a major airline as a sponsor of the recent Stanford University Centennial Celebration which attracted nearly 50,000 of the school's alumni and friends—primarily business people and, thus, the right audience for the airline's message.

Communities and organizations large and small are aggressively pursuing special events of all kinds because they know the economic benefits implicit in them. And there is always room for one more successful event; one organized and run by people with the know-how to do the job efficiently and correctly.

ACKNOWLEDGMENTS

The authors would like to thank the great many professionals, both in and out of Ernst & Young, whose insights, guidance, and contributions helped make this volume possible.

Unlike other guides, this work has few (if any) precedents and it fell to the authors to create a new state of the art for a field that is assuming ever greater importance on both the national and global scenes. In accomplishing this, we were fortunate to have the help of many partners and other professionals at Ernst & Young, as well as friends outside of the firm, who have had years and often decades of experience in creating and managing special events from Olympics to award ceremonies, whether local or global in scope.

In particular we would like to salute the contributions of Mark Nelson, whose knowledge of the financial management of event management is nonpareil, and Richard Perelman, with his wealth of meaningful anecdotes about all kinds of events.

We would also like to thank Mort Meyerson, who first conceived this work and helped get it off the ground. Appreciation is also due to Ron Tepper, for his writing and interviewing skills, and Richard Sasanow, whose tenacious management of the project assured a successful completion.

There are also many others who contributed significantly:

Larry Anderson	Sandy Knapp	David Simon
Jim Andres	Art Kraus	Jim Taylor
David Bloom	John Leemhuis	Harry Usher
Bob Graziano	Mike Mangan	Mark Wallinger
John Gula	Bill O'Malley	Bob Walsh
Hugh Holbert	Chase Revel	Jim West
Richard Johnson	Mike Sammis	

C O N T E N T S

CHAPTER ONE

Understanding the Market—An Overview

GETTING STARTED

Vision is vital to the success of any event of any size: It is the grand scheme of how the event will be perceived before, during, and after it takes place. It is a view of what the event should be—who will attend, what they will buy, what the financial goals are—and, in general, what it should hope to accomplish. The most important task for any promoter/manager is to create a reality from this vision. Webster defines a *promoter* as an "active supporter, and a finance and publicity organizer," while he describes a *manager* as "one who is in charge of business affairs, of the training of a person or group," and someone who "has skill in managing." A *promoter/manager* is, indeed, a rare breed, able to expect the unexpected and know how to handle it, because he or she knows that with special events, Murphy's Law (anything that can go wrong, will) is particularly true. A promoter is able to hurdle all obstacles in order to achieve the goals of predetermined visions.

Without such a vision, an organization will never be able to attract the larger event, since it is integral to the bid plan that you will have to submit to site selection committees or artist management so as to attract them to a proposition. Vision is just as important for the smaller event, for unless an organization is aware of its goals—for example, to raise money to send the local Little League team to the playoffs—the event will never get off the ground.

VISION: A MANAGEMENT TOOL

Vision is not just important in getting the event started, it also plays a major role in seeing that it moves toward its goals. It is the best form of control in managing those involved in the event because it gives them a shared goal. No manual of policies and procedures can accomplish as much because vision will allow people to work independently toward a common end.

How do you put together a vision statement for your event? While you will certainly have some ideas of your own for beginning the process, it is best to articulate and develop a shared vision among all the parties involved in planning and staging the event. Involving your people in this team effort right from the start can only add to their commitment—something you cannot buy.

THE 10 KEYS TO SUCCESS

In assembling the vision for the event, there are many matters which must be considered, but most importantly is the question, "What makes an event successful?" Whether it is a world class event, special gathering, a one-night concert, or an afternoon barbecue put on by a local service organization, the success of the event is impacted by a number of different elements. These elements are important for every promoter/manager to consider when going after a top event. Each element can make a significant difference. The promoter/manager and staff should begin by asking 10 questions:

1. Is the event a good idea?
2. Do we have the right planning and marketing skills available?
3. Are we in the right community?
4. Who will perform? (What class of athletes or performers?)
5. Do we know the infrastructure of the community?
6. Where will it be held? Can we get the venue we need at a price we can afford?
7. Is there a "hook" or "angle" in the event that will attract an audience? Will it pique their interest?
8. Will we attract media support?
9. Are advertising funds available? Can we attract strong sponsors? Will publicity/promotional programs attract the crowds?
10. Are our "success" criteria reasonable?

If you are able to answer these questions, your vision should be in place and you are in a position to move forward.

ASSEMBLING THE TEAM

Once a bid has been accepted and the plan has been adjusted to the realities of the constraints built into the bid process, it is time to assemble the key members of the team that will see the project through to the end. The key players needed will encompass four basic kinds of expertise:

1. *Financial*—to help determine sources of revenue, expected expenditure level and timing of expenditures versus revenues, and to establish a system of financial accounting and control.
2. *Marketing*—to see that you get the best audience possible, and the best sponsorship and support available.
3. *Operational*—to guide the overall operation of the event, including the management of any technology needed.
4. *Legal*—to advise on and negotiate the many contracts involved in an event, as well as to handle any lawsuits that may arise.

Depending on the size of the event, these advisors may be from within or from outside the organization. (The bigger the event, the more likely it is that consultants will provide a more cost-effective way to provide the required skills.) You will need your team to determine the policies that will be followed from start to shutdown; a process which could take months or years. Because of the many aspects involved in events management, your team should begin with some basic guidelines. For example:

- Will you function with volunteers or have a paid staff?
- Will you try to get special rates from venues or accept the going rate?
- What kinds of group discounts will be offered?
- How will ticketing be handled?

USING PLANNING TECHNIQUES AND TOOLS

Because of the unique nature of each special event, planning is a process that must continuously occur from the start of the bid until the end of the event. It is crucial to have as a foundation for this ongoing planning a vision, a statement, or concept that can be easily articulated and understood. As the development of the event unfolds, management will need to keep the group working toward this vision by continually monitoring all progress toward the milestones and goals that must be met in order to successfully stage the event.

Each person brings his or her personal management style into play during this period. There is no single management approach or technique that has been universally successful. However, certain tools and techniques have proven helpful in many cases:

- *Gantt Charts.* This bar chart is a basic graphic scheduling technique, yet it is useful for simple as well as complex events where more complex charts often prove too cumbersome. It is a valuable tool in laying out sequence and duration of activities.
- *Work Breakdown Structures.* This is a technique for identifying and grouping all the elements of work to be completed, allowing for the isolation of tasks that may have been overlooked in the planning process. It is particularly useful for large events where details are more easily forgotten.
- *Critical Path Charts.* This is the modern version of PERT (Program Evaluation and Review Technique) which was developed in the 1960s. It identifies the time required to complete a series of activities, taking into account duration and sequence dependencies (i.e., what activity must happen before the next activity can begin). In order to reduce time in the process, activities on the critical path must be shortened.
- *Policy Statements.* Policy statements are developed to help guide decision making and the fulfillment of commitments. Such policies are crucial because they will be followed from the plan's inception to the final shutdown—a time period which may entail months or years. Some of the areas where policies need to be set down are:

—human resources;
—procurement;
—ticketing;
—accreditation;
—sponsorship;
—security; and
—transportation.

Having correctly formulated policy statements will prove useful in dealing with all kinds of questions. Policy statements provide the framework for the continued development of detailed operating, marketing, and financial plans for the event. Once the event is securely scheduled, it is never too early to establish a policy statements framework. Such a policy framework provides a tangible reflection of the underlying vision that has been developed for the event.

UNDERSTANDING INFRASTRUCTURE

It was summer, 1977. The downtown Los Angeles office was crowded with some of the best-known entrepreneurs and sports afficionados in the country, and although the air-conditioner was on, most of those in the room felt warm. For the past hour they had been scrutinizing a bid; a bid that would soon be presented to one of the most prestigious bodies in the world; a bid that would put them on the map; a bid that would change the face of the Olympics forever; and, in fact, a bid that would revolutionize the approach and attitude that promoter/managers had towards the Olympics and other special events.

Those in the room were all members of an elite, 40-member group: The Southern California Commitee for the Olympic Games (SCCOG). The detailed document they were going over was going to be their submission to the United States Olympic Committee (USOC), which, in turn, would submit it to the IOC (International Olympic Committee), the governing body that decides which city shall be awarded the Olympic Games.

The SCCOG's bid—which was targeted at the 1984 Olympics—was unique in several ways. Most notable was the tight, cooperative infrastructure SCCOG had put in place. *Infrastructure* not only encompasses venues, it also means that the most powerful people, whose support and cooperation is vital to getting anything done in the community, were ready to go. In this case, the promoter/manager had successfully done his pre-event organization, lining up everyone who could have anything to do with bringing a world class event to a city; seeing that it has the proper venues and

FIGURE 1–1. *The Makeup of the Infrastructure*

1. Politicians and political power/influence
2. Civic and community groups
3. Governmental bodies
4. Social and cultural "movers and shakers" in the community
5. Key business leaders
6. Local media

backing of every necessary group. Some members of such a group would include politicians, civic and community groups, private-citizen influencemakers, and the area's governmental bodies. (See Figure 1–1.)

After such organization of the infrastructure has been accomplished, the promoter can approach the governing body or international organization running the event with a key part of his bid being the backing of the community's infrastructure ready and willing to do everything in their power to bring the event to the community and ensure its success.

So, infrastructure means more than determining whether a community is right for an event—and whether it can hold one. It means more than just the availability of venues. It means political clout. Do the powers that run the city or community—the movers and shakers as well as the politicians—back the proposition? Is the chamber of commerce president and the board behind the event? Are the business interests all for it? Is the councilperson in whose district(s) it will be held behind it? Will the homeowner groups and other activists support it? If the answer to all those questions is an unqualified "yes," the promoter has an excellent chance of succeeding with his bid.

For the prospective promoter/manager of a major event, infrastructure is as important an ingredient as reputation and financing. The one-night rock concert is not going to happen if a group of angry citizens presents a loud enough protest to city hall and their representative. Nor is the venue going to be built if the infrastructure isn't solidly behind it. Regardless of the event, whether it is cultural or athletic, promoters and managers of events need a solid infrastructure.

Infrastructure and the Promoter

Infrastructure dictates the way promoters/managers run special events. For example, on most concert tours, well-known national acts have a "national" promoter. The national promoter—although capable of promoting the show—always seeks out a local counterpart to stage the event. The reason—infrastructure. The national promoter picks someone who knows local politics and customs; someone who knows the problems that can develop on a local level. Relationships impact every promoter, regardless of the size of the community and the event.

In one small West Coast town, a company, the town's prime employer, decided to put on a "thank you" concert to show its appreciation to those in the area for all the help the people had given to them over the years. The company brought in a promoter to stage the event which was to take place in the city park. The tickets were to be given away, and the amount of tickets available depended solely on the discretion of the fire chief and how many spectators he thought the park could hold safely. The promoter, although an out-of-towner, realized the importance of infrastructure, and from the moment he arrived in town, he worked diligently with the fire chief as well as other city authorities. Because of his relationship, he was able to convince the chief that an increase in seating from 4,000 to 5,100 would not endanger anyone. As it was, the additional seating was a wise move because of the huge number of people that showed up the night of the event. Without the extra capacity, the promoter, fire chief and police chief might have found themselves in the middle of a difficult crowd, with a sponsor getting a black eye for poor planning instead of kudos for a well-done thank you concert.

RECOGNIZING LOCAL CONDITIONS AS KEY IN OBTAINING EVENTS

Governing bodies and international federations (the groups responsible for the awarding of different athletic and cultural events), involve promoters/managers in cities and communities far removed from their headquarters. These prestigious international bodies put their faith entirely in the hands of local promoters/managers, and seldom (if ever) make an attempt to have their own personnel impinge on the local organization.

Why? Because they know when it comes down to it, the smooth functioning of any event is going to depend entirely on the local people and the infrastructure of the community. One of the things these federations and organizing bodies demand before they award any event to a local promoter/manager or group is a solid infrastructure. That starts with the elected officials, and goes on down through the community. Everybody must be in sync.

If there was one thing Los Angeles had in abundance when it bid for the 1984 Olympic Games, it was a solidified infrastructure. Everyone from the mayor to state senators and assemblymen were behind the proposal. They gave shape and direction to the way the proposal was constructed, and the result was a memorable event—and a profitable one.

PRIVATE PROMOTERS AND MAJOR EVENTS—A REVOLUTIONARY CONCEPT

Let's take another look at our Olympic Games examples to best explain the role of private promoters. Another difference that the ambitious Los Angeles organizers brought to the International Olympic Committee (IOC) was that, for the first time, a *private* group would be promoting the Games. Although the Games had been going on for nearly 100 years, never before had a group of private citizens proposed to put on an event this massive. It was always a public/government project, and understandably so. It takes enormous funds to build facilities such as stadiums and housing for the athletes, and private promoters had never come up with that kind of backing. The Montreal Games, which preceded the Los Angeles Games by eight years, cost hundreds of millions of dollars, involved the building of venues all over the city, and would have been impossible to stage without government aid. But the SCCOG members proposed a Games that would:

1. require minimal construction; and
2. would not require any federal/government funding.

Both were shocking and innovative ideas. The SCCOG had carefully thought it out, perused existing venues, and had complete cooperation from the political structure, both in and around Los Angeles. It was a daring, radical approach.

Normally, the IOC would have turned thumbs down on such a proposal, but there was not an overabundance of cities bidding for the Games. The enormous expenditure of funds exhausted to stage the Games in Montreal had scared away most potential bidders. The economic health of many potential host nations was not robust in 1979. Couple that with the Montreal deficit, and no one was overly anxious to host the Games. That opened the door for this unusual bid. The SCCOG bid, although unorthodox by Olympic standards, was accepted by the IOC a year later.

Most of the nearly 100 members of the IOC had doubts as to the ability of Los Angeles to put on the Games without government funding. Six years later, the 1984 Olympics closed with the largest surplus in the history of the Games—$230 million. The TV revenues coupled with the sponsorship dollars are two elements that helped produce a surplus that other Olympics will most likely be unable to match.

Part of the phenomenal ratings success was due to the fact the event was held in the United States, which is not only the number one TV market in the world (in terms of revenue generated for an event), but also because most of the events could be televised live (there was no radical time difference from East to West Coast). Viewers did not hear the results beforehand, thus the suspense element remained. They were able to turn on television without knowing the winners in advance. This led to a larger audience. (The Atlanta Games in 1996 will have the same advantage—at least insofar as television viewing is concerned).

Peter Ueberroth and Harry Usher, the president and general manager of the Los Angeles Games (The SCOOC evolved into the Los Angeles Olympic Organizing Committee (LAOOC) in early 1979), and company revolutionized the way the world's premier special event was managed, and the way promoters and cities thought about these events. Their success inspired many other cities in the United States to compete for special events, even if they did not have the funds to build new facilities. Communities discovered that new venues were not the magic drawing card when it came to attracting special events. Everything could be done with existing venues—as long as the community was behind the effort.

Although the success of the Los Angeles Games did not exclude government participation for future Games, the effort made everyone aware of the value of an efficient, privately run organization that knew how to market events and knew the value of volunteers over cash.

TAPPING INTO THE GROWTH OF POTENTIAL MERCHANDISING AND MARKETING

Ueberroth, Usher & Company merchandised, marketed, promoted, negotiated, and made the 1984 Olympics the envy of every promoter and event manager in the world. The 1984 Games piqued the world's interest from the very onset. The dramatic and historic torch run, which took place shortly before the Olympics opened, initially created a furor in the media because of the fees charged to each runner. But by the time it was over, it earned the admiration of people throughout the country, and was looked upon as a brilliant marketing and promotion stroke—and it was. It electrified spectators and participants alike, generated millions of dollars worth of free media-exposure, and introduced promoters to one of the most effective marketing devices ever created for a special event.

The run introduced "emotion" to the event. Up until that time, it was a group of well-meaning businesspeople trying their best to bring a special event to the United States. At the time of the run, there were a number of events that had not been sold out, but the torch and the political interference caught the imagination of Americans and sales were off and running on the remaining events. Even non-sports fans began buying tickets. With increased ticket sales came increased sponsor product sales. Sponsors not only sold enormous amounts of current product lines, they also successfully introduced new products through this very special event.

SPONSORSHIPS AS POTENT MARKETING TOOLS

Of all the innovative ideas that the organizers of the 1984 Games introduced, the one that has had the most lasting impact is the emphasis the group put on sponsors. Ueberroth, Usher & Company insisted that firms that put up money to be an Olympic sponsor should get more than an Olympic logo on an in-store product merchandiser. Up until 1984, sponsorship was viewed as a charitable endeavor by companies. They pulled out their wallets and wrote the check. It was a community obligation and, in return, the companies received few tangible benefits.

The 1984 Games ushered in a new era. It showed that sponsorships were potent marketing tools, and that companies could not only promote established products but introduce new ones through special events.

The Games, for example, provided a launching pad for a relatively new and unknown product in the United States—Fuji Film. (See Chapter 3 for a discussion of the impact of sponsors and the Fuji story). By the time the Games were over, Fuji was not only known but had made inroads into Kodak's dominance of the domestic film market in the United States.

The LAOOC's emphasis on helping sponsors market their products opened the eyes of many promoters/managers across the country. Suddenly, they saw the potential and the opportunities for generating national sponsors even in markets previously considered too small for interest. If sponsors in smaller cities received the same type of marketing assistance given to companies at the 1984 Games, the opportunities for convincing corporations to become a sponsor would be dramatically increased.

And that is exactly what has happened. Communities anxious to stage major events but shy of revenue have seen the door of sponsorship opportunity open. (The reasons corporations are more interested in sponsorship today than previously are covered in detail in Chapter 4.)

WHICH COMMUNITIES SHOULD HOST EVENTS?

As a result of this increased sponsorship, smaller communities, which had counted themselves out as potential hosts for these special events, saw that they were still in the running. International federations and other governing bodies no longer concentrated on awarding events solely on the basis of a community's population. They were more interested in staging a smooth, well-run operation in which the participants enjoyed themselves and were treated well. The key was not population, because the ticket buyers, for the most part, could come from outside the community. The critical element was organization and a solid infrastructure. That has opened the doors to communities of all sizes.

Los Angeles put on a spectacular, unified show. But it also showed the IOC—as well as other federations—how a unified community with one goal or event on its mind could put on a magnificient event. For one brief period, all of Los Angeles, with its many suburbs and ethnic mixes, was unified. It was, in fact, for a short period, a mirror-image of a small community, working together as a team.

The Small to Mid-Sized Community Advantage

Many cities, particularly small to mid-sized ones, can do the same. In small to mid-sized cities, the diverse groups and interests present in larger communities are not as prevalent. They can more easily focus on one event and work together. They can be a "Los Angeles, 1984" every day of the year. The international federations understand this capability, and they have come to look on mid-sized American cities as ideal venues for world class and special events. Today, promoters/managers in Oklahoma City, Indianapolis, Kansas City, and even Wheeling, West Viriginia, are attracting significant events to their towns.

That's the exciting facet of the business of special events, and the good news for mid-sized and smaller cities throughout the country. International governing bodies are no longer just looking at mega-population centers. They understand the value of the smaller community and the attention such an area may heap upon an event. Indianapolis has, in fact, become host to many major attractions that larger cities have little chance of attracting. They have always had good fortune with the Indianapolis 500, but they have acquired many more prestigious and profitable events. For example, Indianapolis recently hosted the Final Four of the NCAA (National Collegiate Athletic Association) basketball finals. From the NCAA's perspective, it was the perfect market because:

1. the community was enamored of the sport (people in the Mid-West do love their basketball!);
2. it would get maximum community and media attention; and
3. it would have no competition in the area.

Would such an event get the same attention in New York, Chicago, or Los Angeles? It's doubtful, because there would be too many other competing events. The organizing committee would almost always have to share the spotlight with some other event. Each of those cities have a number of professional teams, as well as a host of never-ending cultural activities competing for media attention. This is not to say that these small to mid-sized cities are void of any other cultural activities during such events, but the competition would be greatly reduced due to sheer numbers.

Oklahoma City offers similar proof of how supportive a small to mid-sized community can be. In 1989, it hosted the U.S. Olympic Festival, a world-class event that features U.S. athletes competing against themselves in non-Olympic years. The event, which lasted approximately two weeks, was an incredible hit, with the opening ceremonies drawing a sell-out crowd of more than 76,000. In other words, one out of every 10 people in the city attended the opening!

ORGANIZATION AND COOPERATION ARE KEYS TO ANY SUCCESSFUL EVENT

Governing bodies such as the NCAA and IOC know it is not difficult to sell tickets to the NCAA Final Four, the Olympics, the World Series, World Cup Soccer, or the Super Bowl. In other words, it does not take a unique marketing and promotional plan to sell out such major events. The ticket demand is built-in. Ask any ticket broker. But, for the event to run smoothly, it takes organization and cooperation. It takes access to venues and a willingness by those within the community to help. It takes the ability to generate volunteers. Any promoter or manager hoping to bring a special event to his/her community has to demonstrate that kind of backing in their initial proposals.

Governing bodies know that followers of certain sports will travel thousands of miles to attend the event. In the NCAA Final Four event, about 80 percent of those who attend the games come from outside the area—and they generate anywhere from $40 to $60 million for the host city, depending upon the size of the arena. The population base in any city may be a moot point when it comes to these events. Realistically, the NCAA Final Four is a plum that many promoters—with civic and community backing—could go after.

The same is true for the Super Bowl, although by its nature the game requires a warm weather community or domed stadium (due to the fact that it is played in January and that audience and player comforts are priority). The event attracts a huge, outside audience and can generate upwards of $100 million for the host community.

A good example of an event where all the right elements came together was the 1990 Goodwill Games in Seattle. For Bob Walsh, whose company promoted the Games, Seattle held few surprises. From the beginning, there were several things that convinced him the area was right for such an event.

- First, the city's attitude. It was relatively close to the USSR compared to other U.S. cities. Therefore, there was a built-in interest about Russia and what was happening there, as well as with other countries.
- Second, Seattle is not a city loaded with activities. It has professional football and baseball teams, but there is not an overabundance of events staged each year.
- Third, Seattle has always been a liberal city, in contrast to some communities that have a more conservative bent. When the city bid for the Games, the Cold War was still hot. The Russian economy had not collapsed and missiles and nuclear weapons were the things that came to mind when the USSR was mentioned. Still, citizens within Seattle were more ready to accept visitors and culture from other countries.

The venues existed and minimum construction would be required, thereby keeping costs down. The size of the Games and the number of foreign countries it would attract virtually guaranteed solid media coverage. Ted Turner's CNN (Cable News Network) would be covering the event nationally, but to draw other attendance, the promoters needed local media help in advance of the Games.

There was an abundance of potential sponsors, many of whom (e.g., Boeing) could see the benefits of getting involved because of the international trade benefits. All of the right elements were in place, as well as an infrastructure that was firmly behind the Games because of the publicity it would bring to this Northwest U.S. city.

The promoters did not wait for the Games to open before building interest throughout the community. Speaking groups were organized and exchange programs between the Russians and Seattle citizens were organized. There were parallel events involving Russians as well. The finals of the World Chess Championship (featuring the Russians) were held in Seattle. When the Games opened with athletes from 56 countries, there were 33 chartered Russian Aeroflot airplanes with more than 3,000 Soviet citizens visiting and living with Americans in Seattle. All this served to keep the media involved, and news of the Soviets and the upcoming Games made page one of the newspapers day after day.

Seattle, then only the 25th largest U.S. city in population, staged one of the most successful international athletic events ever. Coverage of the Games and related events continued to make headlines in the Seattle and outlying town newspapers for more than a year. When Seattle won the bid for the 1990 event, the city knew it had to do more than duplicate the Moscow show. The promoters split the activities, 50 percent cultural and 50 percent athletic. They also brought the cultural activities in first: a full five months before any athletic contests were even staged, the cultural events were taking place.

More than 800,000 tickets to sports events were sold, with 600,000 to cultural events. Only a few events in track and field failed to sell out. In all, promoters estimated the Goodwill Games generated $325 million for the community. The credit goes to the promoters and managers who not only knew the elements needed to succeed, but how to implement them as well. (See Figure 1–2.)

Seattle's accomplishments illustrate another important concept: promoters/managers have to know their community. What will people buy? How much will they spend? What will the event be competing against? Outsiders to a community do not usually have the ability to judge and answer these questions without proper research.

When it comes to planning events, promoters have to take careful stock of events that might draw attendance away from theirs. In Dallas, Texas, for instance, year after year, when the Washington Redskins played the Dallas Cowboys in an NFL football game, nothing else of importance

FIGURE 1–2.   *The Six Keys to Seattle's Success*

1. Built-in community interest
2. Few competing events or activities
3. Existing venues
4. Solid media coverage
5. Abundance of potential sponsors
6. Adequate pre-promotion

went on in the town. Shopping centers and cultural events may just as well have never opened on those Sunday afternoons. Any other special event slated for that day would have been disastrous. A promoter/manager who knew the market would have realized that anytime those two teams were scheduled to play, any other event just couldn't compete.

TURNING ON THE POWER OF THE MEDIA

At about the same time the Goodwill Games were going on in Seattle, thousands of miles from Seattle in Wheeling, West Virginia, radio station WWVA was wrapping up its 15th annual, sold-out, country and western "Jamboree in the Hills." Ninety thousand consumers (30,000 a day) jammed the rural site outside Wheeling to listen to Barbara Mandrell, The Judds, and The Charlie Daniels Band. The venue was an open field with a stage built in the center. WWVA promoted the event round-the-clock, as did WOVK-FM. Every country and western music publication in the country previewed the event and, as a result, the "Jamboree" was, once again, a sell out.

The "Jamboree" is not only a good example of how a special event should be staged, but it also illustrates the drawing power of shows that develop a national reputation for quality. Wheeling, of course, does not have a large enough population to pack the "Jamboree" for three days. In fact, while the show is on, most of those from Wheeling are working it in some way (e.g., selling tickets, programs, merchandise, and so on). The crowds come from as far away as Tennessee, Ohio, and New York.

Wheeling also demonstrates another fact of life in the special event arena—the power of the media. Osborne Communications, a sizable media conglomerate in New York, promotes the show. Osborne owns radio station WWVA, the country and western music station in Wheeling that is the official host and promoter of the show. Osborne, an aggressive media-oriented firm, continuously promotes the "Jamboree" on its station. It buys significant time on 18 other radio stations as well as saturating country and western publications with ads. So, the promoters of the "Jamboree" used research, community involvement, a good reputation, and the power of the media to create a profitable and successful special event. (See Figure 1–3.)

FIGURE 1–3.   *Keys to Wheeling's Success*

1. Powerful media backing
2. A well-researched market
3. Local community fully involved
4. Infrastructure in place
5. National reputation for quality production

How to Avoid Lost Ticket Sales—Keep A High Profile

The extensive campaign Osborne conducts illustrates that, with enough media support, the crowds will materialize. Most promoter/managers of events will testify to that. But what happens if an event does not get enough support? What happens if the promoter runs short of funds? What impact does he/she have in the market at that point? Many promoters will automatically cut their marketing efforts if they run short of cash. But cutting back on ads for a special event is a big mistake. Without advertising, how will people know about the show?

If a market has been properly researched and deemed viable for an event, then it is a mistake to pull back the portion of the campaign that focuses on selling tickets. Some promoters take their cue from the way many businesspeople operate during a recession, pulling in their marketing horns and trying to preserve cash. While they are protecting their reserves, aggressive competitors hit the marketplace and take market share.

The perfect illustration of this phenomenon occurred in the real estate market. In 1990, the real estate industry was having a difficult time. Sales dropped for most real estate companies. But a number of firms not only increased sales, they had all-time high years. In surveying these companies, it was found that in every case they continued to advertise and market aggressively while their competitors kept a low profile. As a result, they generated business, while many of their competitors went out of business. Similar results were experienced by other service businesses and many retailers. Granted, the shoppers (and event ticket buyers) may diminish in numbers, but those who are shopping and buying will go to the high profile (or highly advertised) stores and events. (Event marketing will be covered in more detail in Chapter 5.)

Tying a Community into an Event

Aside from the superior marketing efforts, Osborne Communications—like other astute special event promoters—makes it a point to involve the local community. Jobs are provided for local residents throughout the "Jamboree in the Hills," and the economic impact, both from employment and tourism, is significant. As a result, Wheeling has always welcomed the three-day event with open arms.

SUMMARY

When a writer sits down to put pen to paper, one of his/her initial considerations is his/her audience (young child, college student, professional, and so on). The work's success depends on the author's ability to tap into the right audience. Just as a writer needs to understand his/her reader, so does a promoter/manager need to understand his/her market. The success of any special event depends upon the promoter/manager's ability to understand every aspect of the event. Who will attend? Is the community right for this event? Who will perform? Do we have the right sponsors? Success can be be obtained by following these 10 simple tips:

1. Plan, plan, plan!
2. Put your infrastructure in place first.
3. Remember that sponsorship is a key marketing tool and revenue generator.
4. Private promoters need public sector support. Go out and get it!
5. Pre-promotion is critical to success.
6. Smaller communities are often equal with larger cities because of their "focus."
7. Involve local communities whenever possible.
8. Remember that economic impact brings communities together.
9. Building venues is not economically feasible in most communities. Use what you have available.
10. The larger the event, the more important the role of volunteers. Use them!

Now that you understand your market and your event is planned, let's move on to discuss the best techniques for matching the event to your market.

Matching the Event to the Market

In the first chapter, we saw how cooperation, organization, and planning all worked together to create a success for the Wheeling "Jamboree." The kind of cooperation found in Wheeling during the "Jamboree" may be contrasted by what goes on in many other communities—especially those in which there may be a difference of opinion between local politicians.

When the Los Angeles Marathon was conceived, one of the plans was to have the competitors run down Rodeo Drive in Beverly Hills. The Rodeo Drive touch would have been perfect for television and it would have given the city of Beverly Hills a plug. Also, it could have been a focal point for selling more ads on the television station carrying the event. Beverly Hills has pizzaz! Many viewers—even though they may not be marathon fans—might tune in just to get a closer look at this exclusive area. Unfortunately, there is no great love between the cities of Beverly Hills and Los Angeles. In fact, there is an intense rivalry. The competition between the two cities was unreconcilable. The promoters found that they could not run the marathon within the two cities at the same time. The Rodeo Drive route had to be canceled in order for the marathon to take place.

HOW TO EVALUATE CONSUMER NEEDS AND SCHEDULE THE RIGHT EVENT

Attracting the Discerning Consumer

Evaluating the viability of bringing events to a community has not changed much in the past 30 years. Consumers, of course, have become more sophisticated and selective; as the cost of entertainment has risen, they have become more discerning about spending their money. When a consumer is spending $7.50 for a movie, he or she does not want to make the wrong choice and, thus, will check reviews and talk to friends before deciding to buy a ticket. If someone is going to spend $30 (or more) for a concert ticket, the demand for quality increases considerably. And, if a two-day ticket to a cultural or athletic festival is $50 or more, the buyer would probably ask for a written guarantee about who is performing or competing if he or she thought it would be forthcoming!

How Does a Promoter/Manager Know Which Event Will be the Right One?

There is no easy answer. The most valuable thing an event can generate is positive word-of-mouth. A hot, multi-day special event can use this tool to build attendance and reviews. On the other hand, if the event is a bore, it can die a quick death. But, what about the event that is only around for one, or at most, two nights? It does not, of course, have time to build positive word-of-mouth. What then? In the words of a well-known comedian, it takes *chutzpah* (or guts and guesswork) on the part of the promoter/manager. Sid Bernstein and Bob Eubanks had both.

Sid Bernstein was a renowned New York promoter and Bob Eubanks was a radio station disc jockey in Los Angeles. The two shared one thing—an opportunity to promote a relatively new group in concert. The musical group came from England and had become a sensation in less than two months. Their manager, however, wanted $25,000 for the right to promote this group's first concerts in the United States (a staggering amount of money in the early 1960s). Most promoters declined. Eubanks and Bernstein dug deeply into their pockets and pulled out the cash. As a result, they were able to take advantage of Brian Epstein's offer to promote the U.S. debut of a group called the Beatles.

Although managing events like a Beatles concert or the Olympics may seem worlds apart, there are similarities. The rock promoters had to determine if their cities were "right for their event." So did the the promoters of the Olympics. The obvious reaction is: "How could either miss?" One was a world-renowned athletic event; the other a group of singers with a big future ahead of them. Still, as is the case with every event, there is no such thing as a "sure thing." There are always pitfalls.

Eubanks and Bernstein booked the Beatles in early 1964, however, the group had only had one hit ("I Want to Hold Your Hand"). What was equally disturbing was the fact the Beatles were not new to the United States. They had released several records in the country prior to "I Want to Hold Your Hand." None sold more than a few hundred copies, which was another reason why many promoters shied away from the dates. Even when the foursome made the first of three consecutive appearances on the Ed Sullivan Show and caused a furor throughout the country, there were doubters. They could be a one-shot, one-hit rock group that faded before the summer and the concert tour. In many ways, Eubanks and Bernstein faced the dilemma that many promoter/managers must reckon with—scheduling an event long in advance of the actual date. In the case of the Olympics, that date can be years ahead. In the case of the Beatles, the two promoters were making a commitment six months ahead of the tour. What would happen if the group released another record before the tour and it flopped?

Neither Eubanks or Bernstein thought about a flop. What stirred them on was their own insight, knowledge of their markets, and an understanding of the consumer/event attendee in those markets. Yet, neither had any way of market-testing the appeal of their events before committing to them. (Eubanks, however, did not take any chances. As soon as the contracts were signed, he put the tickets on sale for the concert, months before the actual date. They sold out in a matter of hours.)

THE RELATIONSHIP BETWEEN SALES AND THE EVENT'S SUCCESS

Promoters soon ascertained that recording acts that were heavy sellers of cassette albums and LPs would also be heavy sellers of concert tickets. There was a direct correlation between the price of the album and the cost of the concert ticket. More than five years after the Beatles' debut, Eubanks' company decided, after calculating the relationship between album sales and concert tickets, that it would became the first to promote a concert by another relatively unknown musical group, the Bee Gees. According to Eubanks' analysis of the most recent release by the Bee Gees, they would be a sure sell-out. And they were.

Today, nearly every event—cultural or athletic—has a yardstick that prospective promoters can use to determine if an act or event will be a success in a community. The easiest technique is to:

- Call another area where the event has taken place;
- Find out how it "pulled";
- Ask what kind of advertising and promotion went into it;
- Determine the similarity of that market to yours;
- Ask about the problems;
- Check the costs, profits, overhead, and economic impact on the community;
- Ask about the political considerations;
- See if there were difficulties with local groups and politicians; Why?
- Ask yourself whether you would have the same problems in your area.

Most promoters will share this information if they know you are not going to compete directly with them. For some events, little research is required. That is, they will sell out simply because of the nature of the event. World-class events fall into this category, as well as many special local events that attract wide community attention.

Forecasting Sales in a Changing Economy

Promoters should evaluate the local economy. Regardless of how attractive the event, if the area is in dire economic straights, attendance will suffer. In the Northeast section of the United States, for example, the economy has been soft for more than two years. In the Southwest, the oil states were in the doldrums for the past two to three years. In the Midwest, however, the economy remained relatively stable in the 1980s, with little shift during the past decade. Regional effects such as these economic conditions can play a major role in the success of your event.

How a "Time Lag" Can Affect Sales

There is a *time lag*, that is, the length of time between bidding and the actual staging of the event. With concerts and many cultural events, this is a short time frame, usually just months. But with many world class events, this can be years (e.g., Los Angeles was selected for the site of the 1984 Summer Olympic Games in 1978). Economic conditions can change. Promoters are not economists, but if a significant amount of time will elapse between the bid and the event, try to determine what economic developments may impact the community during that time period.

Conditions are not, of course, always obvious. To get a closer look at what to expect, consult the local chamber of commerce. The chamber can give promoters fairly accurate information on who is moving in and who is heading out, which companies are cutting back, and which are hiring. They usually know about legislation that will impact business, which, in turn, will impact hiring—and that, of course, is going to impact the paychecks of those in the community (i.e., the ticket buyers).

Generating Excitement To Sell Tickets

Certainly, staging events takes a certain amount of "G&G" (guesswork and guts). But there are techniques that will help cut down the uncertainty. The major questions: Does the event generate excitement? An Olympics will involve everyone, but what about the staging of the gymnastic trials, soccer, weightlifting, or ice skating? Do consumers in the area feel strongly about any of those events? The legendary Ed Sullivan was once asked how he kept his national television show going for so many years. "It's simple," he answered. "The one emotion I try to generate in an audience is excitement. As long as I can excite the audience I will be able to keep them."

Staging world class and special events is no different. People seldom attend events out of an obligation to the community. They come to be entertained and thrilled. But, what may be exciting to people in Cleveland or Indianapolis may be a bore to the folks in New Orleans and Pittsburgh. Anyone who wants to promote and manage a special event in their community, must keep that in mind. Communities differ, sometimes radically.

FRIENDS IN HIGH PLACES—HIDDEN AGENDAS

Promoters should keep one point in mind when staging events—it is important to have someone with political clout on your side. A contact inside city hall or town government is important. Without a contact, your proposal could can take weeks—even months—to get through the bureaucracy.

The following story of "Conejo Valley Days" is an illustration of how clout and hidden agendas can make a difference.

Conejo Valley, which is a small, rapidly growing community in a Western state, has a group of highly motivated individuals who belong to service clubs. Each is anxious to raise money for a worthy cause. Several years ago, one of the clubs came up with an idea to hold an outside event that would feature entertainment, food, and rides. At first, the event was small and it was held in a local shopping center. As time went on, however, the following grew, and people from outside the area—hearing how much fun it was—decided to take advantage of the event. Eventually, the service clubs (15 of them ranging from Kiwanis and Rotary to the Elks and even the Chamber of Commerce) talked to the local Parks & Recreation Committee. The city organization agreed to let them move "Conejo Valley Days" to a park site which had sufficient acreage for the entertainment and much more.

There was one condition: the sponsors would have to repair any damage to the grass or the sprinkler system. The sponsors readily agreed, and the event was moved to the park location. The event—although it only lasted a week—required the park to be closed for a total of four weeks. The closure was necessary so temporary stands and a carnival could be moved in (and out). The stands were for consumers to view a rodeo, which had become part of the festivities. Consumers complained about the park closure, but the city had the perfect excuse. The park needed reseeding each year and that would have required a two-week closure anyway. By allowing the service clubs an extra two weeks, the city not only obtained its reseeding, but it got someone else to pay for it as well. In addition, because of the moving of heavy equipment, the promoters of the event almost always wound up replacing the sprinkler system as well.

The Conejo event, which generates more than $500,000 for charity during its short run, would never have happened if the service club members did not have significant influence in the community. Nor would it have come off if the Parks & Recreation Committee did not see an opportunity to save money and get the job (reseeding) done at the same time.

This is a perfect example of friends in high places and, of course, hidden agendas. Everyone—and every community—has at least one hidden agenda. Staging of events can be facilitated by promoters who are aware of these agendas. For example, if a promoter can solve a political problem for

---

FIGURE 2–1. *Keys to Conejo Valley Success*

1. Recognizing hidden agendas
2. Complete community cooperation
3. Civic group involvement
4. Political influence
5. Charitable cause

---

a dignitary (i.e., get them recognition and credit) they can go a long way towards getting approval for a special event. Learning how to time and use agendas can make any event a success. (See Figure 2–1.)

Examples of Promoters Using A City's Agenda To Stage Special Events

Entire communities may have agendas. Barcelona, the site for the 1992 Olympics, may be celebrating the 500th anniversary of Columbus sailing to America, but it is also taking advantage of a once-in-a-lifetime opportunity to show itself (and the rest of Spain) off and sell the country to tourists and businesses worldwide.

Atlanta, Georgia is doing more than hosting the 1996 Olympic Games. The city views the event as an opportunity to showcase Atlanta as "the leading city in the South." Astute promoters are aware of community agendas, and they use them to their advantage. If a community is anxious to improve its cultural image, that desire presents the perfect opportunity for a promoter to propose the staging of a special event along the existing cultural lines.

Indianapolis decided to host the 1982 National Sports Festival to show the world they could host a special event. The city fathers wanted to not only prove the city's togetherness and worldliness, but they wanted to prove to federations throughout the world that Indianapolis was a place that should be considered when it came to top flight athletic and cultural events. It worked! The 1982 Festival showcased the city and set it up as one of the premier communities for hosting special events. (In fact, in 1987, Indianapolis hosted the Pan Am Games.)

Knoxville, Tennessee is a relatively small market, but the community opened eyes throughout the world when it successfully hosted a world's fair that consisted primarily of communications and technology in 1982. The effort put forth by the community not only put the spotlight on the community but showed federations and groups that Knoxville was a city that had its infrastructure and promotional muscle in place.

Using Agenda Priorities

Some cities have an agenda with priorities. In Los Angeles, according to the Los Angeles Sports Council, those priorities are:

1. professional championship events;
2. NCAA championship events; and
3. events that are on the Olympic calendar.

That's a hefty agenda, but one that most federations realize is a priority for any West Coast city. For other communities, the number one priority is to attract an event that is prestigious. By promoting an event of this type, the prestige rubs off on the community.

For some communities, the priority is to remind the rest of the country (and world) that the area is rich in tradition and culture. Such was the case in Philadelphia, during the mammoth bicentennial celebration of the U.S. Constitution in 1987. A huge parade, featuring 25,000 people and 30 horse-drawn floats, came through the town in a two-and-one-half mile display that was televised nationally on CBS-TV.

The Pioneer Priority

Some promoters/managers want to simply be known as pioneers. For example, there is a group of promoters/managers in the Northwestern United States who are planning to stage the first world/special event in Vietnam, in Ho Chi Min City (formerly Saigon) when the U.S. State Department lifts its embargo. The group plans to enlist sponsors from throughout the United States who are interested in increasing trade overseas. When the wall came down in Berlin a group determined to "unite the world" began planning a rock concert that would bring groups from the United States, Russia, and Japan together for the first time.

THE ECONOMIC IMPACT—COMPETING FOR THE PRIZE

Regardless of the motivation and agenda, most communities know that a special event will have significant economic impact on an area. That fact alone has created intense competition among cities to attract events. For example, so-called "freebies" or inducements that are offered to the NFL (National Football League) if it will stage the Super Bowl in a particular city average more than $2 million. (See Appendix C for Super Bowl Requirements.) Cities offer everything from chauffeured limousines and free stadium rental, to concession and parking control. Not a bad investment for an economic impact of more than $100 million. Even one-night concerts impact a community economically. The Michael Jackson Victory Tour, which traveled the United States a few years ago, had an entourage that included 18 semi-trailers. The money spent in each community by the show's performers, plus the funds that were generated for everything from security to souvenirs was significant. Being awarded a major event is indeed like receiving a prize for any community. But is it a trophy or a booby prize?

SUCCESSFUL VERSUS UNSUCCESSFUL EVENTS— READING THE COMMUNITY

While it may seem as if a Michael Jackson concert or some other special event doesn't have a chance to lose, it can. Some can be financial traps for promoters and managers. Obviously, if the infrastructure is not in place, the event can be unsuccessful. Or, if the 10 keys to success we have mentioned are poorly executed, there can be problems.

One other element plays a role in determining whether or not an event can make it in a market—an understanding of the community itself. Some call this *market research*, others just gut instinct. Taking it to the lowest common denominator, the neighborhood retailer understands that his customers come from a market that is no farther than three miles from his door. Thus, everyone within that circumference is a prime customer, and the retailer must understand their desires. He must sell them what they want and need—not what he wants to sell.

With special events, a promoter must have an understanding of a wide area, often involving numerous cities and counties. In the case of the Goodwill Games and the Olympic Festival in Los Angeles, good promoters understood that either Los Angeles or Seattle could host a major event, but the customers within those two markets are radically different. Seattle is primarily a "homogeneous" market while Los Angeles is "heterogeneous." What do those terms mean, and what do they have to do with predicting whether a community is right—or wrong—for an event?

Heterogeneous versus Homogeneous Communities

Although Seattle has recently had an influx of people from other parts of the country, it remains primarily a *homogenous market*. That is, the majority of people who live there were born in the community, grew up there, and have worked in the area all their lives. Most share the same interests and desires. Obviously, a community that has similar characteristics is easier to analyze and research than one that does not. For example, an event that is appealing to consumers in one part of Seattle will most likely carry over to another part of the city.

There are many homogeneous communities in the Midwest where ethnic groups and cultural tastes have remained stable for years. Des Moines, Indianapolis, Milwaukee, Minneapolis, Kansas City, and other markets in the Midwest have a homogeneous population; what they buy on one side of town can usually be sold on another side. This characteristic cuts down the guesswork for promoters.

But, take Los Angeles, Miami, New York, San Francisco, and many other communities that have become melting pots, and promoters suddenly find themselves in a society with a number of different cultures, tastes, and preferences. In multicultural, *heterogenous communities* events stand a much greater chance of being unsuccessful because of the diversity of the groups, their varied interests, and what they may or may not oppose. There is often fragmentation between cultures and they differ in what they prefer insofar as cultural and athletic events. In many cases, they are more outspoken, too.

The Roles of Religion and Nationalities

Religion plays a role in the success of an event, as do nationalities. In Miami, for instance, there is an eight-day festival (Caja Ocho) put on by the Cuban-American Chamber of Commerce, celebrating the success of the Cuban-American community in that city. Although Los Angeles has a huge Latin population, it does not have an abundance of Cubans. Los Angeles Latinos celebrate another festival. Cinco de Mayo celebrations are popular in Los Angeles, but they would not go far in a city like Phoenix. Miami, because of the great influx of immigrants, has become a heterogeneous community. A promoter/manager familiar with the market knows an event that appeals to the Miami Cuban segment of the market can be enormously successful. Still, the promoter/manager has to be sure they are staging it in a part of town that is frequented by Cubans. That means studying the Cuban media and past events that have been targeted at the Cuban audience. How did they do? Where were they held? How were they promoted?

If the event involves the African-American community, promoters should get a feeling for those within it by reading and listening to African-American media, instead of white, middle-of-the-road publications and media. In New York, that means the *Amsterdam News*, and in Los Angeles the *Los Angeles Sentinel*. Both publications are written by and cater to the African-American audience.

Reading different cultures can be difficult. Promoters would do well to visit the local chamber of commerce, Kiwanis, Rotary, and other organizations in order to bounce their idea off these local groups, which frequently have a good feel for the pulse of their neighborhoods.

Recognizing the Differences Between Communities

Even communities that seem similar can be deceptive.

In Dallas, one of the most popular recent special events to be developed was a basketball tournament that featured 400 teams from the area. Attendance was beyond expectations and the promoters thought about taking the concept and utilizing it in cities throughout the country. They looked around at other communities that were fond of basketball and had given the sport exemplary support. They picked Los

Angeles and New York. The results, however, were far from satisfying. In fact, the event in both communities was a near disaster.

Why? Dallas is a community that is virtually homogeneous in its makeup and tastes. A large segment of the population considers itself Dallas Cowboy fans. Los Angeles and New York, of course, are mixtures, melting pots. The idea of pitting the best teams in either area against each other is not novel. The event also competed with dozens of other athletic and cultural activities happening that same day. The market was limited. Competition was tight.

In Los Angeles, the 1991 Olympic Festival faced stiff competition in the media: news of the Los Angeles Dodgers and California Angels, news of the upcoming football season (Los Angeles Rams and Raiders), news of whom the colleges (USC and UCLA) were recruiting. In New York, it would be the same story. But, when Denver and San Antonio (two cities that will host upcoming Olympic Festivals) stage these events there will be much less competition for attention.

THE UNKNOWN QUANTITY IN ATHLETIC COMPETITIONS—WILL "THEY" SHOW UP?

In promoting/managing an amateur athletic event, there is a problem that every host must face—which athletes will be there? Will the "big" names show? Controlling this aspect of any event is difficult, unless the event, by its rules, requires certain athletes to compete. This seldom happens unless the event is an Olympic or similar competition. The 1991 Pan Am Games are a good example of well-known athletes deserting for another event. While the Pan Am Games were going on in Cuba, many of the top athletes in the United States (and the world), were competing in events in Europe. On the day the track and field competition opened in Havana, a four-man U.S. 400-meter relay team broke the world's record—in Europe. The absence of these athletes did not hurt attendance in Cuba, but it could have been devastating in the United States, where consumers are used to seeing the best and turning out only for name athletes.

THE IMPORTANCE OF KNOWING THE AUDIENCE

If there is one clear lesson that all promoters/managers should hear, it is "know your audience." Although many smaller communities can hold a successful Olympic Festival, it is often more difficult for large cities (e.g., New York, Los Angeles, Chicago) to compete. Why? In key population centers, numerous athletic and cultural events hotly compete for the consumer's dollar. In these communities, promoters need to offer something "extra" (i.e., big names, head-to-head competition among the best in the field, or a chance of a world record) to get the crowds excited.

Although sports festivals have worked well in many communities, it's no guarantee of success in others. In order to determine if it will work in another, the promoter first has to pinpoint the audience: Who saw it? What age? How far did they come? Was there a competing event? If not, what might have happened if there were? Once those questions are answered, a promoter can look for pockets of consumers with similar tastes in other markets.

THE IMPACT OF SPECIAL INTEREST GROUPS

Even when a promoter finds an event that seems like a natural, has broad appeal, and could be a success in more than one market, there can be obstacles.

> Americans love to eat. In fact, all-American barbecues and eating events have been a mainstay of mid-America for decades. In Chicago, the "taste of Chicago," an eight-day food festival, has been a bonanza for the city. In Cincinnati, there is a similar festival. A promoter, eyeing these two events, thought a natural would be an "All-American Barbecue," staged Labor Day weekend, which is traditionally the close of summer and the finale of the barbecue season. The event, of course, had to be outdoors. Thus, the venues that would appear to be the best were city park and recreation facilities. It is difficult to get public employees and politicians to agree to the closing of a public facility, especially during the season when it is most utilized. The promoter, sensing this reluctance when he talked to officials, decided to generate another venue. He went after a college, knowing the institution had the ground and could use the rental fee that would be generated. Everything was set until it came down to the final planning of the area. The president of the college surveyed the plans and shook his head with a firm "no." The reason: the college had plans for expansion, and hoped to build a new structure almost exactly where the barbecue would be held. The president was fearful that the barbecue might be noisy, and irritate residents. Thus, when it came down to their agreeing to his expansion plans, they would say no.

Every area has special interest groups, and while a promoter may get the blessing of one, he may run afoul of another.

THE VALUE OF SPECIAL EVENTS

While many communities realize the value of special events to the city, and they go out of their way to help the promoter proposing the event, cities such as Cincinnati, Cleveland, and Indianapolis have established special event committees and policies to help the promoter work his way through the power structure. These groups concentrate primarily on major events that have demonstrated they can have an economic impact on the community. But what about new events that have not yet proven their viability? Can they generate community support? An example is the "International Chili Cookoff."

> In 1967, a group of Texas landowners decided that they needed to do something in order to sell 2,000 acres of land they owned. Their idea was to hold a special event, and they came up with the "World's Champion Chili Cookoff," a competition that would pit the best chili cooks against each other. The idea, of course, was to call attention to the land—and it did. Although there were only two contestants that first year it provided grist for the news mill, particularly when the judges (three) outnumbered the contestants, and especially when one of them claimed his "taste buds were wrecked" from the concoctions that had been brewed.
>
> From the start, the event was a tongue-in-cheek cookoff, with people ending up with more laughs (and promotion for the land) than quality chili. The event caught on and spread. It was even held one year at the posh Balboa Bay Yacht Club, where it drew more than 200 people who paid $2 each for all the chili they could eat. One of the 14 participating chili cooks would win a trip to Texas to vie for the "world" title. Eventually, the event became so big that it was moved to an almost-ghost town in the desert called "Tropical Gold Mine." The first year in Tropical, the cookoff drew more than 14,000 people. This year, the crowd will be in excess of 20,000. And more than 300 other local chili cookoffs are now staged throughout the year. Each purchases a license from the national event so they can utilize the name, and some— such as the Malibu (California) cookoff—generate more than $300,000 for charity each year.

The success of this cookoff illustrates several points. First, in order to have an event you need an idea. Second, if it's unique and offers consumers two other elements—fun and entertainment—it can be successful. People must be able to enjoy themselves. Third, fun and entertainment can lead to feelings of goodwill by attendees—which can be transferred to a sponsor and the sponsor's product.

Although it is difficult to predict exactly how much revenue an event will generate for a community, one thing is becoming abundantly clear—the competition among U.S. cities is growing and the stakes are getting higher. To international committees responsible for awarding these events, the United States is a lucrative market because of its economic guarantees and the potential TV market.

HOW THE UNITED STATES IS VIEWED BY INTERNATIONAL COMMITTEES

Interestingly, many international committees have a distorted view of the United States—a view that benefits many of the smaller communities. For example, Europeans have a difficult time differentiating between our markets and the various cultures within them. They view America much as they view countries in Europe: homogeneous. They look upon the United States in the same manner, and believe there is little difference between Seattle, San Francisco, Miami, Los Angeles, and New York. We're all Americans, so we must all be the same. Obviously, the culture differs radically in these markets. In some cases, they could even be different countries insofar as tastes go. Europeans, for instance, cannot conceive that breakfast in New York is eggs over easy, while it is grits in Atlanta and a muffin in Los Angeles.

This misconception works in favor of U.S. cities competing for international events. Many governing bodies view cities in the East, West, North, and South as equal when bidding for events. They do not see the differences in Houston and Boston, or Charlotte and Portland. To many international bodies, population in a community is not the factor that determines whether or not the area gets an event. It is the infrastructure and venues, the cooperation and organization that is displayed in proposals. Thus, smaller population centers, such as Indianapolis and Kansas City, frequently have an equal chance to attract major events. And that's what makes the promotion and managing of world class and special events a possibility for more communities in this country than most imagine.

SUMMARY

Matching your special event to a particular market is not an easy task. But if you follow the following 10 simple tips, you should be successful:

1. Remember, consumers are more discerning than ever.
2. Positive word-of-mouth is critical.
3. Market knowledge is a must for the promoter/manager.
4. Measure your event's potential by the previous performance of a similarly located event.
5. The local economy is a key indicator of success.
6. Utilize local information sources, such as the chamber of commerce.
7. Consumer motivation is entertainment.
8. Beware of hidden agendas.
9. Communities differ—heterogenous versus homogenous.
10. The international view of the United States differs from our view of this country.

CHAPTER THREE

How Communities and Promoters Are Selected

Although we begin this chapter by using only sporting events to illustrate the selection process, we will discuss other special events later on in the chapter. Some aspects of the process are the same for most events but others are quite different, as you will see when we discuss the entertainment industry. For now, let's focus on attracting a sporting event such as the NCAA Finals or the U.S. Gymnastics Championships.

HOW TO BECOME A FINALIST—DEALING WITH THE GOVERNING BODIES

There are governing or sanctioning bodies for virtually all sports, and each of these organizations sets the rules for where and how they will make a promoter and site selection. For example, there is a national governing body for most amateur sports in the United States (See Appendix A). When it comes to collegiate athletics and events, the National Collegiate Athletic Association (NCAA) decides where to locate finals and other major college events. Within the NCAA, there is a committee for each sport. It is this committee that ultimately decides the location for major, national championship competitions.

Typically, these organizing bodies work in the following manner with a timetable (typically five to six months) similar to this one:

- An RFP (Request for Proposal) may come out in June.
- The bid has to be submitted by September.
- A decision is made in October. The October choice actually focuses on three of the *bidders* or *finalists*.

THE IMPORTANCE OF RESEARCH

How does a promoter/manager representing a community become a finalist? The finalists are determined by numerous factors ranging from the condition of the venue to the guarantee (cash) offered to the federation for the event. Gymnastics, for instance, which has enormous appeal on television, has become a hot item with promoters (and communities) vying for events. In 1990, three cities—Baltimore, Memphis, and Columbus (Ohio)—were finalists to hold the 1992 U.S. national championships. Baltimore won the bid based upon the highest guarantee—more than $350,000.

Get to Know the Site Committee Members

The U.S. Gymnastics Federation is a case in point. It has a large board but it typically delegates the site decision to a *site selection committee* consisting of three to five people. Seldom is the site selection recommendation rejected by the Federation. Promoters/managers of these events have to know the site committee members. Who are they? Where do they live? Have they ever been to your city? What is their track record? Are there venues, special amenities, or features of a community that they favor?

Study Prospective Events for Profitability

Gymnastics, for example, will make money for the promoter. But, not all events do well. One of the most prestigious events is the Olympic track and field trials for U.S. athletes. It is hotly contested and an expensive event to stage. The governing body will probably generate a six-figure guarantee from the bidding promoter and city. Unlike gymnastics, however, track and field has become an enigma. In many cities, it loses money for both the city and promoter. This is an event that requires careful study by prospective promoters before bidding. There is one saving grace about track and field trials, though. When they are held in cities where there is little or no competition, they usually do well. But, when they are brought to a major, metropolitan city that has distractions and a myriad of events, they usually do not do well. Yet, there are many cities waiting to bid on it because of the image and prestige.

In the case of gymnastics, every community wants it, and the promoter will pay dearly for the rights. It has become one of the hottest sports in the country, and the number of young Americans entering it are astounding. Some of the credit for this event's appeal belongs to the 1984 Olympics. It was a sport dominated by foreign countries prior to the Los Angeles Games. But in 1984, the American presence was felt for the first time. The success of the American team captured the imagination of people throughout the country, and the enthusiasm has not yet died.

Know What's Hot and What's Not—Choosing the Right Attraction

Not all international and national sports can command high guarantees. In fact, many do not command an advance at all. Others may only generate a small guarantee. It all depends upon *supply and demand.* Much of the demand is generated through the simplicity or difficulty of the sport when it comes to the fans' comprehension of the rules. For example, many people have trouble with hockey because they do not understand "icing" and other terms used in the game. Usually, the more difficult an event is to understand, the smaller the following, and the easier it becomes to negotiate dates but the harder it is to achieve profits.

FOUR FACTORS TO CONSIDER WHEN SUBMITTING A BID

Adding Quality Control Guarantees to the Bid

Regardless of the popularity of a particular sport and the muscle the governing bodies may have, the winning bid is not always the highest. International bodies want more than a good price and profit. They want the people they bring to a community treated well. World-class athletes and performers are celebrities and the federations like to have them dealt with in that manner.

Part of that preferred treatment means that the event must be thoroughly organized and trouble-free. Those two elements weighed heavily in Baltimore's favor when it bid for the gymnastics championships. It was perceived as a community with a solid infrastructure and world class potential venues. The competitors would be treated royally, and they would have the city's undivided attention. They were well organized.

Propagating the Event's Main Theme

Aside from community awareness and togetherness, Baltimore offered the gymnastics federation another opportunity. Federations want to propagate and expand the influence of their sport. Baltimore presented the federation with this chance because it was not known as an area that contained an abundance of support for gymnastics.

Unlike such markets as Los Angeles, where gymnastics had attracted huge crowds, Baltimore was a community that did not have much of a track record when it came to the sport. But the undivided attention the championships would receive from the community and media was a plus. To the Federation, that meant there could be a huge, potential audience of non-gymnastic fans who might tune in and turn on to gymnastics. This increased support would translate to increased future ticket sales.

Guaranteeing Future Fans Equals Better Bidding Potential

Expansion of the sport carries weight with federations when it comes to awarding bids. The organizing committees know the importance of spreading their sport and making as many converts as possible. International governing bodies know that if they return to the same market all the time, they will eventually reach a point of diminishing returns; each time, they will find fewer people to introduce to the sport.

The same thinking goes into "Kids Days" at the baseball or football game. Kids are future fans. These events not only reach established fans, but potential ones. The future of the sport—and the revenue it can generate—depends upon demand. More fans and followers translate into growth. When bidding, the promoters who take that into consideration and make it part of their proposal are ahead of the game.

Taking Advantage of a Sole Bidder Position

Not all international federations are as organized as the U.S. Gymnastics Federation when it comes to bidding. Some are unsophisticated and have only recently found themselves in a situation where more than one promoter (and market) is interested in their event. The International Weightlifting Federation was recently approached by a U.S. promoter who wanted to bid on having the world championships in America. To his surprise, the promoter found he did not have any competition.

Being the only bidder has significant advantages. One of the most important advantages is TV rights (discussed in Chapter 9). With most well-known, international sports, promoters have little chance of negotiating for TV rights. For lesser known events, though, there is an abundance of opportunities. Weightlifting is one such event, but it is not the only one.

THE KEY TO ATTRACTING AN EVENT

For communities that have never hosted an international event, the key to attracting one is to first decide what event the community will support. Initially, promoters/managers do not have to go after Super Bowls, Olympic Trials, or Pan Am Games. With the multitude of international and national federations, plus the NCAA, there is an abundance of events available.

If a promoter decides to shoot for an international event, the critical thing is not to understand the sport as much as the governing body. Judgments have to be made as to the event's appeal to the community, but in order to bid effectively, the infrastructure and workings of the federations should be understood.

Attracting and promoting events is similar to marketing a product. Before a company can be successful, it must know the audience (customer) and what the buyer wants. With manufacturers of products, there are two markets—the distributors and retailers who buy the product to sell and the consumers, the ultimate buyers. Both must be understood. The same is true when it comes to events. There are, once again, two markets; the federations or organizing committees who control the events and the consumers in the marketplace—the people who will ultimately decide whether they are going to the event.

To market products, companies must research two items. They study the end-user (the consumer), and develop and test theories as to why those consumers will buy their product. They actually go out and test the product with consumers. The test may only be in one small portion of the market, but they do test. They get opinions. Once they find what the consumer needs and will buy, they develop marketing plans that appeal to those needs. They show the studies—and their plans—to distributors and retailers. The more thorough the study, the easier it is to convince the distributors and retailers that consumers will buy the product.

Federations need the same support. Promoters need to research both their market and their consumers. What will they buy? Why? Will they buy tickets to a world weightlifting championship? Will they buy tickets to a figure skating championship? Once the promoter has developed practical evidence (via surveys or studies of similar markets), he is ready to present his case to the governing bodies. But first comes the research.

In many ways, bidding for a Super Bowl is less work and requires less guesswork than bidding for a weightlifting event. With the Super Bowl, Olympics, Pan Am Games, or Final Four Basketball, promoters have the benefit of looking back at previous proposals. Many federations will supply promoters with copies of those proposals. Or, if a city has hosted an event and knows it will not be able to host the same attraction for years, there is a chance the promoters will share information as well.

When the Indiana Sports Federation was launched a decade ago, it had little to go on. But, in 10 years, the organization has built a catalog of information and contacts throughout the world. Their promoters/managers called federations, cities that hosted previous events, and even talked to politicians and promoters in other cities. They built a substantial resource base. This is one of the reasons it has been successful. Today, Indianapolis has good reason to be proud. The 1992 Olympic Swimming trials were awarded to the city along with the diving event. The city also played host to the 1991 World Gymnastics Championship and is bidding for the 1994 World Soccer Cup.

SEVEN RULES TO FOLLOW IN SUBMITTING A PROPOSAL

Indianapolis has been enormously successful because it has followed the key rules when it comes to submitting a proposal. A *Request for Proposal* (RFP) is a simple document in which the bidder lays out the answers to a number of questions raised by the governing body. (We will discuss the Request for Proposal [RFP] document in greater detail in Chapter 4.) Here are seven rules to keep in mind when outlining your proposal:

1. *Do Your Research.* Promoters should not write a word in a proposal until the event is thoroughly researched. This may involve interviews with those at the international (or national) organizing body, as well as conversations with previous event promoters. It means finding out what went right and what went wrong with the last event. Most importantly, discover the mistakes that may have been made by the previous promoters/managers.
2. *Use Objective Writing.* Adjectives and flamboyant prose do not belong in proposals. Factual writing is the language of the winning proposal.
3. *Be Creative.* Promoters/managers should develop creative ideas that will appeal to the organizing committee. For example, the pre-Super Bowl party, with its nearly $2 million in income for the NFL, was an idea that had much merit—and certainly could influence the awarding of the game.
4. *Address a Unique Selling Proposition.* Every winning proposal should have a unique selling proposition. With it, the promoter sets his

city/community apart from the competition and tells what it can do that no other area can. This can range from previous experience (e.g., with a similar event or an infrastructure that cannot be matched) to a new, improved venue with a community that is willing to give their utmost attention and dedication to the event. Promoters should take a hint from previous winning proposals. What elements in the proposal attracted the international governing bodies? Search them out and repeat them!

5. *Handle the Competition.* Promoters or managers should never point out a competitor's weakness, but should just concentrate on their own strengths. If, for instance, a promoter has access to a new, ultra-modern, state-of-the-art venue, stress that availability. It does not take long before proposal readers begin to see that other venues do not match up. Leave it up to the awarding and governing bodies to compare strengths and weaknesses. When they do, they will undoubtedly be able to see the differences.

6. *Organize Properly.* Proposals should be well-organized with evidence that the promoter has a firm grasp of the event and how it should be staged. Organizing committees look upon someone who fails to follow their questions in sequence as a promoter who obviously does not know how to fill out a bid properly. A bid should not ramble. If a bid cannnot be submitted properly, the ability to promote an event properly will be in question.

7. *Summarize Key Points.* The key selling points must be reiterated in a management or executive summary that is placed at the beginning of the proposal. This summary contains all the pertinent information so that the committee receiving it can easily see the outstanding points the bidder is making.

NEGOTIATING WITH AGENTS/MANAGERS

Recognizing the Agent's Position

Requests for Proposals, of course, are vehicles that are identified primarily with special events involving international or national governing bodies or organizations (namely, sporting events). For the promoter/manager seeking to stage a one-night concert or a weekend cultural event, the procedure differs markedly. A promoter who wants to stage a concert with a contemporary rock act will be dealing with agencies and managers. Usually, the artist's manager contracts with the agency overseeing the booking of a tour and who is responsible for selecting the promoter.

The agency is a go-between, a buffer between the promoter and artist and his/her manager. It is up to the agency to pick the right promoter and the right cities. If a date blows up and the crowd is not on hand, the agency is one of the first to be blamed because they booked the date. In return, the agency gets a percentage, usually around 10 percent. While 10 percent of a new, untried artist does not amount to much, 10 percent of a hot attraction can amount to hundreds of thousands, even millions, of dollars. With that kind of revenue at stake, agencies are careful and tough. They don't want to lose a money-making performer or event. To protect their investment, agencies can be tough with promoters. In some cases, they may even tell a promoter that he cannot have a certain attraction unless he takes Artist X and Artist Y—two newcomers—along. In other words, the agency forces the promoter to book two or three new or average acts in order to get the superstar.

Dealing with the Artist-Driven Industry

But, simply wanting an act and having the finances to promote it does not guarantee that the promoter will get the date. A smaller community, for example, may have little chance of booking a big name act unless the manager and agency have:

1. decided the group is going to tour; and
2. the city is on the schedule.

The days of calling an agency and negotiating for the appearance of a top artist in a city when there is no tour slated are gone. A decade ago, independent promoters could, for instance, watch the music charts, pick a hot act, and call the agency to book a date. The agency would try to fit the city in on the artist's tour, and if it meant a detour of several hundred miles, it could be, and most times was, done. Events were promoter driven.

Today, however, they are artist driven. It is the era of the superstar. There are fewer big name artists around, but the name acts make more and demand more. Once again, booking a one-night concert in any city that is not on the proposed route does not make economic sense. The cost of that one date would exceed the generated revenue. What does make sense is a planned, lengthy tour which involves numerous dates across the country.

The artist's equipment and gear can be carried via truck, while the performer travels by air. The distance between dates is normally no further than 500 miles, thus it is possible for the band to pack up and break down the equipment following a date, and for the equipment to be moved to the next venue between midnight and 3:00 or 4:00 P.M. the next afternoon.

The Roles of the National and Local Promoters

Usually, to coordinate the tour, the agent and artist's manager select one national promoter whose job is to select all local promoters. Aggressiveness, organizational skills, and knowledge of the business and the market are the characteristics the national promoter searches for in a local promoter. No one, of course, wants to fail. One-night or weekend concerts that

---

FIGURE 3–1.　*Points To Remember About Agencies*

1. Agencies act as go-betweens between the artist(s) and his/her manager(s).
2. The agency oversees the booking.
3. The agency usually gets a percentage (usually around 10 percent).
4. Agencies want to book tours, not isolated dates that are out of the way.

---

do not do well have a direct impact on an artist's or event's appeal—and on the price that is paid for them down the line. Experience counts.

This does not mean a local entrepreneur who is interested in getting into the business will be automatcially disqualified. If the new promoter can demonstrate he knows the business, the complexities of promotion, and the market itself, he has a good chance of getting the event.

If you keep in mind a few basic facts about agents, your negotiations with them, whether you are the national promoter or the local promoter, will go much smoother. (See Figure 3–1.)

What Publications to Read in Order to Stay Current

New, as well as old, promoters need to keep abreast of what is happening in the industry. In music and related fair events, promoters should be reading *Billboard* and *Amusement Business*. With other international sports and cultural events there are publications such as the *IEG Directory of Sponsorship Marketing* and *Special Events Report,* both out of Chicago. A promoter/manager scanning, for instance, *Billboard* would soon find that a major artist may have sold out six nights in a row in Philadelphia, but, a few days later, sold 8,000 tickets in a 14,000 seat arena in Florida. Obviously, this artist does well in one part of the country, but not in another.

With musical attractions, promoters/managers have to judge if a recording act will do well in concert. Not all record sellers generate concert ticket sales. The promoter should be tracking the act's performance and checking with local distributors and retailers. If the act is hot nationally, how is he/she doing in the promoter's local market? Attendees at a concert are not at all like those who come from miles around to see a Super Bowl, national gymnastics meet, or world-class soccer event. Concertgoers are locals, and if the music is not selling locally, the concert tickets won't either. The same is true of non-music events. Promoters should have an inkling of how well the ballet, a particular art show, or other cultural event will do. It is relatively easy to check with venues and examine the past performance of previous or similar events.

Never Assume Anything!

When a promoter/manager is about to sign an artist or event, the rule is "never leave something to be worked out. If it is not spelled out in the agreement beforehand, chances are it will never work itself out." Never assume anything! If a promoter is assured that a venue is available, he should not count on it until the date has been firmed up and the agreement signed.

In the case of universities/colleges, available dates can be deceptive. Universities have their own programs and promoters are usually secondary. The date may appear to be available, but, in most cases, it does not officially belong to the promoters until all departments within the school have had a chance to approve it. A promoter's event can be bumped if the drama or speech department needs the auditorium for their own use.

Renegotiation can be another pitfall. All-pro linebackers and quarterbacks, all-star pitchers and hitters, are not the only ones who are asking that their contracts be revised. The problem is one for special events, as well. Typically, the longer lead time, the more surprises a promoter can encounter.

In the 1984 Olympics, the organizing group had contracted with the Los Angeles Coliseum Commission for the entire venue during the run of the Games. A short time later, the committee was astounded when it discovered that the Coliseum Commission had also contracted (at a later date) with Al Davis, one of the owners of the Los Angeles Raiders football team, to build luxury boxes in the venue. The boxes and ticket revenue for those seats would also belong to Davis during the Games. This would have been an unacceptable situation for the LAOOC. The problem disappeared when the Coliseum boxes were delayed until after 1984. (Actually, the boxes were still not built by the end of 1991.)

MERCHANDISING: THE WINNERS AND LOSERS

Merchandise (e.g., souvenirs, programs, and other similar goods) can produce significant revenue at special events. Promoters generally do not share in these receipts and, for the most part, promoters prefer to stay away from program and food sales. Merchandise and novelty items are another story. The artist or event, though, is not going to give the promoter a share of the profits if they own the goods.

In some venues, promoters may be able to negotiate a share of the revenue from parking, concessions, and programs, especially if the promoter ends up with the responsibility of selling the programs. This typically happens in venues where there is not a strong union presence. In others, they will hit a stone wall. Dodger Stadium will rent to a promoter for a flat fee, but the promoter has no chance of getting any profits from concessions or parking. One exception is in the program area. In Los Angeles' Dodger

Stadium contracts, for example, there is an organization that sells products for the promoter within the stadium. The promoter works a profit split with this organization and the organization gives Dodger Stadium a piece of the pie as well. This kind of arrangement can be found in many stadiums across the country. Each stadium will have its own policy and there are almost as many policies as stadiums. In markets where there is an abundance of venues and a signficant number of open dates, promoters have additional leverage in negotiating splits with program and other merchandise sales.

NEGOTIATING WITH UNIONS

Some of the most challenging negotiations promoters run into are with union vendors. Unions are usually strongest in the Northeast and Midwest, and less strict in the South and far West. It's a fact of life that in the Midwest and Northeast, unions have been entrenched for years. Nothing moves in or out of any venue in New York City without a union participating. In some cases, exhibitors cannot even carry a small box in the door without a union's permission.

Whether it is a strong or weak union town, promoters should get into the venue early and meet with the union. The weaker the union venues, the more flexible they will be when it comes to vendors carrying in their own goods.

MAKING THE MOST OF COMMUNITY NEGOTIATIONS

Some cities are anxious to establish an image as a community that is in the forefront of presenting new events. In many cases, these cities may offer everything from free (or reduced) rates in hotels to discounts on arena rentals. The city will also bend over backwards and help the promoter get licenses or anything else needed. They may even help the promoter negotiate with the union insofar as merchandise is concerned. Where the city controls the venue, they may let the promoter (if he desires) handle all his own merchandise and keep the proceeds.

Negotiating is never cut-and-dried or black-or-white. A promoter/manager who wants to set aside a stadium date for x years down the line may find himself without a venue if the stadium operators have the chance to put in a bigger, more profitable event. The promoter who negotiated two or three hotels for an event may find himself in trouble if a bigger (more profitable) convention contacts the hotel for the same dates. For instance, there are numerous conventions that were booked in Atlanta for the summer of 1996. Now that the Olympics are coming to town, many of those conventions will have to look elsewhere for a more accommodating venue.

Negotiations and renegotiations are part of the reason infrastructure is important. If all the politicians, hotel operators, and public and other officials are aligned behind an event, the promoter/manager has less chance of being burned.

LAYING OUT THE BUDGETING ELEMENTS— REVENUES VERSUS COSTS

Regardless of how shrewd a promoter/manager is when it comes to negotiating and bidding, one of the key elements for success is a carefully prepared, thorough, and understandable budget. Budgeting is not only for accountants. Any good manager will have worked up a budget that is a financial reflection of the event's vision statement and the resources required to bring that vision to life. Successful development and use of budgets involves thorough planning based on common sense and the discipline to monitor and track against the amounts and schedules in the budget. The bid should include a complete listing of the key revenue and expense items expected for the event.

What to Expect in Revenues

The revenue elements will vary, depending upon the nature of the event, but could include such items as:

- Ticket revenues (admission);
- Television/radio;
- Advertising revenues;
- Sponsorships;
- Merchandise/licensing revenues;
- Concessions/food revenues;
- Transportation revenues;
- Donations; and
- Special programs (e.g., coin sales for major events).

Although revenue projections may not be required for the bid itself, no promoter/manager should submit a bid without knowing what the anticipated revenue stream will be.

Budgeting for the Cost of the Event

The cost elements for an event can usually be grouped into four main categories:

1. *Operational/production*—personnel, security, licenses/permits, construction, contractors/consultants, insurance, administrative support, and so forth.

2. *Venue/site rental*—flat fee, percentage of ticket sales, or percentage of ticket sales against a minimum flat rental.
3. *Promotion*—flyers, banners, public relations, and other forms of advertising.
4. *Talent*—the costs to obtain the performers or participants.

As an integral step in preparing the bid, the promoter/manager must identify all the major areas of expected cost as they fit into his/her vision of how the event will be developed and staged. It is important to remember that costs will be incurred before any significant revenues start flowing and that cash flow must be considered in developing both the financial plan and budget.

The price of the venue. The promoter/manager must think everything through. What will it cost to stage the event? Will it require fencing, building a stage or props? What will the city charge if it has to block off streets? (In today's tight economic environment, cities do not hesitate to charge and ask for as much as they think they can collect for events.) Other considerations include how much of the work will be done by volunteers versus paid staff, contractors, or consultants. Also, will some of the expected costs be covered by "in-kind" goods and services you expect to get from sponsors?

Don't forget the insurance. An expenditure that should not be overlooked, and which is by no means a small cost, is insurance. There are two kinds of *liability policies* promoters should seek. The first insures the promoter in the event someone is injured at the venue. The second insures for accidents that may occur after the event (for example, a person drinks too much at the event and is injured in an auto accident on the way home). Surprisingly, the second type of insurance is much more expensive.

In the bidding process, promoters can often get very creative in describing how they will respond to the questions in a Request for Proposal. It is important that, no matter how creative the promoter gets, there is a solid financial plan, expressed in the form of a planning budget and planned cash flow that will provide a roadmap for financial success of the event.

Realizing the marketing costs. When it comes to costs for marketing the event, promoters include a broad range of items, from flyers and banners to radio/TV advertising and publicity. Flyers can be utilized on everything from car windows in parking lots to doorknobs at residences. Also, they can be included in packets of discount coupons that are frequently delivered to neighborhoods by direct mail companies. Banners are not just produced for the day of the event. Promoters contact cities and other nearby communities and investigate the possibilities of having banners produced and hung over bridge abutments, streets, and highways wherever possible. If the infrastructure is in place, the promoter/manager will have an abundance of cooperation from officials. If not, countless hours can be spent trying to convince someone at a local zoning commission to let a banner hang over a railroad crossing.

Radio and television advertising is costly. In large, metropolitan markets, for example, it can cost anywhere from $600 to 10 times that and more for a 60-second TV spot in non-prime time (before 7:00 P.M. and after 10:00 P.M.). Radio can come close to that TV figure as well. Television is increasingly difficult to buy because it has become fragmented. There are not only commercial stations, but now every market is flooded with cable. What does the promoter buy? (See Chapter 9 for a further insight into media buying.)

What softens the budgetary blow in both these areas are *tradeouts* (the swapping of air time for tickets, promotions, and the like). A station could be given *x* number of tickets for on-the-air promotion. Or, maybe there is a contest that generates more than commercial time for the event. Dovetailing into this area is publicity and promotion. Publicity and promotion can make or break an event. For example, consumer interest is piqued by personalities and names. This is especially true when it comes to athletic events. Consumers like to root for people and teams—but they can only cheer for a team if they "know" someone on it and have a reason to scream for that person (i.e., a Daryl Strawberry, a Michael Jordan, or the like).

Obtaining "free" or low-cost marketing. Publicity is a key element in this budgetary mix. Generally, such PR does not require the promoter to expend as much money as advertising, but it can provide enormous media exposure. For example, setting up a radio interview with one of the major stars of a gymnastics meet or basketball game gives the public some insight into the people involved and not just the event itself. The Super Bowl does a superb job of promoting itself via publicity. Notice the number of "personality features" that are done by the media on coaches and players in the days leading up to the game.

Consumers—or attendees—get emotionally attached to people, not just events. A clear example of this is *The National Enquirer,* a gossip publication that is sold in supermarkets. Although *The National Enquirer* and world-class events may seem worlds apart, they are related. *The National Enquirer* sells five million copies a week because it offers people an insight (exaggerated or not) into what they are most interested in reading about other people. The organizers of the Super Bowl do the same thing. Suddenly, Joe X, the linebacker, becomes Joe X, husband, father, and someone who has problems aside from playing ball. Smart promoters always look for the human interest element in their events.

Estimating talent costs. The last element to consider in budgeting is the cost of the talent. What does it cost for the performers? In the case of international federations, the talent is usually free. The wrestling federation provides the competitors at no cost; the gymnastic federation provides the performers at no cost. And, in fact, the Olympics and Super Bowl provide their performers at no cost. But, when it comes to concerts, cultural events, and other outdoor activities that do not involve sports organizations, one of the highest costs for a promoter can be the talent. It is not uncommon to see a well-known musical group take $50,000 (or more) for an afternoon concert at a venue. Neither is it unusual to see an act take a hefty guarantee against a percentage of the gate, even though the gate may be admission to a fair where there are other acts and activities for which the promoter has to pay.

Of course, there are some events that do not have high talent costs. For instance, the chili cookoff provides its own entertainment in the form of a beauty contest and the wild and wierd dress of those who attend. People who come into the cookoff expect entertainment supplied by the customers and participants. Hence, the chili cookoff has a low entertainment payroll. Most of the bands that play are local and inexpensive.

RECOGNIZING THE IMPORTANCE OF CASH FLOW

The adequate budgeting of cash flow is going to be critical in determining whether the event is financially successful or not. How much money does the promoter have up-front for advertising, promotion, advance payments, and other fees? Take the following scenario:

> A promoter is staging a week-long fair at a local park. His costs will include talent, insurance, venue fencing, security, promotion, publicity, and marketing. The promoter's costs may break down as follows:

> 1. Talent: $50,000 for bands.
> 2. Insurance: $3,500 for liability.
> 3. Venue: $35,000 rental, or $5,000 per day, plus fencing costs of $6,000.
> 4. Advertising: radio ($5,000) for the week preceding the event; TV ($7,500); print ($30,000).
> 5. Flyers/billboards: $8,000.
> 6. Publicity: $8,000 for the hiring of a firm to specialize in the area.
> 7. Promotion and giveaways: $5,000.

> The promoter has costs of nearly $160,000 to stage the event. He also has $60,000 in capital. He anticipates he will sell a total of 40,000 tickets at $6 a head for a total of $240,000. Ignoring the other areas of revenue (e.g., licensing for

merchandise being sold, booth rental, souvenirs, and so on), the promoter seemingly has things in hand. But does he?

Suppose the venue asks for its entire rental in advance ($35,000) and he has to put out half the talent fees ($25,000) in advance. Suddenly, his $60,000 is gone. More important-ly, the promoter now lacks funds for advertising and promo-tion, the two key areas that will draw people and help sell tickets. Without proper advertising and promotion, advance sales may be in jeopardy and, without advance sales (and rev-enue), the promoter is not in a position to advertise even more in an effort to draw more attendees.

From this brief scenario, one thing is obvious—cash flow is king for an event because there must always be sufficient cash on hand to promote the event. To solve this problem, the promoter needs to negotiate as many back-end payments (after the event is over) as possible or obtain additional capital. Can the venue payment be put off until the end of the event? If not, will 10 percent down suffice? Will the artists accept the minimum down with a guarantee of a certified check the night the event closes?

This next example discusses an event that was actually staged. It shows the importance of cash flow.

It was a three-day carnival slated over a holiday weekend. The venue was not fenced, so the promoter was going to have to rent fencing and have it put up especially for the event. The cost for talent, venue, and promotion was $150,000. Where would the money come from; how and when would it be distributed?

The gate—the number of paid admissions—was estimat-ed at 35,000 over the three-day period. In the immediate area, there was a population of approximately 250,000 peo-ple. The promoter projected, based upon past events he (and others) had held in the area, that he could draw at least one to two percent of this potential audience per session if his pro-motion and marketing was sound. The admission was $5 a ticket for a total of $175,000. (The promoter arrived at the price by figuring that the entrance fee should not be high be-cause there would not be big name entertainment inside. In fact, most of the entertainment would be supplied by the vendors and local bands.)

The show hours were 10:00 A.M. until 10:00 P.M. With those hours, promoters can usually divide a crowd into three segments. The first crowd (10:00 A.M. until 2:00 P.M.), the afternoon group (one until 5:00 P.M.), and the evening or late crowd, 5:00 P.M. until 10:00 P.M. Dividing the 35,000 into the three days and these time periods, meant that each of the three daily segments would draw 2,500 to 3,000 people.

In order to draw the crowd, the event has to have an appeal. What's inside? What kind of enjoyment can people expect? The promoter planned on local bands supplemented by unusual exhibits and displays. The promoter staged a vintage car show; open barbecue pits with vendors selling everything from chicken to barbecued pork; rides that ranged from a ferris wheel to a kids' roller coaster; unique shops and some of the latest in technology.

With 35,000 admissions ($5) plus the sale of booths, the promoter estimated a gross of around $250,000. His expenses would run around $150,000, and he would be giving approximately $20,000 to the owner of the venue for its use. Thus, the promoter would be left with a gross profit of $80,000. Not bad for three days—if the event goes according to plan.

Planning An Appropriate Cash Flow

As you can see by the above example, the promoter has to push as many costs to the back end as possible. His advertising can be billed and paid three to four weeks after the event, and security can be paid following the event. However, some costs may be up front. For instance, the fence surrounding the venue required 50 percent down. The promoter estimated his advertising and publicity expenditures to be in the neighborhood of $50,000. Once again, most of this could be paid afterwards.

With most tickets being sold on impulse (at the gate) there is no need for a computerized ticket agency or other similar firm. The challenge for the promoter is to come up with enough cash flow so he can pay those bills which require advance payments so he can "open" the event. The promoter generated a portion of the funds through booth sales. He sold them for $300 each, and required 50 percent down. With 30 booth sales he generated approximately $4,500 prior to the show.

Using Sponsorships

How else did the promoter in our example generate funds? Through an area that has impacted world class, special, and local events more than anything during the past five years—*sponsorships*. For today's promoter/managers, sponsorships have become a lucrative and relatively new source of revenues; a source we will cover in-depth in Chapter 5.

SUMMARY

After reading this chapter, you should be aware of the basics of the promoter and site selection process. Keep the following 10 tips in mind when putting together your initial proposal:

1. Each international or major national sport has a governing body that sets the site selection rules.
2. Not all international/national sports generate high guarantees. It depends upon supply and demand.
3. International federations want more than a profit. They want their athletes to be treated well.
4. International federations are interested in propagating their sports.
5. Promoters/managers have two markets to sell—the international federations or national governing bodies and the consumers who will (hopefully) attend the event.
6. Promoters/managers need to keep abreast of activities in the international/national arena by reading trade journals that specialize in reporting on events.
7. Promoters/managers should remember that a date scheduled at a university is not definite until every department in the school approves it.
8. Venues vary and promoters/managers will find that in some they can negotiate for a portion of the parking, concessions, and programs.
9. Unions are usually stronger in the Northeast and Midwest, and less strict in the South and far West.
10. The most critical element in promoting an event is budgeting properly so that cash flow does not become a problem. Without the cash to support the right promotion effort, it is almost impossible for the event to be a success.

In this chapter, we discussed the basics of the selection process for various events. Once selected, bidding for a special event takes both experience and creativity. Chapter 4 discusses the ins and outs of the bidding process by providing both real-world examples and tips to present a well-organized and professional bid.

CHAPTER FOUR

The Ins and Outs of Bidding

Imagine an event that needs 425 buses, 65 limousines, 16,000 hotel rooms, 70 suites, a 70,000 seat stadium, the rights to all novelty sales for the event, 750 working spaces for the media, and a 10,000-square foot interviewing facility for the press.

If you can, you have just put yourself in the place of the promoters/ managers who bid on behalf of communities for the Super Bowl, professional football's world championship game, a game that has become such a popular attraction that Super Bowl Sunday is as much a holiday for football fans as July 4. The written bid that is submitted is a mammoth document that typically runs more than 100 pages, detailing everything from the number of suites that will be available for NFL personnel to letters pledging support and cooperation from every community and politician in the area.

The game, which is traditionally played on a Sunday toward the end of January, has such a large viewing audience that retail stores resemble ghost towns on the day of the event. Super Bowl "sales" and "Super Sunday Promotions" can be held any day of the week—except for Super Bowl Sunday.

In an effort to attract this premier event, promoters/managers and the cities they represent offer everything from free stadium rental, all parking receipts, and catered parties to free helicopters that will shuttle VIPs in and out of the stadium the day of the game.

This one-day event actually consists of more than a week of parties and celebrations that have to be bid, planned, and negotiated—and have their infrastructure in place—three to four years before the game is played. The demands and requirements laid down by the NFL are enormous, but international federations and governing councils can be just as demanding.

Even less celebrated special events can cause a promoter to wring his/ her hands and pull his/her hair out. A case in point—the Michael Jackson Victory Tour. As part of Jackson's contract, the promoter had to fulfill a requirement that a portion of the stage be glass, and underneath it—beneath the stage—a disco had to be constructed.

While Jackson sang and frolicked on the glass above, his friends and entourage danced beneath it. If audiences wondered why the talented artist sometimes laughed in the midst of a song, it was because he frequently glanced down at the group below in the disco. The demands put on the promoters for the Jackson tour were so great (and expensive) that the concerts—although mammoth box office winners—turned out to be a unprofitable for the promoters.

Glass stages are not, of course, everyday requirements, but promoters should be aware that the fees and percentages paid to artist's agents and federations are only part of the price tag for a special event. The Bolshoi dancers may require only certified fresh mountain spring water in their dressing rooms, while the Joffrey Ballet may insist that there be no smoking in any part of the theater or lobby, and that limousines must be available between the hotel and venue whenever needed.

Most perks do not come out of left field without warning. Promoters usually know about them ahead of time because they are spelled out in bids and/or contracts. They are negotiated and added to the agreement. Some perks (e.g., free helicopter rides to the venues, limousine service for 60 people, a party for the performing artist's friends) can represent whopping financial expenditures.

WHAT IS AND IS NOT NEGOTIABLE

Every artist, event, and/or manager representing a special event is going to ask the promoter for as much as they can get. In an effort to sign the attraction, some promoters may go overboard and promise everything that is asked. That can be a disastrous mistake. Promoters have to carefully analyze what they can and cannot afford based entirely on projected revenues (see Chapter 3). The trick is for the promoter to understand what is and what is not negotiable. Checking with previous promoters and/or hosts of the event can provide significant help in this area. But some special events are in such demand that the organizers and agents know they can ask for virtually anything and probably get it. When was the last time, for instance, that a promoter turned down the NFL's request for another perk for the Super Bowl? That turndown has not yet occurred.

When San Diego hosted the Super Bowl a few years ago, the promoters/managers of the event came up with a clever revenue-generating event, designed to offset some of the staging costs. The city, which promoted and managed the event, constructed a private hospitality area adjacent to the stadium, and entertained more than 6,000 guests at prices ranging up to $289 per person. The gate was in excess of $1.6 million—a figure that did not escape the shrewd eye of the NFL.

When it came time for the next city to bid on the game, the NFL had written into the contract a hospitality area requirement so it could hold a party similar to the one thrown in San Diego. Seeing an opportunity to dangle another perk before the NFL, nearly all the bidders mentioned that they would turn all revenues from the area over to the NFL. As a result, a tented hospitality area was constructed prior to the Tampa, Florida game. More than 7,000 people paid $295 (and more) to attend the pre-game event. In the 1991 bid from Los Angeles and Pasadena (the first combined entry by the two cities), the NFL was offered free use of more than 1.5 million square feet of space adjacent to the Rose Bowl for such a hospitality area.

A hospitality area is just one example of a negotiable item. Agreements can be extremely creative. The most important factor to remember, though, is that all items should be negotiated and bid on before the agreement is signed. If some simple steps are followed, the bid will cover all of the most important negotiable points of any agreement. But, first let's discuss how an organization or city (represented by a promoter/manager) qualifies to bid on a special event.

THE BID LIST

Most cities that have staged events are on a *bid list*. That is, the national or international organizing committee has been requested (by the community and/or promoter/manager) to add them to a list, and notify them whenever an event is coming up for bid. Many cities still do not make the list, even after they request it, because the organizing committees are overwhelmed with their own activities and forget to add the new name. Thus, any promoter who is interested in being kept abreast of the activities of these international groups has to keep tabs on the organization.

Even cities that have successfully put on major events find themselves left off bid lists. This is not a snub, it just happens. That's why promoter follow-up and constant contact with these groups is imperative. For promoters who are anxious to find a more tangible way of following up, there is a book published in Monaco by the international federations which outlines events and tells where they will be held. The reference book may have a 10-year rundown; it all depends how far in advance the event is awarded. For instance, if a federation has a policy of awarding a world championship in a sport to communities six years in advance of the competition, the book for that sport will show the five cities that are slated to host the event prior to that date.

In some cases, there is an extensive time gap between the bidding process and the actual event. It may be years from the time a city first bids for the Olympics, for example, and the start of the actual Games. Why so long? First, it takes *politicking*. The promoter/manager or organization representing the hopeful community initially may wine, dine, and host members of the U.S. Olympic Committee (USOC). The USOC then selects the American city that will vie internationally for the event. This is by no means a reflection of this politicking. It does not mean that the city who does the best job of wining and dining the USOC is going to get the bid. On the contrary, sometimes too much wining and dining can turn off an organizing committee. It suffices to say, promoters/managers have to tread lightly and be able to "read" the members of the USOC and any other federations and organizing committees.

The pre-Olympic tug-of-war among U.S. cities can take up to two years. Once the USOC has made its choice, the IOC (International Olympic Committee) may spend another 18 months making a selection. For a city seeking to win the Games in 2004, the bidding process starts in 1996 and ends in the year 1998.

Maneuvering for every big event may not take six or eight years, but it can be filled with pressure. The 1994 World Cup of Soccer is a good example. The 1994 event was awarded to the United States by the international federation. The International Federation designated the U.S. Soccer Federation (USSF) as the organization responsible for selecting the American cities that would host the event. In turn, the USSF formed an organization called World Cup USA, 1994. This body was given the duty of evaluating bids and making the selection from cities that applied within the United States.

Not surprisingly, 27 cities submitted written bids for the 1994 event. The 1984 Olympics, with its massive soccer crowds, accelerated the appeal of the sport in this country. Couple that with the number of immigrants from Europe and Latin America—where soccer is king—and it is easy to see why bidding was so competitive.

In most cases, the organizing committee visits each city that has been named a finalist; however, in the case of the 1994 Cup, the USSF decided to have all 27 cities present an oral bid in Los Angeles in May of 1991. Delegations from more than two dozen hopeful U.S. cities made presentations—and waited. Approximately eight to 12 of the 27 cities will be selected to host at least one of the soccer games.

Interestingly, a number of the cities brought along local politicians as part of the oral presentation to verify, in person, what the written bid disclosed. This approach can have a tremendous impact, particularly if the politician on hand is a high-ranking official from a major city. The final impact of these outside parties will be determined when the USSF makes its recommendation and the cities are selected.

THE BIDDING PROCESS

The Request for Proposal

Oral bids are only one side of the bidding process. The written agreement for many special events involves responding in writing to a Request for Proposal or RFP. RFPs are simply documents in which the sanctioning or governing body specifies the guidelines and procedures for submitting a bid proposal. RFPs usually contain specifications for form and content, and often include a list of specific questions to be answered by the bidder. Often the RFP will contain information on the evaluation process as well. For the most sophisticated events, bidders try to present their case in the most attractive fashion, sometimes spending lavish amounts on graphic designs and presentations.

RFPs in the Public Sector. For many years, the RFP was a vehicle used only by public or government agencies. For example, if a city wants a new sewer line installed or a stretch of highway constructed by a private firm, it opens the work up to competitive bids from previous vendors as well as new ones who prepare and submit a proposal. When it comes to the government, RFPs are written in a language that often can be understood only by vendors who have dealt previously with such beaurocracies. In many cases (especially when it comes to things like ordnance, the defense industry, and other technical products), the RFP can be technical and difficult to follow for any company that has not been previously involved in the process.

RFPs in the Private Sector. RFPs have made the transition from the public to the private sector. Prior to the widespread use of the RFP process governing bodies were forced to look at a myriad of proposals, each organized in a different way. They were difficult to compare and evaluate. With the introduction of the RFP, the bidders were all instructed to answer the same questions and provide similar data. Today, the RFP is a vehicle through which promoters/managers submit bids and compete for major events in a more standardized form. Within the RFP, both the NFL and the IOC can state their varied requirements, but each can expect similar proposals from competing bidders. Thankfully, most of these RFPs are written in practical, how-to terms so that any promoter will be able to answer the questions.

Limiting the Competition

Just as RFPs in the public sector can be slanted, so can those in the private arena. An organizing committee may request venues that only a certain city can supply, or it may ask for housing that only exists in one city. The federation responsible for awarding the World Cup Soccer games, for example, has a requirement that the host city's stadium must have natural turf. Serious bidders with artificial turf in their stadiums, must answer the bid by pledging to remove the artificial turf and replace it with natural grass.

The Super Bowl RFP requests that cities have a certain temperature during January. Within the answers to the RFP, the promoters/managers have to document mean January temperatures for their city. If they do not meet the NFL's criteria, then the only way the community will get the game is if it has a domed stadium.

RFPs often have long and involved questions that spell out requirements ranging from logistics and the type of venues required to financial requests (e.g., advance monies) and housing, transportation needs, and other event-related requirements. The Super Bowl RFP, which contains anywhere from 10 to 12 pages of questions or requests, poses a plethora of items to be addressed by the bidder. The following are just a sampling of the questions and/or requests for information:

1. Firm and binding (not tentative) advance commitments, including a statement on maximum room (rack) rates and minimum length of stay required from area hotels (three or four days recommended).
2. Firm and binding commitments, including guarantees on rates and total number available from transportation companies, including availability in numbers of buses, limousines (limited guarantees),

taxis, and rental cars. (The NFL needs 425 buses, 65 limos; exclusively signed agreements on these should be noted). A detail of the access and costs for up to 100 school buses for use by the pre-game and half-time shows.

The first question reveals how complex a Super Bowl can be. When the NFL says "firm and binding," it means the promoter has to have the rooms lined up when the bid is made. That takes cooperation from all the hotels, as well as a solid political infrastructure. This one request is an indication of why Super Bowls take the effort of an entire, united community.

The second question indicates that additional community cooperation and effort is going to be needed. Some promoters in evaluating this second question see the possibility for a cost-saving opportunity. For example, although buses are part of the bid process, what would happen if the community offered to pay for a portion of the transportation required? This brings us to the difference between implied and required costs.

Implied versus Required Bids

Promoters have to weigh what is implied and what is required. There are two kinds of *implied requirements*—things that actually decrease the federation and/or artist's costs, and those that make the performer's visit more comfortable. An example: Live Aid, the concert that was held a few years ago in London and Philadelphia to benefit the starving people in Africa, would have benefited significantly if the promoter/manager of the event had arranged for free hotel or a transportation discount for the performers. This assistance would have shown up on the bottom line immediately. It would have lowered the cost of doing business and, of course, increased the profits.

On the other hand, suppose the promoter had arranged for limousine transportation from the airport to the studio instead of a special bus. Either way, the promoter was picking up the tab, but in the former case it would have made the artist's stay more pleasant but not necessarily more profitable. Or, perhaps the promoter was able to arrange for the artists to clear customs without going through the terminal or waiting in line. It may not add dollars to the bottom line, but it can be an implied requirement that means a great deal to the performer.

Astute promoters carefully analyze what is implied versus what is required in an RFP. The organizing body or an agent may not ask for certain perks, but the RFP may offer the opportunity to present them. The Super Bowl RFP is loaded with possibilities for implied requirements. They can, of course, be ignored but that will not help the promoter's bid. Astute promoters are also aware of their competition and develop strategies to "do one better" wherever possible.

Returning once again to the list of questions on the Super Bowl RFP, still other areas give promoters/managers an indication of how massive the

Super Bowl promotion is going to be and how critical it is to have community interaction and cooperation. Look at the following question, for example:

3. Provide a statement of cooperation from game-related services, especially police agencies.

This, of course, would never happen without the complete backing of the political infrastructure within a community. Some of the other questions in the NFL RFP ask:

4. Provide adjacent or nearby hotels (total rooms needed 900) to media headquarters for spillover of related groups (200 to 400 rooms each)—indicate meeting space. Press rate needed at the same or lower rate than headquarters. All spillover hotel recommendations must be accompanied by a signed letter from that hotel confirming block, rate, deposit, cancellation, cut-off date, and guarantee policies.
5. Provide accommodations including 60 to 70 suites and 600 rooms for NFL officials' family members in top quality hotels (i.e., club owners, top club personnel, and their parties).
6. Provide top facilities for the TV network covering game (750 rooms including numerous suites over that which they place at the headquarters hotel) ideally in three hotels—sales, production, and technicians. Also top quality rooms for the networks not covering (75 to 100 rooms each, including suites).
7. Provide arrangements for half-time show production staff, field preparation crews, and the like at a property near the stadium or rehearsal site (property similar to Residence Inn) at a reduced rate for a 10-day to three-week stay (50 rooms).

Suddenly, it becomes much clearer why a Super Bowl (or Olympics) has such a great economic impact. While many cities can supply these accommodations, how many will offer incentives (e.g., a portion of the rooms free, free or low-cost transportation, and so on)? That's where the shrewd promoters and committees with negotiating know-how and the ability to read the "implied" requirements excel—and win the bid.

Demanding? Yes. Worthwhile? Yes, especially when events of this type can pump millions into a community. Although economic studies on the Super Bowl impact may be flawed, it suffices to say that the influx of funds can reach $100 million or more. When Phoenix bid for the game, the promoters/managers estimated that there would be a $225 million influx to the local economy. The city won the event based on its competitive bid, but later lost it for political reasons.

FIGURE 4–1.   *RFP Guidelines*

1. The RFP (Request for Proposal) poses questions in the order the sanctioning organization would like them to be answered.
2. The RFP was originally utilized in the public or governmental sector; however, today they are used by virtually every special event committee to find the best community, venues, and promoters/managers.
3. The RFP is almost always written in easy-to-understand, practical terms.
4. The RFP spells out everything from logistics to the type of venues required.
5. Don't hesitate to have direct discussions with the sanctioning organization if you have any questions concerning the RFP.

The RFP, although only previously used in the public sector, has "come of age" in the private sector. Become familiar with the types of questions asked and learn the difference between what is implied and what is required. (See Figure 4–1 for a list of guidelines concerning today's RFPs.)

The Real Bottom Line

For cities that understand the bottom line—prestige, notoriety, and image building—special events can be a bonanza. The Super Bowl brings hordes of free-spending visitors to a city. The communities involved may not receive any gate revenue, or concession or parking fees, but the area comes out a winner because, in many cases, more than 80 percent of those who attend the game are from outside the area. This increase in tourism will be a significant stimulus to the local economy.

Equaling the benefit of the increased tourism dollar figure is the increased TV exposure for an area generated by an event (world class, major, or special). A chamber of commerce could save its membership fees for 100 years and it would never be able to match the media coverage and notoriety that a Super Bowl generates. When it comes to bidding and negotiating for these high profile, glamorous events, the governing bodies hold the cards. Super Bowls do not have to negotiate contracts, cities do.

GENERATING THE BIG IDEAS

Imaginative promoters do not have to wait for RFPs to come from federations before orchestrating an event. International governing bodies are not only interested in regulating their sports, but in making money as well. They are open to proposals from promoters.

Ideas for other events can come from trade journals (e.g., *Billboard* and *Amusement Business*) and the many conventions that are held for fairs, carnivals, and sports. From Chicago, there is a *Special Events Report* that promoters can subscribe to, to keep abreast of events that may be looking for bidders.

Developing Events

Competing with other cities is not the only way for promoters to attract a special event. It is possible for a community to develop its own. That's what the international chili cookoff did for one small Texas town and one small ghost town in California. In fact, the 300 communities that license the chili cookoff name have accomplished the same type of development. Promoters in large communities are in a position to develop events that can turn into major attractions as well. Most of the time, these self-developed events require no negotiation with any governing bodies.

There is always a chance to develop something new. Let's look at what some creative promoters involved with Los Angeles sports came up with. The idea was for an international baseball game and tournament that would be held in Dodger Stadium. Teams from North and South America would compete against the rest of the world. Cubans, North Americans, and South Americans would compete side by side on the same team. On the other team would be Koreans, Dutch, Italians, Australians, and everyone else willing to compete. The appeal was more than just countries competing against each other in baseball. Part of the lure was that Cubans and Americans would be teammates; an interesting concept that would draw thousands of curiosity-seekers as well as baseball fans. The idea also had an element that could give the promoters/manager a solid hook for TV coverage.

This idea was for one event that might be "made for Los Angeles" because of the area's diverse ethnic groups. Instead of running head-on into other competing events being held in the city, the concept of the international baseball game, complete with competing nations on the same side, could be an event that promoters of other attractions being held during the same time period might dread.

At one time, an event of this type may have been a longshot at best. How could the Cubans and Americans be brought together? But the world is changing along with international competition. It is possible to negotiate anything, particularly where some countries—hard-pressed for dollars—can see a payoff.

Be creative! Think big! But remember, planning means everything. Even the simplest event requires a good plan, a well-researched bid, and professional negotiations.

THE BIDDING AND NEGOTIATING DIFFERENCE

When it comes to bidding and negotiating, there is a big difference between major events—an international baseball tournament, Pan Am Games,

Super Bowl, or Olympics—and the one-night concert or cultural event. Major events involve cities and entire communities in what can turn into months of arduous negotiations. The key difference is that events that involve a promoter negotiating on behalf of an entire community are usually not private sector events. The public is going to foot the bill if the promoter errs. There are taxpayer dollars at stake.

These promoters are in the business to enhance a community image and generate a positive economic impact. Profit is usually not the prime motivation. On the other hand, the special events that are put on independently by private promoters have to be money-making ventures. The promoter of Guns 'N Roses has to make a profit. Every dollar they spend to rent venues, hire security, and arrange transportation comes out of their pocket. They cannot—as in the case of cities that bid for the Super Bowl—give too much away simply to obtain the date. Even major event promoters and managers representing cities and communities conduct a thorough financial analysis before agreeing to provide an event organizing committee with perks that may cost thousands—or millions—of dollars. This is particularly true in today's economic climate, which finds local governments short of funds and not anxious to hear taxpayer complaints about spending money frivously on a "game."

Before giving the NFL free use of the Rose Bowl for the Super Bowl, the cities of Los Angeles and Pasadena studied the impact, the loss of revenue, and the advantages to the community for such a event. They found that both their financial and civic image would be improved by such an event. Although Los Angeles is known throughout the world, hosting a Super Bowl once again would put a bright spotlight on the community. The additional exposure would be well worth the cost of staging the event.

THE FUNDING DIFFERENCE

The private promoter/manager has to go for the dollars and, in doing so, he or she often will back an event that a governmental agency would not be equipped to handle. The private promoter/manager has more latitude and creativity. He or she can focus on special events that the public sector would avoid. Astute private promoters know that not all major events involve athletics or culture. One of the hottest special events in the country today is the appearance of personalities or celebrities as speakers. These name personalities/celebrities draw significant audiences and can be used to bolster an event or even headline one. Most belong to a speaker's bureau. The following is a recent example:

> General Norman Schwarzkopf, the hero of the Persian Gulf War, became one of the hottest speakers in the country during 1991. With his appeal, he could headline an event or be part of a larger one. The General's fee is roughly $70,000 per

engagement, or $20,000 more than former President Ronald Reagan commands. With the right size auditorium, a promoter could stage a one-nighter with the General and come away with a signficiant profit. The advantage of the one-man show is he (or she) is less expensive, the overhead is better controlled, and the negotiations with the speaker's bureau are relatively easy, as compared with dealing with a rock group's agency or trying to bring a cultural attraction to an area.

However, there are items that involve the General's appearance that can mount up to significant expenditures. These include the General's airfare (first class, round-trip) and room requirements. Wherever the General speaks, he normally gets an entire floor of a hotel for security reasons. When these items are added to the speaking fee, the cost of staging a one-night event with the General can be increased almost 30 percent. Thus, a promoter has to plan on direct, speaker-related expenses of nearly $100,000 and not just a $70,000 speaker fee.

The General is the type of "act" that promoters find fits in perfectly when it comes to providing an event for a corporation or for a company that may want to impress its clientele. Although it is usually not part of the contract, frequently the promoter has to ask such speakers to stay around after their speech for a private reception.

There is no question that the General brings the media and publicity with him wherever he speaks. Unfortunately, as with most well-known speakers, the media is only allowed in if the speaker/attraction permits it. Former President Reagan's advisors did not permit the media in on his talks. General Schwarzkopf is highly selective as well.

Part of the prohibition is due to the speaker's agents knowing that a great deal of the charm of a former President or General is the mystique that surrounds them. What will they say? Once an audience knows, the aura begins to dissipate, and their value as a speaker diminishes. Neither Reagan or the General say anything of shattering consequence. But, if the word got around as to exactly what they talked about during these speaking engagements, it would enable groups to evaluate the speaker based upon the content of a previous speech. That is not what agents want. They prefer the speaker's value to be determined by his reputation as a former President, former General, or as a personality.

It does not take a General or former President to attract crowds either. Notre Dame football coach Lou Holtz generated approximately $25,000 for an hour-long talk and for more than a year was the hottest commodity on the speaker's circuit. Basketball coach Pat Riley pulled down $15,000 for a similar address. Most of the time, these speakers develop quickly. For instance, Pat Riley was a hot attraction when he took the Los Angeles

Lakers to a world championship. Lou Holtz was in demand when he coached Notre Dame to a national championship. There are always new-comers—the public can be fickle.

Promoters/managers should be constantly evaluating new faces and personalities. The promoters who calculated Schwarzkopf would be a big draw as a speaker were able to save thousands of dollars if they negotiated his speaking fees early on. Those who waited until the General donned his civilian clothes, were in for a rude shock worth $70,000 for a 45-minute talk.

World record-holders, famous authors, psychologists who tell companies how to run their firms, and other speakers with a growing identity make excellent headliners for a special event or, depending upon their appeal, can be a special event themselves. Following the 1984 Olympics, there were few speakers more in demand than Peter Ueberroth. (Ueberroth, however, limited his engagements and donated most of his speaking fees.)

Despite the price and some of the fringe requirements asked by such parties as Schwarzkopf's agent, the negotiations may simply involve a five-minute (or less) telephone call. The lengthy RFP or complex bid is replaced by a simple letter of agreement. Obviously, good communication skills are imperative when negotiating this type of agreement. Again, plan in advance of all the aspects of the event to be covered in the letter of agreement.

BEHIND-THE-SCENES LOBBYING

Obviously, not all international events require lengthy answers to RFPs because they are not very complex attractions. In fact, for most sporting trials and events, the proposals submitted by promoters run only five to 10 pages. Often, the real effort is in the lobbying that surrounds the event. Smart promoters do their homework and study the competing cities and communities. They find out who the decision-makers will be. As is the case with many events, the members of the federation may defer the actual decision making to a small, site selection group. The committee, which functions as a staff, may only consist of three to five members even though the governing body may have a large board of directors. Astute promoters/managers recognize this organizational structure and know that the challenge is to impress those individuals because they are the real decision makers.

SUMMARY

The bidding process requires both oral and written negotiation skills. In order to stage a successful event, keep the following 10 tips in mind during the bidding and negotiation process.

1. Perks are either spelled out in an agreement or negotiated and then added to the agreement.
2. The more demand there is for an event, the less chance there is of negotiating concessions.
3. Promoters/managers and communities should be on bid lists to keep abreast of international events and opportunities.
4. Oral presentations may be required along with written bids by international governing bodies.
5. "Implied" language in a bid gives a promoter/manager an opportunity to outbid competitors.
6. Although some special events may not make money for a community, the bottom line is often prestige, notoriety, and image building for the area.
7. Promoters/managers do not just have to bid on established events. In many cases, their community affords them the opportunity to stage and develop events that are entirely new.
8. Ideas for events can come from industry trade publications.
9. A thorough financial analysis of an event is a must before promoters/managers commit to anything.
10. Behind-the-scenes lobbying is often more effective than a well-written proposal or bid.

As with all stages of special events management, planning plays a major role in the bidding and negotiation process. A well-researched bid, a professionally presented proposal, and the proper negotiations will not only help to ensure the award of a special event, but will aid in the smooth execution of all aspects of the event itself.

Once the bid has been accepted and the negotiations are finalized, the hard work begins in earnest—staging the event itself. Chapter 5 discusses how to get started.

CHAPTER FIVE

Preparing for the Event—Setting Up Basic Operations

As anecdotes, the following stories are amusing. But for those promoting the 1984 Olympic Games, two occurrences—the "incident at Lake Casitas" and the "Libyan Connection"—were anything but funny.

It all started with the site selection for the 1984 Olympic rowing competition. The 1984 Games in Los Angeles were noted for the myriad venues that were utilized—from San Diego in the south to Ventura County in the north (a distance of approximately 200 miles).

Lake Casitas, which is located just north of Los Angeles, is a picturesque, sprawling waterway that is used by fishermen throughout southern California. Activities on the Lake are controlled by the Ventura County Department of Fish & Game, which, along with the city, was proud to showcase the charming spot. Everything went smoothly until a little-known law suddenly became an issue. In Ventura County, any waterway that is used for drinking water cannot be used for swimming, and although those Olympic competitors on the Lake would not be donning their trunks, they did have a tradition of tossing the winning coxswain in the water following a match. To the Ventura County Fish & Game people, that was akin to swimming. The Olympic Games and the small Fish & Game department found themselves in a standoff.

The International Rowing Federation did not demand a change of venue or anything drastic when the problem developed. Instead, the officials left the solving of the problem to the local organizing committee and the community.

Not to be outdone by this watery dilemma, officials in Washington, D.C., were about to introduce another problem: A Libyan journalist accompanying his country's athletes and coaches to Los Angeles ran into a government roadblock. The U.S. State Department denied his entry on the grounds he was a "high risk" visitor. The Libyans retaliated and pulled out of the Games.

No one, of course, will ever know the real reason the Libyans pulled out. Was it true political indignation or just a political maneuver designed to increase its visibility with other Third World countries? Nor will anyone ever know if there was a particular agenda behind the State Department's giving a "high risk" classification to the journalist.

DEALING WITH THE PUBLIC SECTOR

The Lake Casitas and the Libyan examples illustrate the problems that can be encountered by promoters/managers when it comes to staging events and dealing with the public and the private sectors. The 1984 Games were staged by a private entity, but they involved officials ranging from local city councilpeople to the State Department, FBI, and CIA. There are, in fact, few events that can be staged without involving some government entity.

Of course, not all events are going to cause stirrings in Washington, D.C., but surprisingly, a local event can cause ramifications at the state level. Once again, take the 1984 Games, for example. Although they were held primarily in Los Angeles County, there were extensive dealings with the state when it came to selecting venues. The Coliseum, where all track and field events were held, was (at the time) governed by a triumvirate—the city of Los Angeles, the county of Los Angeles, and the state of California. (Los Angeles is not the only city to have a venue with this type of unusual arrangement.) Each entity had three votes and nothing happened without a majority approval from the nine members.

Obviously, dealing with three different government bodies takes *time*—and that is a critical factor that must be considered when dealing with a publicly owned venue Remember, if dealing with the public sector, allow extra time. The government moves very slowly. It sometimes moves inexplicably, as well.

How to Handle Government Bureaucracy

With the layers of beaurocracy frequently encountered in government, it behooves promoters/managers to develop a list of who controls the venues (e.g., is it a private or public promoter?). Which agencies are involved? The public sector is going to be involved regardless of whether the venue is privately or publicly owned. And when it comes to dealing with the government, the key to minimizing problems and misunderstandings is adequate communication. There must be a continual flow of information to every public organization that conceivably could be involved in the event.

Public officials tend to be extremely sensitive about activities that are planned for their jurisdictions as they are a direct reflection of their judgment, clout, and so on. If, for instance, a promoter is bringing an event to a venue in a community, the councilperson or local politician who represents that area must hear about it first! Promoters should make every effort to see the local politician in person and explain the event and its benefits to the community. The politician or his staff should be consulted on an ongoing basis. Political figures do not like surprises and if the venue or date is being changed, they should know about it. Failure to communicate is the prime cause for delays in issuing permits and licenses.

The First Steps in Staging an Event in the Public Sector

Staging any event is going to require at least:

1. securing a venue; and
2. obtaining permits.

For promoters, one of the first steps should be to determine what public agencies might be involved in the permit process. For example:

- If an event is going to involve food, the health department may be involved.
- If it involves securing a city recreation facility, the parks and recreation department will be involved.

If possible, the meetings should be in person. There is nothing like a face-to-face meeting to clear up misconceptions and solve potential problems. Early contact and communication with the proper agencies are a must. If the channels have been opened properly, when it comes time for the promoter/manager to obtain a permit, waive a fee, or obtain some other form of approval, the process will move more smoothly.

Underestimating the Complexities of Dealing with Public Sector

The most common mistake made by promoters/managers is underestimating the complexity of dealing with government—an oversight that can lead to a misstep that may come back to haunt the promoter. If, for instance, a venue is controlled by more than one public agency, the promoter should make sure that all parties concerned sign the contract. If just one entity signs, the other can always (later) claim they did not agree. Where does that leave a promoter, especially if the event is only weeks away and tickets have been sold?

Dealing with agencies requires constant follow-up as well. If a permit was granted but not delivered, the promoter must make sure he obtains it before the event opens. If not, the entire event can be shut down by one aggressive inspector. Many events take place at night when it is impossible to reach anyone at a public agency. If the event is shut down then, it might as well be cancelled.

Sometimes, public agencies have a difficult time making a decision, hence the importance of getting them information early. One of the most graphic illustrations of what can happen belongs to a recent Olympic Games. The Games, of course, use multi-venues and it is relatively easy for the promoter to miscalculate, especially if they have been verbally assured that everything will be alright. At this particular Olympics, the organizers had been promised the availability of a specific venue, but nothing was signed. Time dragged on and still nothing happened. As a last resort, the frustrated organizing committee made an appearance before the committee in charge of the venue. He explained to them that time was growing short, and his crew had to begin work immediately if the venue was to be ready in time. The committee continued to vacillate.

Additional time went by. Just a few months before the opening of the Games, the committee had still not voted approval. The public agency had a difficult time making a decision about when the organizing committee could bring in bulldozers and other equipment to start the changes. They controlled a public entity and were concerned there would be a backlash from taxpaying citizens if a public venue was shut down and remodeled.

The delays continued up to 90 days before the Games' opening. The organizing committee knew they would not be able to finish the changes if they did not start within the next two to three days. At the meeting of the agency that afternoon, they took a chance. The organizing committee announced to those in the room that the bulldozers would be arriving the next morning. With that announcement—and an additional fee—the agency suddenly made a decision and with only hours to spare, the workers were given approval to start. To the promoters, it offers a clear lesson: Never underestimate the time it takes for a public agency to issue approval.

Dealing with Agencies

The "Taste of Chicago," the "National Rib Cookoff" in Cleveland, and the New York and Boston Marathons are all smooth-running private or quasi-public events that offer insights into the complexities of dealing with political figures and agencies. Two of these events involve food, which means that the promoters not only have to obtain permits from health departments, but from the sanitation departments (since they must clear the refuse). The promoter may also find himself dealing with the food vendors' union who may claim that the event threatens to take away sales from unionized operations.

Even in the non-food events, the impact of the public sector can be surprising. Take, for instance, a marathon. Streets have to be blocked off, which requires fire department approval. Transportation departments may also be involved because the course may disrupt traffic patterns, bus routes, and other forms of public transit.

The 1993 Super Bowl, which will be staged in Pasadena, California, is, of course, a private event (i.e., the National Football League). But few events, whether they are staged by a private or public organization, involve more agencies or require the cooperation of virtually every department within a city.

In this case, two cities (Los Angeles and Pasadena) are involved. Both have to agree on everything from how traffic problems and sanitation will be handled to security and police protection. Even the FAA (Federal Aviation Authority) gets involved because private helicopters are utilizing airspace to transport VIPs to and from the game.

Early communication with these agencies makes all the difference when it comes to granting permits in a timely manner. Obviously, in the case of the Super Bowl, agencies are going to make the path extremely smooth because the event has the backing of every political and public figure in the area. Things will get done, and quickly!

But, when it comes to smaller events that will not attract wide notoriety or an abundance of political support, promoters should do their homework and get opinions from commissions and departments long before final plans are drawn. Asking people for their help and opinions not only generates input, but it helps develop rapport between the public agency and private promoter. Everyone is flattered when they are asked for their opinion, and if those in an agency feel their suggestions were seriously considered and utilized by the promoter, the agency may grant faster approvals and permits.

SETTING UP SECURITY: A CRITICAL PLAN

Equally as complex as dealing with government agencies—and even more perplexing—is arranging security for substantial special events. Promoters need it, but they hope they never have to use it. And when it does have to be used, there is nothing that can drive a promoter/manager's blood pressure up higher or faster.

With any Olympics, there are many concerns. Security for the Olympic Village is an issue that ranges from what nations are going to be housed next to each other to protecting the Village. At the Los Angeles Games, concerns centered on the Village location, transportation of the athletes, and airport arrivals and departures. In Atlanta, similar concerns are being felt as they prepare for 1996.

Security, however, is not something that just applies to the Olympics with its world-famous athletes, or to art exhibits, with their valuable paintings, or to rock concerts, with legendary performers. It applies to every event—and every event must deal with it.

Usually there are two levels of security:

1. The security supplied by the venue. In the case of a theater or a major league baseball game, this may simply consist of the normal complement of ushers, supplemented by a few off-duty police officers.
2. Professional law enforcement and security personnel.

If a baseball game were to suddenly become an international event with competing teams from nations around the world, security would have to expand to include everyone from the FBI and CIA to a competing team's own internal security force. Security not only becomes a matter of protecting the performers/athletes from any possible outside problems, but from themselves as well. Typically, if security involves athletes, the international governing body will set the rules and requirements because they have the responsibility for the safety of the performers.

If the event involves a musical act, the venue may have its own security. Often, additional protection requirements stipulated by the agency representing the act will be written into the contract. The performers may also have their own internal security.

Who is in Charge?

Which security takes precedence? Who gives the orders? There are usually "layers" of security personnel. If, for instance, the event is a major league baseball game, the home team is going to be responsible for security. If the game becomes an international event, the FBI, CIA, State Department, and other government agencies take precedence over local security. There may also be security people from each of the international teams.

A promoter may find himself dealing with an international event that has all three layers. In this case, the government (e.g., FBI) may make suggestions to the performer's security staff. Between the two, they will decide upon the appropriate procedures. At the bottom of the pyramid will be the venue's security. Usually, they will take orders from the host government's entity.

Security for One-Shot versus Ongoing Events

For events that are repeated night after night in the same venue, there is an obvious security advantage—the promoter and security people get used to procedures. The mistakes made during the first performance can be eliminated during subsequent evenings. The major league baseball team with 81 home games can certainly hone its procedures within a few games, as can the pro football team that has eight or nine home games. Ongoing events have a definite security advantage. But the one-shot, one-night concert, the special trade show, or convention does not have such an advantage. Each event differs and each has varying requirements. A jewelry show may require inordinate security while a business opportunity expo requires only minimal protection. The jewelry show may have security after-hours and throughout the night, while the business expo may utilize security only until closing.

Security in Different Venues

An artist may tour across country and give the same show in every city; however, venues differ as do the crowds. Security has to be adjusted because of the configuration of the stadiums and the psychological bent of the crowds. Younger audiences can be more boisterous and threatening, while older people may be well-mannered with few problems. Rock concerts can cause mammoth security problems, while country concerts and festivals, which usually have an older audience, may offer only a fraction of the problem. The following are a few of the better-known examples of security plans gone awry.

Perhaps no performing group has encountered (or caused) more security problems than the legendary Beatles. Initially, they were a group that attracted young teens. But, by the time they embarked on their last tour in the late 1960s, their audience had grown to a cross-section of old and young alike.

During their last tour, the media had changed its focus, and instead of asking about music, they were asking the foursome about their political and philosophical beliefs. By the time they came to the final week of the tour, their every movement was headline news. Stories about crazed rock fans storming arenas were commonplace.

To avoid the security headaches, the group decided to hold its last press conference on a Sunday morning at a recording studio. Only the media would be told about it. As an added precaution, an armored car was assigned to pick the group up from its hotel and drive them to the gathering. The promoter, anticipating that word could leak about the group's appearance, took additional precautions. He hired 15 burly security guards to handle any possible disturbance.

On the day of the press conference, the security guards looked out from the glass doors of the studio where the press conference was to be held. Outside was a growing crowd of fans. Instead of dispersing the crowd before the group arrived, the promoter let it grow, feeling that the security force would be able to handle any minor problems. The promoter also knew that the armored car was not going to stop in front of the glass doors. It would continue past the door for another 50 yards, stopping eventually at a pair of steel firedoors. Behind those doors were 14 of the 15 guards.

A security plan had been worked out. As soon as the armored vehicle pulled up, its doors would open, the act would jump out, and the 14 guards would simultaneously open the fire doors and let the foursome inside where the press waited. It was a perfect plan with one, slight flaw. When the armored car pulled into the lot, the driver made the mistake of stopping at the glass doors, 50 yards shy of where the fire doors and security force waited. Instantly, the doors to the armored vehicle opened, and the famous group jumped out—as they were told to do—and landed in the midst of 300 screaming, clawing fans.

Somehow, with the help of the one guard who was left at the glass doors, the group managed to struggle through the violent crowd and get inside. Clawed and bleeding, the four young performers experienced the most traumatic encounter with fans that any artist could have. And the fans who waited outside the studio would never be the same again, either.

Another example of security problems took place in Chicago, at a relatively small theater (2,800 seats). A promoter watched a young rock act perform before a screaming audience. Satisfied the audience would not do anything, he made his way to the box office where he would do a final accounting with the theater's personnel. Within 15 minutes after arriving at the box office, he heard screams and shouts that sounded relatively close. He exited the back of the box office into the theater and was astounded at the scene. Virtually every fan in the audience was charging the stage, and many had already managed to get behind the curtains and backstage. The artists had taken refuge in one of the dressing rooms and locked the door. Outside, the bus driver who had driven the act throughout the tour had a six-foot long two-by-four, and was stationed outside the dressing room door. Within minutes, Chicago police were on the scene, and much to the relief of the promoter, there was no need for the bus driver or his two-by-four.

Crowds and Mob Psychology

What went wrong in the above example? Why did a crowd of seemingly harmless fans suddenly become life threatening? Mob psychology is the answer. Understanding the causes of such behavior is a science unto itself, but usually there is a specific catalyst. In the case of the Beatles, it only took two screaming girls to charge the four as they stepped out of the armored car. The rest of the crowd followed at full speed.

In the case of the group in the Chicago theater, the problem was with inexperienced security. When the group was almost through with their show, a small contingent of fans charged the stage. The ushers, who were doubling as security guards, took one look at the descending crowd and bolted. If they had stood their ground, they would have stopped the group and the incident would have ended. But they did not.

Crowd Behavior and Marketing Approaches

In neither of the above cases did the gathering have to turn into a riot. Promoters/managers can control crowds, but first the groundwork must be laid. *Control the crowd before it becomes a mob*. Eliminate the problem before it becomes one. To do that, promoters have to realize that several elements contribute to crowd behavior.

The first is the way the event is marketed to its audience. Every crowd and event differs. Promoters must know the audience and its pyschology if they are going to properly staff security and handle an event without incident. A case in point: The Los Angeles Dodgers. The baseball club greets more than three million fans through the turnstiles every year, with an average attendance of 40,000 or more. In 81 home games, seldom is there any mention of fights or a riot. Yet, there is a professional football team that generates more disturbances in one game than the Dodgers do in a year. Why? Primarily because of the marketing techniques utilized by the promoters.

The Dodgers—and many other baseball teams—market their product to families. As a result, a crowd of 40,000 may consist largely of husbands and wives, sons and daughters. The football game is a different story. The promoter's marketing thrust is to the rough-and-tumble fan, the bellicose individual who is there to scream, yell, and taunt the opponent. The pro game is marketed to a relatively young, raucous crowd, the single male joining his buddies for an afternoon of whooping it up. It's an event where beer sales are cut off at half time.

The following Saturday, a college team takes the same field that the pro football team occupied, and the mixture of fans—and their behavior— is radically different. This time, it is couples, some families, lots of students, and alumni. The crowd may be as loud as the pro fans, but much less volatile. The product of all three competitions is that generated by the marketing thrust for those events.

Controlling the Fans

Promoters/managers have the ability to tailor the type of crowd coming to their event. They also have the ability to change or modify the fan's behavior by acting quickly and decisively. If someone is inciting problems, he or she should be removed, and quickly. If it's tolerated, it will spread.

The psychology of the crowd, however, should never be a surprise to a promoter. Aside from designing the marketing approach—which helps shape the crowd and its behavior—the promoter generally knows who is going to come to an event. A Jewish Festival in an ethnic part of a city is not going to attract rowdy groups. The promoter who brings the circus to town will be drawing families for the most part. The promoter who brings the Bolshoi Ballet to town understands that mobbing the stage, screaming and yelling will not be part of his crowd's psyche. But each event will need security.

Unexpected Security Problems

Promoters may know their audience, but they do not always know the performers. A few years ago, the Rolling Stones toured the country with a popular, well-known opening act. Although the security had been put in place with the Rolling Stones in mind, it turned out the prime security problem was the opening act and not the crowd.

Crowds can be difficult to judge as well. The classic case is that of a well-known rock act that agreed to do a charity garden party for the president of their record label, at a posh hillside home. The crowd consisted entirely of celebrities and industry notables. Each paid admission to meet the group, and the funds went to charity. At the last minute, the record label CEO decided that he wanted to generate publicity from the event. To do so, he had his publicity department invite photographers from publications throughout the world. The day of the event there were more than 100 photographers on hand, as well as the celebrities and industry people. The publicity chief of the label took one look at the photographers and knew there would be trouble. Photographers are notorious for "getting the picture" they want. In an effort to contain them, the publicity chief had a corral constructed out of sawhorses. The photographers were restricted to the "pen," and would only be allowed to take pictures after the musical group had entered the party, sat down, and had a chance to meet the celebrities. Reluctantly the photographers agreed.

Both the publicist and the record label president thought they had the problem solved and the event ready. The publicist instructed the seven security guards to concentrate their attention on the "pen" and to make sure no photographer left it until the proper time. Finally, the group arrived and chaos broke out. Instead of the photographers causing the problems, it was the celebrities. They were so enamored with the group and had heard so much about them, that the celebrities could not be restrained. Instead of waiting in line to meet the group, they rushed the area set aside for the act and mobbed them. An amused group of photographers watched and laughed. They took some of the best shots on record.

Should Security Be Visible?

How visible should security be? With an artistic, international group such as the Bolshoi, security is best utilized when it is low key. The problems, if any, may come from protestors outside the hall. Of course, there always is the possibility of someone in the crowd running up onto the stage. In the event there is someone in the audience who plans to rush the stage (in the past, anti-Soviet demonstrations were a problem), the plainclothes, low-key security person is going to have a better chance of stopping the perpetrator than someone with a uniform. The uniformed officer stands out, and the demonstrator who is determined to reach the stage can better plan his/her moves if they know exactly where security is stationed.

Visible security at a raucous pro football game, however, may serve to tame the crowd. Many pro football and other events that get fans charged emotionally utilize private security guards who are stationed on the field. These guards, who may be spaced a few yards apart (usually in front of an entrance tunnel), are definite deterrents to fans who contemplate charging the field. The fact that there are so many of them (i.e., one at each tunnel) creates a physical barrier that most fans would not want to tackle.

Security at a rock concert may be a combination of the visible and the invisible. At the same time, security for WWVA's three-day "Jamboree in the Hills" (discussed in Chapter 1) consists of professionals and locals. Everyone from the Boy Scouts and the youth football team to the Ohio State Highway Patrol and Belmont County's Sherriff's Department is on hand. The officers are, of course, professionally trained, but the youngsters are not. They are there to watch for disturbances and if they see any they are to notify one of the professional law officers. Although the professional peace officers have rarely been called upon during this event, their visible presence is a form of insurance that the "Jamboree" cannot do without.

THE INSURANCE FACTOR

For events of every size, an element that is equally as important as security is *liability insurance*. In fact, in today's litigious society, there is not an event that can be staged without it. Every policy will vary in cost depending upon the event, the potential exposure for injury, and the previous interpretation of the courts.

The most vulnerable area for promoters is the liability attached to liquor and liquor laws. In some states, if a promoter is serving alcohol at the venue and an attendee gets drunk, leaves the venue, and injures someone in an auto accident, the event's promoter may be liable. Each year at the International Chili Cookoff, the promoter has the two most common (and required) liability policies in place. One is to protect against someone injuring him or herself on the grounds, while the second protects against someone injuring him or herself after they leave the event (e.g., the policy covering someone who may get intoxicated at the venue and injuring someone outside).

Liability policies covering injuries within an event are relatively inexpensive; however, when it comes to liability outside the venue, the fees can be exhorbitant. To obtain a more favorable rate from companies *for off-venue liability policies*, many promoters/managers control what happens inside. The Cookoff's "beer-drinking contest" is typical of the precautionary measures that are taken inside and evidence of the concern promoters have for the liability they may incur should a drunk person leave the venue. The beer-drinking event is held with contestants drinking out of a baby bottle and through a nipple, which cuts the flow and amount of the alcohol.

Lowering Insurance Costs

Aside from monitoring what is going on inside the venue, there are administrative techniques that promoters/managers can use to lower insurance costs. If an event is nonprofit, a promoter may be able to tie into another nonprofit organization that already has a liability policy in place. The organization with the existing policy can name the promoter (and his event) on a rider. This is a common procedure with *product liability policies.* The prime manufacturer purchases the policy and names distributors of the product on a rider. The promoter of the Chili Cookoff has developed a similar approach. The local chamber of commerce is a nonprofit organization that has a license to sell alcohol, and it uses it at events. The chamber also has a $1 million liability policy and its insurance rates are cheaper because it stages more than one event per year, gets a volume discount, and has instituted safety procedures (e.g., a ride home for any attendee who drinks too much).

Since the Cookoff benefits the local community as well as its charities, the chamber has allowed the event promoter to be named on the policy. The promoter pays for the insurance, but he is able to obtain a lower rate because of the chamber's volume discount.

There are national organizations that make the same arrangement with their local branches. The national group obtains the policy and names the local entity on a rider. The Kiwanis Club as well as many other civic organizations operate in this manner.

Still, liability insurance is an expensive proposition. Because of the propensity of many to sue, the required policies and the premiums have soared. Liability insurance represents a major problem for many local promoters.

Insurance from Public Entities

The high cost of liability insurance has hindered many cities when it comes to staging special events. Some, in an effort to escape the exhorbitant premiums, have opted for self-insurance. They stage the event, insure it themselves, and provide the funding if there is a suit. The city may escape high premiums, but, in several instances, cities have found themselves without sufficient funds to cover suits. If a promoter/manager represents a city in an event that utilizes self-insurance, it would be wise to examine the policy before proceeding.

Venue Supplied Policies

With more than one venue involved in one event, the promoter will find that he/she cannot stage an event without a liability policy. For example, most convention centers require a promoter to provide a $1 million liability policy before an event can be staged. Most of these venues have studied the issue and usually have an insurance agency or broker that is ready to supply the required liability coverage to the promoter.

Usually, promoters will be asked (by the venue) to supply a comprehensive general liabilities policy for a combined single limit of $x. The *comprehensive general liability* policy is a product of the insurance industry with a so-called "combined single limit." This means you can get up to $x for one incident, but that is the limit that the entire event can be insured for. In other words, the limit of any one incident may be $1 million, however, that $1 million may be the total amount of liability insurance for the entire event. A problem develops if there are a numerous incidents totaling more than $1 million.

During the past decade, liability insurance has been one of the prime stumbling blocks for promoters. It is expensive and it is getting more so every year. For any promoter staging an event, a reliable insurance broker who knows general liability insurance should be signed on. Although the venue can usually supply a company and/or agent, it is wise for the promoter to shop around before deciding on a specific broker.

Prevention, Security, and Insurance

With special events, the insurance question always gets back to other issues—prevention and security. It is up to the promoter to police the venue carefully. Wherever abuses occur, they must be stopped if the promoter ever hopes to return to the venue with the event. Excessive drinking invariably leads to accidents and increased liability.

The Conejo Valley Days promoters are well aware of this factor. (The Conejo Valley Days Festival was discussed in Chapter 2.) They have off-duty police stationed at every beer-drinking station at the venue. If anyone gets out of line—or even has the appearance of doing so—they are not served alcohol. In many cases, they are asked to leave. As a result, the promoters have never had a lawsuit and they have been able to keep the "family image" for the event, an image that allows them to raise more than $500,000 during the event.

The Venue Selection Affects Liability Insurance

Another major factor having an impact on the cost of liability is the venue itself: Where is it located? Does it have a history of trouble? Of course, before the promoter can answer these questions he has to select the venue, and that choice is usually going to be based upon the event's requirements. The Final Four Basketball Tournament, for instance, requires an arena that seats somewhere around 15,000 (or more) fans. If there is only one venue in the community that can provide that seating, the promoter has little choice or guesswork involved if he wants to bring the contest to the community. Many world championship tournaments require promoters to supply an arena as well as a similar practice venue within close proximity.

SELECTING THE VENUE

Selecting a venue is more than just finding an arena that will hold a crowd, however. Promoters/managers must consider convenience and location. While the latter influences insurance costs, both influence attendance. Some cities have convention centers and arenas in locations that have become obsolete because population shifts have occured and consumers no longer frequent the area. The promoter should check the venue and its history.

- Has it had an event similar to the one he or she wants to bring to the area?
- If so, how has it done?
- If it did not do well, why?
- Is the target market for this event close by?
- If not, how far do they have to travel?
- Is parking readily available?
- Is the cost reasonable?

CHECK OUT THE COMPETITION

The promoter/manager should check competing events for the proposed dates of the event. Every city has a visitors and convention bureau—an organization that tracks and lists every incoming convention and meeting slated for the area. The bureau can supply a list of events scheduled to come into the community before, during, and after the promoter's proposed event. The promoter should look at each of these and evaluate the competitive strength. Are they drawing from the same crowd?

Some events may even help. For instance, a promoter staging a show at a convention center may find another show—at the same center—catering to the same or a similar audience. The advertising impact of the shows may enhance the attendance at both. But promoters should be wary of attractions that detract from their event. For example, an athletic event staged anywhere in the country on the day of the Super Bowl may be in for difficulties, because the Game has a major following and many consumers will not leave their homes (and living rooms) to attend something that conflicts. Some promoter/managers have taken advantage of the Super Bowl by staging events prior to the Game. "Super Bowl 10K" runs are commonplace.

Often, it does not take an event with the magnitude of the Super Bowl to detract from other special competitions. In Dallas, for instance, when the Cowboys play the Washington Redskins, the entire community comes to a stop and they are all glued to a TV set. Any shows that are staged in Dallas during the game invariably do poorly.

PLANNING EVENTS ON OR AROUND HOLIDAYS

Occasionally, it may be a factor other than a competing event may have an impact on attendance. Special events staged on certain holidays may not do well. Take, for instance, "Mother's Day." Most people are spending time with mom or they have planned something special. An event that runs that day—unless it is geared toward mom—will not do well.

This does not apply to all events, because some holidays and attractions go well together. One interesting example is that of a promoter who decided to put on a business show between Christmas and New Year's. December, aside from the first six or seven days of the month, is a bad time for most shows because everyone's mind is on Christmas and shopping. Few are oriented towards business. The exceptions are Christmas-oriented productions such as "Nutcracker" ballets and "Scrooge."

But between December 27 and December 30, most people are not working and they have time to attend a show. The promoter looked at his calendar and selected December 28 through December 30. He excluded December 26 since it was the day after Christmas and too many potential attendees would be returning goods or shopping. He also eliminated December 31 since it was New Year's Eve and he calculated most people would be thinking about or getting ready for a New Year's celebration.

Usually, the promoter ran his three-day business show on a Friday through Sunday. December 27 fell on a Tuesday; however, he went ahead with the show because he felt the entire week between Christmas and New Year's was one in which an event could be staged and the day of the week would not matter. Why? Because people have time. Even if they were in the office there was little activity between the two holidays.

In researching the period, he found that many companies closed down for the week and there were few competing events. It was also a relatively "dead period" for the media so his advertising would have little competition. Most consumer print and spot radio ads appeared prior to Christmas during December, with the exception of ads that focused on December 26, traditionally one of the busiest retail days of the year. Ads focusing on the sales for that day would be appearing on December 24 and 25. His advertising would start on December 26. The promoter rented a convention center, put his three-day show together, opened it on December 27, closed it on December 29, and ended up with nearly 30,000 attendees and a net profit of more than $100,000 for the three days.

Not every show, of course, is going to do well during a holiday period; however, if a promoter carefully researches the market, determines what has and has not been staged, and how the shows did, the odds for success increase dramatically. Research is critical.

HANDLING THE TICKET SALES

How to Price Tickets

Along with careful analysis of the market, the venue, and the competition, another major challenge for a promoter/manager staging an event is the pricing or scaling of tickets. Ticket pricing is, as one veteran promoter said, more art than science.

On the surface, all pricing represents is the promoter's desire to get the highest price possible for each ticket. But before he arrives at a price, the promoter has to evaluate a number of things. How "elastic" are the prices and at what point will people refuse to buy? In the case of the Super Bowl, there is much *price elasticity*. Even at $125 a ticket, demand far outpaces supply. With the "Taffy Festival," an annual, two-weekend event that provides entertainment and performing arts for children (pre-teens), the promoters charge $9 for adults, $8 for children (ages three to twelve, the prime audience) and free admission for those under three. The event has nearly doubled in attendance each year with parents more than willing to spend $8 for a youngster (plus many more dollars inside) because it is the only performing arts/cultural festival of its type that visits the community.

For most events, however, the promoter relies upon the consumer's discretionary income. In tight economic times, people are more cautious and discerning about spending. Even when the economy is bounding along, virtually every event has a point where the price is no longer elastic and consumers will refuse to buy.

Whether times are good or bad, the challenge for the promoter is to find the maximum price for every ticket. That requires research and a certain amount of guesswork or "art."

One organization that proved itself adept at judging price elasticity for an event was the Los Angeles Olympic Organizing Committee. The group had to determine pricing for events that were held in more than 30 venues. Although the Olympic Games are atypical special events, the procedures followed for pricing by the LAOOC at the 1984 Games provide an excellent guideline. More than $120 million in ticket sales were generated from tickets ranging in price from $5 to $200 for a single event. The average price was approximately $25. How did the LAOOC decide one event would only generate $5 while another would be worth $200? First, LAOOC researched comparable events and prices.

For instance, the opening and closing ceremonies were special. They were considered to be on a par with other one-night, one-time spectacular events such as a major concert or world championship boxing match. Events in these categories were studied and the promoters decided there would be three ticket prices—$50, $100, and $200—for both the opening and closing ceremonies—in the Los Angeles Coliseum (a venue that would hold more than 90,000). The events sold out via mail. Months before they were even held, ticket brokers ended up selling $50 seats for as much as $500.

Obviously, there is enormous price elasticity for events that are perceived as once-in-a-lifetime events or attractions that people may not have the opportunity to see again. Aside from the Olympics and the Super Bowl, other events in this category would be the World Series and the Final Four of the NCAA Basketball Tournament.

But, what can you charge for a field hockey game between the women of India and Afghanistan? If the event took place in an area where there was an abundance of immigrants from both countries, pricing would be much higher than it actually was at the Olympics. In Los Angeles, there was not an abundance of either nationality, thus the field hockey seats were priced low at $5. In soccer, there were seats as low as $7 and the event became one for the entire family because of its relatively inexpensive price. As a result, the soccer venues surprised the promoters by attracting huge crowds. The combination of a low price plus the fact the southern California area has an abundance of Latins—a prime audience for soccer—provided the impetus for the large soccer crowds. The promoters gave nearly every consumer a chance to see a once-in-a-lifetime special event. The promoters made money and the consumers were happy—the ideal marriage.

How do other promoter/managers emulate this kind of marriage when it comes to other special events and pricing? The promoter has to evaluate several things: From a scientific standpoint, he looks at the cost of the venue and the cost of the talent.

Most venues (stadiums) can be divided into three tiers. That is, there is a high-, mid-, and low-priced seating area. In some cases, the amount of high-priced seats may exceed the others or vice-versa. It depends upon the venue and how it is configured.

Analyzing a typical special event at a typical stadium reveals the following figures:

- The Event: Major football bowl game
- The Stadium: 90,000 seats
- Configuration: Oval
- Rental: $1 million, including all mainteance, security, and other help required.
- Costs: Each team gets one-third of gross ticket sales.

What does the promoter charge? At $30 a ticket, the gross will be $2.7 million, which will not cover all costs. The stadium costs $1 million and another $1.8 million is split between the teams. This runs the promoter into the red by $100,000. The tickets have to be scaled higher. But how high?

A major bowl game is not the Super Bowl. On the other hand it ranks above a typical game. The average college football game may charge $25 to $30 for a premier attraction. Assuming the promoter has one (and he should with a bowl game), what might he charge?

If the promoter charged $38 he would add $720,000 to his revenue for a total of $3.42 million. Once again, each team would earn about $1.4 million (a total of $2.28) and another $1 million for rental—a total of $3.28 million. The promoter would have a margin of just over $140,000. Is that enough? Only the promoter can answer that question and determine whether the tickets have to be priced higher. And only the promoter can determine if he could get more for the game. What about parking, concessions, and merchandising? What kind of effect will they have on profits? That is, once again, where "art" plays a role in pricing. Just arbitrarily putting a price tag on a ticket does not work. The promoter has to know the market, competition, and what similar events are getting.

Take the "Jamboree in the Hills" again, for instance. The venue is an open field (125 acres) with rent virtually free; however, assume the promoter has expenses in the form of talent and the tremendous amount of help it takes to run a festival with 30,000 people in attendance. Still, the "Jamboree" is an extremely profitable event. Let's take a look at its figures:

- Stadium configuration: Field, level.
- Rental: Minimal, but promoter has to pay for security, maintenance, and all other costs associated with event. The costs associated with the rental may run $200,000 to $300,000 per day.
- Seating: 30,000
- Costs: Talent gets approximately $200,000 for the one day.

At $30 per ticket, the promoters could generate $900,000 with expenses of around $500,000. An excellent profit! But will country music fans pay $30 per ticket? Once again, that is where the "art" and promoter's expertise enters the picture.

Distributing Tickets

Once a scale has been established, promoters/managers have to make a decision about how tickets will be sold. Will they be sold strictly through the venue or will a computerized ticket operation be utilized? There are advantages and disadvantages to each.

By controlling the sale of tickets through one central box office, the promoter/manager maintains control over tickets. He/she knows exactly what seats are available, and if they want to distribute them in a certain manner to specific people, they can. By controlling the tickets, the promoter also controls the price. There is no service charge attached to the ticket.

Promoter control over the tickets is particularly advisable where there is a multitude of events, such as was the case with the Olympics. With sellouts and oversubscriptions to some venues and lack of sales on others, the promoter has better control—and is able to respond more quickly—if he maintains the sale through his own location(s). Computerized ticket outlets have a definite role, however. They offer a promoter mass distribution, but the price of the ticket (to the consumer) is going to be higher. Organizations such as Ticketmaster generally ask the promoter how much they want to net from each ticket. If a ticket is $7, and the promoter wants the $7, then the ticket outlet will tack a service fee on top of the face value of the ticket.

Obviously, this increases the cost of the event to the consumer, which many promoters prefer not to do. This is particularly true for an event that is a first-timer. It is is difficult to get consumers to buy into the inaugural of an event, and adding a service charge to the price of admission does not enhance the appeal of the event in the consumer's eyes. Usually, promoters handle the event themselves the first year and once it is proven they go to a ticket outlet in subsequent years.

HOW TO SUPERVISE MULTIPLE VENUES

In addition to pricing tickets, another challenge for larger events is running multiple venues. Although this does not happen frequently, it can happen more often than some might imagine. If, for instance, international federations are staging a world championship, there is often a need for a second venue in which competitors can practice. Or, additional venues may be needed for preliminary matches.

With the Olympics, multiple venues are, of course, the norm. But in the 1984 Olympics, the venue selection was complex and involved more than just finding a facility with the proper seating. The fact that the promoters did not build any major venues put additional pressure on the group to find the right location for every event. First, there were the obvious events (e.g., track and field which, of course, would have to be staged in a stadium with a track). The Coliseum was the obvious (and only) answer.

But when it came to other events, the choice of venue was not easy. Take, for instance, weightlifting. It could be held in a variety of auditoriums but the requirement set down by the international body says there must be an adjoining space where the weightlifters can practice. Not every auditorium offers this type of arrangement.

There were numerous venues that would hold the judo competition as well, but the promoters tried to fit the event to a venue in an area where there might be some appeal. For instance, judo is a major sport in the Orient so the promoters tried to locate a venue in a section of Los Angeles where there was a large Asian population.

Scheduling Multiple Venues

Promoters have to think about one other thing, especially when it comes to events held in multiple venues—scheduling. How much time will it take to hold the event? Will the venue be cleared out afterwards and will another competition or event come in at that point? If so, how much time is needed to clear the parking lot as well as the arena? Is the event conflicting with other events in other venues? If so, can the conflict be avoided?

Selecting the correct venue and managing it applies to every world class and special event. A promoter in New York puts on a new product exhibit and series of new product seminars every year. The products are exhibited in Madison Square Garden, and the seminars are at a midtown hotel. At each venue, he has a management team. Each team is responsible for costs and revenues at their venue. They maintain separate books and accounting as well.

Each venue should be treated as a separate entity. That's the way the organizers of the 1984 Olympic Games handled the 30-plus venues under their control. It was impossible to have one manager to supervise all the venues. For tighter control and quicker decision making there was a management team put in place over each venue, with a Commissioner put in place over each sport. Each venue virtually became a stand-alone mini-event.

Authority and responsibility were localized with every venue operating as an independent entity. For major problems, the commissioner was able to communicate directly with top management at the LAOOC. Breaking down each venue allowed the organizers more flexibility and the ability to handle localized problems with a minimum of delay.

THE COMMUNICATIONS LINK

Organizing an event the size of the Olympics (more than 80,000 paid workers, volunteers, and sponsor staff people) requires communication. A good portion of the work was done in the preparation of the Olympics and, at first, the LAOOC tried putting together a critical path chart with *milestones*. (A milestone ranged from the installation of a computer and the negotiation of a venue to start of the torch relay.)

Tracking more than 600 milestones can create confusion and ultimately the Committee switched to manually driven milestones involving weekly sessions with department heads discussing what was going on in their areas. Once a week, each department head and the commissioners (those in charge of each sport) met to discuss developments in their areas. As the event came closer, management switched to semi-weekly meetings.

As the Olympics came closer, written reports and paper became superfluous. Things would change before the updates could be dictated and typed and/or printed out via computer. The most valuable communication tool between venue managers and staff was the face-to-face meetings. The interchange at these gatherings frequently brought a point to light that someone did not know about.

THE ROLE OF TECHNOLOGY

The 1984 Summer Olympics were not only the most profitable in history, but the smoothest running, thanks to the high level of technology used for communications. Every special event will make use of technology in one form or another. With the rapid development of new, more powerful and compact electronics, there are many options available to support an event's needs for communications, data processing, scoreboards, sound, and lighting.

Technology has become integral to any special event. The media expect timely results and reliable communications support. Officials expect computer-aided timing and timely, accurate results. Spectators expect accurate ticketing information and quality sound and lighting, as well as informative and entertaining scoreboards at athletic events. And, for very large events, the sheer volume of activity requires the use of sophisticated data processing and communications equipment.

Microcomputing: Technology for Any Event

Fortunately, the development of microcomputing power has made it feasible for events of any size to benefit from technology. Even a one-person operation can benefit from using a microcomputer for accounting support, mailing lists, text processing, desktop publishing, and other needs.

Large, complex events make use of microcomputers and standardized software packages to meet a number of needs (e.g., seeding athletes, spreadsheet analysis, and scheduling). Of course, large events many also use mainframe computers, thousands of terminals and personal computers, and complex voice and data communications networks to meet the needs of the officials, spectators, media, participants, and organizing groups.

One of the fundamental technology needs is for data processing. No major sports or entertainment events take place without some degree of automation. The basic approaches to automation include:

- The purchase (and possibly modification) of application software packages available on the market.
- The design and development of customized applications.
- The use of standardized general use software (spreadsheets, graphics, and text processing).

Basic Business Support Functions

The types of data processing applications which are found in special events include basic business support functions and specialized uses related to the specific event. The basic business support applications include:

- Accounting systems (general ledger, financial reporting, accounts payable and receivable, inventory control, payroll, and so on).
- Planning systems (scheduling and project management).
- Human resource systems (recruiting, personnel records, job classification, and so on).

The types of applications that are related to particular events incude:

- Staffing systems (skill needs and volunteer data banks).
- Transportation systems (bus scheduling, VIP transportation, and fleet management).
- Accommodations (talent, media, officials, support staff, and spectators).
- Registration/accreditation (access control, rosters, and privileges).
- Ticketing (mail order, seat inventories, seat assignment, gate sales, and so forth).
- Scoring and results.
- Scoreboards (displays, data retrieval/display, replay, and so on).

Many of the event-related special data processing needs are best met by custom software which has been developed for a similar purpose at a like event or by custom software developed specifically for your event. The key to cost-effective use of data processing is to minimize the expense of developing or modifying the application software you will use. It is usually better to use software already developed at or for another event than to incur the expense of new development for short-term or one-time use.

Communications Support: Vital to Any Event's Success

Communications support is vital to the success of any event because things happen quickly and often unexpectedly during special events. Fortunately, there are several relatively inexpensive ways to keep in touch. These include telephone systems (including "voice mail" systems), short-range radios, pagers, beepers, and electronic mail systems.

An important part of planning is the *communications plan*. Communications requirements and objectives must be identifed and a system must be designed to meet those needs. Usually, you will be better served by using systems that bring enough new technology to make the systems very user friendly, since your training time for staff and others will probably be minimal or very limited. Also, in the communications plan, you should have back-up systems included for those inevitable times when your primary communications system goes down. As an example, radio systems may serve as backups to basic telephone coverage.

Technology plays a major role with virtually every special event today. Technology is not just the use of walkie talkies (between venues and departments), but it also involves everything from scoring gymnastic and other events to providing a main scoreboard at each venue.

At the 1984 Games, instant information had to be supplied to the thousands of media people who came from throughout the world to cover the event. Printed results of events had to be available to the media within minutes of an event's ending. Wire services were fed results on-line and the media had instant access to results through inquiry terminals that were placed at every venue.

Technology: Making Events Simpler

Technology has been utilized in accreditation, accounting, payroll, measurement and timing devices. More than any area, technology played a key role once the Games got underway. It would have been impossible to run the Olympics without it. The most important role of technology is the ability it gives to promoters/managers to access people wherever they happen to be. Security in a 100,000 seat stadium is difficult but, thanks to technology, a promoter/manager or supervisor in charge of security can be instantly notified of a problem and its exact location. Additional security can be sent without delay.

Major and special events have become more complex. But thanks to technology, their administration has become simpler. Earlier in this chapter, we spoke of the near-disaster the Beatles found themselves in when they mistakenly stepped into a crowd of admiring fans at a press conference. This could have been avoided if the guard inside the press conference had had the ability (and technology) to communicate with the driver of the armored car.

Ticketing and Control

If there is one other area in which technology has played a major role it is at the box office. Computerized ticketing has not only sped up the operation but it helps ensure accuracy at the gate.

Historically, ticket management activity consisted of maintaining hard copy stocks in vaults, along with manually developed financial records which caused significant problems relating to the physical inventory of the tickets and the cash receipts from ticket outlets. Today, when it comes to major events, this kind of ticketing is considered antediluvean. The system of choice is computerized, which works well for many reasons:

1. There is no storage problem, since the tickets are printed as they are used.

2. Discounts and other variations in price can be reflected as the tickets are issued.
3. There can be daily balancing to the general ledger.
4. Each seat sold has an accompanying financial transaction record.

Of course, small events do not require such complex systems and may prefer to have rolled, numbered tickets. Ongoing events that will be repeated each week or month might consider using a sophisticated system, like those used at most major concert halls and sports arenas. These automated systems, many developed by professional services firms, operate on minicomputers such as the IBM System 38 and AS/400. Their costs are often less than those for manual systems.

GENERATING VOLUNTEERS

Volunteers play a key role with most events. There were more than 30,000 at the 1984 Olympics, and Indianapolis generated an equal number for the Pan Am Games. Volunteers play a part in events from golf tournaments to the Macy's Thanksgiving Day Parade.

They are generated in several ways. First, when news of the event comes out, many prospective volunteers will immediately call the promoter. Some come from the junior chamber of commerce, others from service clubs, and still others from the community itself. For the most part, they are interested in working for the community although, at times, a volunteer simply wants to donate services to get closer to the performers. There is nothing wrong with that; however, if that is all the volunteer has on his mind, the promoter will never get any work out of them. Others volunteer in hopes of landing a full-time job with the organization—and that happens.

The main problem with volunteers is that their minds are not always on the job. Often, they are thinking about something else—and the promoter has to make it clear that he needs 100 percent concentration from the volunteers on what they are doing.

If the event is charitable or non-profit, additional volunteers can be generated through *public service announcements* (PSAs). The PSAs, which run anywhere from 30 to 60 seconds when read, usually have a telephone number at the end of the message so that the volunteer will know who and where to call. The spots may be aired by local radio and TV stations. News releases with the same slant should be sent to local print media, as well as any publications that may be published by civic groups or the local chamber of commerce.

SUMMARY

In this chapter, we have discussed the basics of preparing for a special event. If you follow the following 10 tips for the staging of your event, your preparation should produce both a profitable and well-managed event.

1. There are at least two levels of security that impact the running of an event. Use them!
2. The marketing plan drafted by a promoter usually dictates what kind of crowd the event will draw. Do your research to ensure a manageable crowd!
3. The most vulnerable and expensive insurance area for events is liability, especially when it comes to potential alcohol-related incidents. There are numerous ways to cut these costs. Use them!
4. Remember, the venue's location can impact insurance costs.
5. Before staging any event, it is advisable for promoters to check competing events.
6. Scaling tickets requires careful analysis of the market and the event. Determine the *elasticity* of the ticket price.
7. Avoiding computerized ticket operations enables promoters to control tickets, but channels of distribution are minimized.
8. Promoter ticket control is desirable when there are multi-venues involved.
9. With multi-venue events, each venue should become a mini-event with separate management and accounting procedures.
10. Technology's prime role at events is that of facilitating communication. Use it!

CHAPTER SIX

Sponsors—How to Get Them/What to Give Them

There are few areas more important and less understood than sponsorships when it comes to promoting and managing special events. Yet, most events, whether local, national, or international, would have a difficult time existing without them.

What is a *sponsorship*? How does it work? What do the sponsors expect? What do they get? And how have things changed?

WHAT IS A SPONSORSHIP?

In its simplest form, sponsors provide funds or "in-kind" contributions to promoters of events and receive consideration in the form of logo usage and identity with the event. Years ago, event promoters would approach potential sponsors and ask for cash to help support a local event. The appeal was based primarily on the fact that the prospective sponsor generated income from the community and was obligated to do something in return. It was a step above charity.

Today, however, there is nothing charitable about sponsorships. When a corporation or individual writes a check to the promoter for the event, they expect something in return. They want to see something tangible that will affect their bottom line. The days of writing sponsorships off as contributions are long gone.

SPONSORSHIPS AS BUSINESS TRANSACTIONS

Recent Trends

Sponsorships have become strictly business transactions—big business. In 1991, for instance, promoters/managers of events were able to generate nearly $3 billion in funds from sponsors, according to *Special Events Report*, the Chicago-based newsletter specializing in reporting on and analyzing sponsorships. A breakdown of these figures shows several trends that will have ramifications for promoters and events in the coming years. In 1988, sports sponsorships accounted for the lion's share of funding, generating $1.2 billion, or 72 percent of the total funds contributed by sponsors. Music events were second with $200 million (11 percent), festivals were third with $125 million (7 percent); arts fourth with $100 million (6 percent), and other causes were last with $75 million (4 percent). The grand total for the year was $1.75 billion in sponsorship dollars. Note how this figure grew in just three years!

First, the good news: Sponsorship involvement by companies is growing rapidly, as are the dollars expended. Second, although sports is still king, companies are beginning to spread their dollars around. Causes, as well as the other categories, are taking a bigger share of the pie. Sports' sponsorships remained number one in 1991, but its share of the market had dropped to 64 percent, while music came up to 13 percent, festivals 10 percent, causes 7 percent, and the arts 6 percent. The figures show an interesting trend, one that provides insight for promoters seeking funds.

Positive and Negative Influences Affecting Sponsorships

The changes are being driven by several positive—and negative—events. (See Figure 6–1.)

The Economy. On the negative side, the economic conditions of the country have altered. County and city governments no longer have the money to fund cultural, art, and sports activities. For example, the Massachusetts Amateur Sports Federation, which puts on summer and winter sports activities for kids between 12 and 17 years of age, used to get state funding for its events. Today, the 10,000 children involved have to rely upon private sponsorship if the activities are to continue. There are 42 other states with similar programs all relying upon private funding.

Reduced Spending. The private sector has cut back, too. Many companies have downsized and must justify every expenditure. When promoters come to potential sponsors, the firms no longer ask what they can do for the community, but what the community (and event) can do for the company (from a marketing standpoint) if the firm were to commit funds and get involved.

The promoters/managers of the nine-year-old Montgomery Volleyball Association (Wheaton, Maryland), know first-hand the problems of generating sponsorship dollars from private industry. The Association, which has a yearly budget of nearly $500,000, puts on more than 30 tournaments a year, many in the high-profile Washington, D.C. area. During the summer, the Association sets up 40 courts in Washington and thousands of people are exposed to the sport and the competition. The Association put together a special sponsor package that enabled a company to back 12 of the tournaments for $60,000. Thus far, they have been unable to sell it. Every potential sponsor has asked the same question—what will our return be?

The volleyball association does manage, however, to generate "in-kind" donations. Instead of putting cash on the line, some companies prefer to supply goods and/or services. A motel chain offers free lodging; a building improvement company offers materials for the event. Either way, whether the company provides cash or in-kind, sponsorships have to show a return on investment.

The Ability to Target Market Segments. Despite the difficulties of obtaining money from companies, most realize that sponsorships are a unique way to market products and services. Markets can be targeted and results measured. The sponsorships also offer companies a method by which they can reach specific customers at a lower cost than they would spend via radio, TV, print, or other media.

The Fragmentation of the Media. The media itself has been responsible for accelerating interest in sponsorships. Newspaper readership has diminished

FIGURE 6–1.   *Five Reasons Why Company Sponsorships Are Growing*

1. Economic changes
2. Ability to target market segments
3. Ability to measure results
4. Fragmentation of the media
5. Growth of diverse population segments

and, with the emergence of the cable networks, TV has become more fragmented. The number of network TV viewers has become static. The networks are feeling the crunch, too, and they have discounted commercial costs in many time slots. TV is a marketing tool to reach the masses, while sponsorships can be targeted at small, segmented audiences.

Radio may provide access for companies to target specific audiences (e.g., country, talk-radio, and all-news stations reach a certain segment of the population), but at an extremely high cost. There are, however, few time-buys or media outlets that have the ability to offer a sponsor as narrow an audience as a special event. When companies buy time they are interested in *cost per thousands* or CPM: How much does it cost Procter & Gamble to reach 1,000 homemakers? Could they reach the same group for a much cheaper price at a special event home show?

Which is better for the manufacturer or distributor of basketball equipment—buying time on a basketball game broadcast or becoming a sponsor at a special basketball tournament or clinic? Which costs more? How many listeners does the radio or TV broadcast reach in comparison to the clinic? What is the CPM?

These are questions sponsors are asking more than ever and smart promoters who are after sponsorship dollars usually have the answers ready.

THE SPONSORSHIP SPENDING SHIFT

The slight shift in spending from sports sponsorships to music, festivals, arts, and causes is indicative of several interesting trends that have emerged during the past decade. Companies have become cognizant of sponsorships being a marketing tool but, at the same time, they also realize that not all of their customers are sports fans. Many can be reached through these other activities. Each year, more than 500,000 people turn out for the Chicago Blues Festival, and firms ranging from AT&T to Mrs. Brown's Chicken view this event as ideal for target marketing of their products.

Mrs. Brown's gets direct feedback. How much of an increase do her chicken sales show? If it's good, promoters can count on her being back the following year. AT&T, however, is not measuring exact sales. Unlike many companies, AT&T is still one that looks upon sponsorship as an investment in an image. It relies upon the fact that most consumers will eventually change long-distance service and perhaps they will remember AT&T when that time comes. AT&T provides a similar program at the Los Angeles Marathon where every runner can make a limited (time) long-distance call. The clarity of the call leaves a lasting impression.

Promoters of causes have been particulary effective in generating sponsor dollars, primarily because companies understand the growing concern in society for issues such as the environment. There are hundreds of issues in the country today that involve more people than ever. Each attracts a specific audience; audiences that many companies want to reach. Whether it be a cause, sport, music, or cultural event, companies look for the logical and strategic fit. They understand that consumers have become more sophisticated. A cigarette company sponsoring a marathon is not the correct partnership. Nor is an alcoholic beverage company sponsoring a youth festival.

THE RETURN ON SPONSORSHIP

Whether they are dealing with sports, arts, or the environment, promoters/managers have come to understand that the sponsoring companies want some "bang for their buck." The emphasis on return for investment can be traced, once again, to 1984 and the landmark special event of the year, the Olympic Games. The success of the Olympic Games gained wide visibility for Fuji Film. Fuji's launching of an extensive marketing campaign in the United States became the model for many other sponsorships that have followed.

First, Fuji obtained an exclusive sponsorship and became the official film of the Olympic Games, shutting out the number-one film manufacturer in the United States, Kodak. Everything Fuji did was tied to the Olympics. On every film package it said, "official film of the Olympic Games." The same line was printed in all their advertising and promotion materials. Fuji's blimp was highly visible during the Games.

Fuji used its involvement with distributors and key retailers as well. One of the fringe benefits of sponsorship is access to good seats. Fuji used these tickets effectively by giving them to major distributors and retailers. By the time the Games were over, Fuji had not only made a significant dent in Kodak's market share, but convinced Kodak not to let another Olympic Games sponsorship opportunity get away.

Fuji showed other companies how a sponsorship, when utilized with in-store merchandising, could be an effective sales tool. It also provided an important lesson for promoters trying to sell sponsorships: When you approach prospective companies, have a marketing plan prepared, outlining how the sponsorship can be used to increase sales.

SPONSORSHIPS ARE NO LONGER CHARITY

Today, every prospective sponsor is asking the promoter how they can get the same benefits that Fuji received. United Airlines, for example, was one of the sponsors for the Stanford University centennial celebration held in late September, 1991 at Stanford Stadium in Palo Alto, California. United shuttled Stanford alumni from all parts of the country to Palo Alto. The airline and the other sponsors received other benefits, such as ads in the program, but the bottom line was sales. Sponsors now expect a return on their investment. If they can expect increased sales, the promoter will have a better chance of signing them on.

CONFUSION OVER SPONSORSHIPS

Regardless of their sophistication, most sponsoring companies are serious when they ask promoters for assistance in structuring a sponsorship marketing program. Companies ask for help because many of them still do not know how they can get the most out of their sponsorship investment. What should they be doing from a marketing standpoint to take advantage of the opportunity? In other words, there is confusion as to how a sponsorship should be handled, how it can best benefit the firm.

In fact, many companies still regard sponsorships as charitable endeavors; therefore, they do not involve their marketing department or advertising agency. They are unsure who should be involved—should it be the brand manager who may have a public relations budget, or the advertising agency?

This aspect of the business is changing, however. More companies are turning to advertising or special event specialty firms and asking them to evaluate and generate marketing plans to go along with the sponsorship. In the long run, this will make it easier for promoters to sell sponsors because agencies and/or special event marketing companies understand the business and what (sales, leads, and so on) can be generated from an event.

Still, there are many firms unsure as to what they should do if they became a sponsor. Successful promoters realize this and before they attempt to sell a sponsorship, they must:

- determine if the event fits the company;
- clarify the company's goal; and
- research its competition.

Initial meetings with prospective sponsors should answer all of these questions. Then it is up to the promoter/manager to come back with promotional ideas that will help the sponsor meet its goals. Selling sponsorships to corporations requires the promoter/manager to know a great deal about the special event, as well as about the prospective sponsor.

SPONSORING A "SMALL" EVENT

Musikfest, a German-themed special event that is held yearly in Bethlehem, Pennsylvania, draws more than one million people to a town that has a population of just over 70,000. The nine-day festival had 141 sponsors for 1991. Based upon its track record, 90 percent of those will be back in 1992. The message: The promoter/manager makes sure every sponsor gets his money's worth.

Do Initial Research

The promoters of the Musikfest spend $3,000 each year on a survey that determines where attendees and volunteers live, work, and shop. Thus, when the promoter/manager approaches a prospective new sponsor, he is armed with information on the demographics and economics of attendees and how a sponsorship can be a profitable investment. The festival always provides sponsors with post-event evaluations as well.

In 1991, the Musikfest, which is non-televised and does not accept sponsors other than local companies and regional or national companies with local franchises or branches, generated nearly $900,000 in sponsorships ($505,000 was cash, the rest in-kind). Sixty-five of its sponsors were in the $10,000 category or below; only one was above $30,000. The lesson: Promoters/managers can find an ample number of prospective sponsors locally without trying to go for large national companies.

Be Creative

Some prospective sponsors resist, though. The Musikfest's promoters/managers, however, have learned to employ unique techniques that other promoters can adapt to convince hesitant sponsors of an event's viability. The Musikfest's promoters convinced a reluctant film sponsor to let them set up a booth, buy the film at a discount, and sell it during the nine-day festival. Musikfest would keep the profit. Sales were so good that the company decided to man its own film booth the following year.

Fit the Profile

A key requirement for the successful sale of any product is that it must fit the profile of the attendees. Trying to sell Mercedes a sponsorship in a local chili cookoff does not make sense, but marketing a sponsorship to Hunt's, a leading tomato sauce manufacturer (a key ingredient in chili) does.

Set Goals

But, even Hunt's would be disappointed in the chili cookoff if it did not have a specific goal in mind for the event. Does it want a thousand people to sample its chili? Does it want to give out 10,000 coupons and have 10 redeemed at local supermarkets? Whatever it is, the company must have a goal and promoters can help them decide on one. The company without a goal for its sponsorship will never feel it received a fair return for its sponsorship dollars. And the company that enters an event that does not fit its image will be disappointed as well.

Recognize the Marketing Opportunities

The chili cookoff illustrates a strong selling point for promoters—special events offer companies "niche marketing opportunities." The Olympics and Super Bowl are mass audiences. Masterlock spends more than 90 percent of its ad budget on the Super Bowl. But for an upscale watch company that makes and sells timepieces in the $25,000 a watch category, both events would be a waste. The promoter of a polo match might be in a much better position than the Super Bowl or Olympics to sell the watch company a sponsorship.

TWO TYPES OF SPONSORSHIP EVENTS

Once a company decides it wants to invest in a special event, it has two options:

1. create its own special event and hire its own promoter; or
2. buy into an existing one.

The Self-promoted/Self-sponsored Event

A good example of a company that has promoted its own special event is Manufacturers Hanover (now part of Chemical Bank) which created the "Corporate Challenge Race," involving personnel from various corporations in short relay races. The financial institution had a clear goal in creating the event: Introduce banking services to corporations or localities not already using Manufacturers Hanover's services. Promoters representing Manufacturers Hanover would go to targeted corporations in key markets and recruit teams of five runners from each firm. Thousands of runners participated from hundreds of companies because it was a fun-filled event. You did not have to be a world class runner to compete. It was designed for the average employee.

The size of the race was such that it attracted media attention and free publicity wherever it went. It fit the Manufacturers Hanover image because it was tying the banking concern directly to prospective customers and employees of companies that could become the bank's clientele.

Initially, Manufacturers Hanover's goal was simply to get its name out to prospective customers. Since then, promoters have become more sophisticated in their approach. Each of the five runners has a team captain and promoters asked them to fill out entry forms with their name and the name of their company. The names, of course, become leads for Manufacturers Hanover salespeople. Later, the banking institution added questions to the entry form (e.g., "Has your company ever considered switching banks?") which enabled salespeople to better target the leads.

The advantage of a company's utilizing its own promoter and sponsoring its own event is control and identity. There is no other sponsor to compete against. The disavantage is the perception that a corporate event is too commercial or too self-serving. And, of course, there is a third problem—money. A potential sponsor who creates and runs its own special event is going to spend many more dollars than if it were a sponsor—along with other companies—in a larger event.

The Traditional Sponsorship Technique

The second type of event, in which a corporation becomes one of many sponsors, has become preferred in today's economy because it lessens the demands on funds and resources. Regardless of a company's choice, it has to be convinced that the event fits its needs and that it will have a bottom line return. That means promoters have to carefully examine the event, the "targeted" sponsor, its audience, the tentative marketing plan, and the possible return if the company were to become a sponsor.

An excellent example of prepared promoters is the recent Cadillac/National Kidney Foundation special "100-Stop Scramble Golf Series."

For years, Cadillac was perceived as the automobile for successful professionals (e.g., doctors, lawyers, dentists, and so on). But, somewhere along the line, luxury foreign imports began to make headway into this market. Cadillac decided to use an event to help improve its image in the high-priced car market.

Cadillac committed funds to sponsoring the "100 Golf Series," benefitting the National Kidney Foundation. The series draws about 15,000 golfers and their families with an average entry fee of $220 (a fee which is high enough to qualify the golfers as potential luxury car buyers). Thus, the event meets Cadillac's criteria: Is it something that fits their image and market, and will it help them with their goal of trying to, once again, penetrate an audience of professionals?

Promoters of the event constructed a full-scale marketing program to help sponsors. Since the event was for charity, the promoters provided public service announcements to radio stations which mentioned the sponsor as well as the tournament. Equally as important, the automaker brought the event to its dealers by mailing 80,000 fliers to prospective buyers in the dealers' area. The mailing piece pledged a $25 donation to the Kidney Foundation in the name of the participant if the direct mail recipient took a test drive.

The event did several things for the sponsor:

1. It enhanced its image because the company did something for a worthwhile cause.

2. It let prospective buyers know about the company's efforts through direct mail and the tournament itself.

The one remaining aspect for the sponsor to structure is measurement—is the promotion working? Did it do anything for us? An easy measurement device is simply counting the number of test drives (and $25 dollar pledges) to determine how many people took advantage of the program. Taking it a step farther, Cadillac can measure one other element—how many of those taking a test drive actually purchased a car. How does this return measure up against other forms of advertising? What is the cost? The return? Is it worth doing again? Should it be revised? If so, how? Again, research is key.

GET TO KNOW THE PROFESSIONALS

The previous Cadillac sponsorship and program were designed by the growing number of agencies that specialize in developing tie-ins between companies and special events. These firms generally act as an intermediary between sponsor and event promoter. Even with the involvement of these professional agencies, promoters/managers seeking sponsorships should be evaluating, in their own mind, the event and how it may fit the sponsoring company's long- and short-term goals. Even with such agencies in place, promoters/managers may find themselves doing a significant amount of selling, especially if the special event is a little unusual. That was what happened with the America's Cup race.

SELLING AN UNUSUAL EVENT

The America's Cup yacht race is the oldest sporting competition in the United States. It began more than 150 years ago when the *America*, a three-masted schooner representing the United States, raced against a British schooner. That first race took place in 1841 and the United States has won every competition since then save one. In 1992, there will be another meeting between the champion (a boat representing the United States) and a challenger (there are eight nations vying for the right to meet the American entry).

The America's Cup Organizing Committee (ACOC), which is staging the event in San Diego, California, has a budget of $30 million, with most of it scheduled to come from sponsors. The promoters/managers of the event have targeted a number of potential companies as sponsors. The challenge facing the ACOC is that the Cup and the race are perceived as a "rich man's sport" in the eyes of potential sponsors. It might be great for upscale products, but would it fit for other items? And would there be enough interest to raise $30 million?

The promoters/managers did not want to lose the upscale image of the race but, at the same time, they wanted to be able to expand it to the point where it was not perceived strictly as a rich man's event. The first move was to drop the word "yacht" from all literature. The event became a "boat race"—a competition in which one, lone American entry would await the winner of a dozen foreign challengers in a final, best-of-seven match race series.

The ACOC promoters also had the TV ratings going for the event. In the mid-1980s, the Americans lost the Cup (for the first time) to Australia. Dennis Conner returned to Australia with his yacht, the *Stars & Stripes,* and won it back. Up until the Australians took the Cup, the race had a modicum of interest. But, once the United States went after its lost prize, the competition caught the imagination of consumers throughout the country. What was once purely a rich man's sport, was now one for the masses. Everyone from Maine to California cheered for the home team—and Conner won. The exciting best-of-seven series also produced TV ratings that far exceeded anything the network or Cup officials expected. It was an event that attracted worldwide attention from every age and economic group.

With viewer ratings and surveys in hand, the promoter/manager's strategy was to bring in levels of sponsors ranging from several thousand dollars upwards of $3 to $4 million. On the bottom of the scale, the ACOC went after local businesses in San Diego where the best-of-seven match race would be held. It developed a non-exclusive sponsorship for $2,500, geared primarily at local retailers and some service businesses. The sales pitch?

- For its $2,500, sponsors would receive logo usage of the America's Cup on all stationery, advertising, and other company materials.
- There would be monthly local "network/marketing" meetings in which all sponsors would get together at an organized program to exchange ideas and meet each other.
- An intensive, three-day marketing session would be held a year before the actual event. During the session, all sponsors would be participating and exchanging ideas.
- A referral network for incoming calls was set up. The ACOC would have an 800 number for out-of-state calls. Any company or prospective visitors calling in for assistance in areas ranging from rentals to flowers would be referred only to sponsors. In the non-exclusive sponsorships (the $2,500 class), referrals would be alternated.
- The ACOC would publish an America's Cup Directory 18 months before the event; a year before the event; and six months before the event. All sponsors and their services would be listed.

The promoters/managers also sold local businesses on the "loyalty" factor. San Diego residents knew the importance of the event to the West Coast city, and they would be patronizing businesses that supported it through sponsorships.

Turning the "yacht race" into a "boating competition" and producing TV ratings that also indicated mainstream America was interested in the event piqued the interest of numerous mainstream U.S. companies, all potential sponsors. These were the companies ACOC targeted with exclusive sponsorship packages ranging from $50,000 to $250,000. For months, ACOC promoters were unable to generate anything other than local sponsors. Then the breakthrough came. The Prudential Real Estate Affiliates, the national franchise subsidiary of the Prudential Insurance Company of America, became an "Official ($250,000) Host." Prudential was the first, non-San Diego company to buy in. The reasons this national organization bought in and the way it promoted the package are illustrative of the motives that promoters should keep in mind when approaching companies for sponsorship buy in.

The commitment was made because the event fit the Prudential's target market and the firm's goal. Prudential bought into the sponsorship because it viewed the event from several different perspectives. It would help the company's high-end (that is, those real estate offices dealing with expensive properties) brokers and agents further penetrate the market. If the promotion was successful, it would also bring in new business to brokers who worked in both the high-end and average market. Those were the two goals.

DESIGNING A SPONSORSHIP MARKETING PLAN

How did Prudential go about accomplishing its goals? First, the company realized it had to get its brokers and agents excited before consumers would get involved. Every company has an *internal* as well as an *external audience*.

Selling to the Internal Audience

The internal audience—the employees, salespeople, and everyone up and down the line—has to be sold on the event if it is going to work. Prudential wanted to introduce the sponsorship in a manner that would impact its entire 900 office network. It chose its national convention to introduce news of the sponsorship because all its key brokers and agents would be in attendance. And it did it with fanfare. On-stage was the 150-year old America's Cup (worth $250,000), flanked by two armed guards. The unveiling of the Cup was preceded by a fast-paced, three-minute video featuring highlights of previous races.

The 3,000 brokers and agents in the audience were told of the massive TV coverage planned, with more than one billion people expected to view the finals worldwide. The company's president briefly outlined four contests that Prudential would run during the next year. There would be three internal sales contests and one consumer contest. Trips to the America's Cup would be among the prizes, and there arrangements would be made so that brokers and agents could even bring key customers to the event if they chose.

The historic Cup was then moved to a special area in the exhibit hall where it remained on display throughout the Convention. During that time, salespeople could have their picture taken with the Cup and it would be sent to them along with a news release for the local newspaper.

Selling to the External Audience

The company continued to promote the Cup internally for more than a year through contests. Its advertising agency then created special America's Cup materials to tie into local offices, and its consumer contest was launched in the Fall of 1991. This contest revolved around a 500-word essay for 11 to 14-year-old children on "What Competition Means to Me." To support it, the company hired professional teachers to create a professional "America's Cup Lesson Plan" that could be taken to teachers for use in their classrooms. The lesson plan included an eight-minute video, complete with a history of the America's Cup and a rock music soundtrack.

Once completed, essays were judged by a panel consisting of the local Pruduential salesperson, the mayor of the community, and the local newspaper editor. Each school had a winner. The national winner was presented with $5,000 and the school was given a matching $5,000. Winners (and the Prudential agents) were also given recognition by the White House.

This tie between the school and agent gave the company what it wanted—community involvement for the salesperson, which is the heart of the real estate business. The America's Cup was a national event, but it also became effective for Prudential on the local level.

POOLING SPONSORSHIPS

Prudential bought a sponsorship from the ACOC promoters, that is, for the event itself. Regardless of who won (e.g., the British, New Zealanders, Australians, or Americans) it would not have mattered to Prudential since they did not back any particular team. Other sponsors, however, did back specific teams.

From the outset, team promoters were actively pursuing sponsors, and for good reason. To build and man one of the boats took somewhere in the area of $20 million. Most captains wanted a back-up boat, as well, in the event something happened to the first. That meant another expenditure of anywhere from $5 to $15 million.

Promoters selling sponsorships in Dennis Conner's or Bill Koch's boats (the two American competitors) faced a dilemma. Only one of those boats would represent the United States and only one could be a winner.

Before getting to the Cup finals, American entries competed against each other. The same was true of the foreign entries. In the end, only two boats would compete—the defending American entry and the best foreign competitor. How do you sell a sponsor on putting in $1 million or more dollars when you cannot guarantee he will be with a winning team?

This problem is not unique to the America's Cup. There are hundreds of competitive sports and events that find sponsors left out when their entries fail to qualify or win. Consequently, many have a reluctance to commit to any one team or competitor. What happens if they lose? No one wants to back a loser.

The ACOC promoters came up with a solution that is spreading throughout the world class/special event industry—*pooling sponsorships.* Promoters approach sponsors and sell them *pooling rights.* For instance, AT&T, which bought pooling rights for the America's Cup for approximately $3 million, has the following arrangement. It is a sponsor of Conner's and Koch's boats, but it is also a sponsor of the America's Cup. If Conner loses, it still has Koch's boat, and if Koch loses the opposite is true. It is sponsoring both. And, if in the event the American entry fails to defeat the foreign challenger, AT&T is still a sponsor of the America's Cup. It has bought an "umbrella" package. It is a sponsor of a competitive event, but cannot lose.

Other sponsors leverage their investments in a similar manner. For example, Saab (automobiles), a major sponsor of the Swedish America's Cup entry, has assurance it will not be backing an under-financed effort. If the promoters of the Swedish team cannot bring in enough funds as co-sponsors to match those of Saab, the automaker is off the hook. The company does not have to pay the sponsorship cost, though. Both the pooled sponsorship and the conditions Saab has built into its agreement have come about as sponsors begin to realize that backing a loser does not accomplish its goals. More of these arrangements, particularly in a competitive sporting event area, are going to be commonplace in the future.

CORPORATE SPONSORSHIP AND THE IRS

A word of caution: The IRS has been evaluating, on a case by case basis, whether the corporate sponsorship fees received by organizers of bowl games, golf and tennis tournaments, and other kinds of special events are taxable, as payments for advertising rather than charitable contributions. Check with your tax advisor to see how this may affect sponsorship of your event.

SUMMARY

In this chapter, we covered the basics and recent trends in event sponsorships. The following are 10 tips for promoters trying to generate sponsorships:

1. The economy and downsizing have made sponsorships a more viable investment for companies.
2. Sponsorships do not always have to be in cash. In-kind merchandise and/or services can be just as valuable a "fee" as currency.
3. Promoters have to show sponsors a tangible "return on investment."
4. Media fragmentation concerns most companies.
5. Some companies look upon sponsorships as image-building vehicles, not sales tools.
6. Issue-oriented events can appeal to certain potential sponsors.
7. Exclusive sponsorship adds value to the proposal and the event.
8. A growing number of "special event" agencies specialize in aiding sponsors get the most for their investment.
9. The event must fit the profile of the sponsor's customer.
10. Marketing plans for the sponsorship are a necessity if the sponsor is going to get the most for their investment.

In the next chapter, we will take the discussion of sponsorships one step further by matching specific sponsors to specific events. (See Chapter 7.)

CHAPTER SEVEN

Matching Sponsors to Events

As we saw in Chapter 6, sponsorship worked for Prudential, AT&T, and Saab because promoters helped the companies put the right program together. It also worked for Boeing in the Goodwill Games. Boeing invested $1 million and received $30 million in new business and it was the first time the airplane manufacturer had ever entered into a sponsorship.

Boeing's goal was not to make sales but to make contacts. It saw the Goodwill Games as an opportunity to open its doors to nations throughout the world. This vehicle would allow Boeing the opportunity to introduce its aircraft to the international market. Boeing's plan was not just to sit back and utilize the Goodwill Games logo. Together with the promoters of the Games, it arranged to utilize Boeing aircraft whenever needed. It ferried representatives aboard a Boeing aircraft in 1987 when the organizing committee for the Games met in Russia. It also provided aircraft for the transport of children requiring treatment from Chernobyl to Seattle. And when the Armenian quake hit, it sent relief goods aboard Boeing planes. Boeing used its sponsorship to travel with the organizing committee and open doors through a cultural and athletic event. As a result, it developed foreign clients who may eventually spend hundreds of millions of dollars with a single $1 million sponsorship investment.

While many companies do an excellent job of marketing their sponsorships, few approach the skill of McDonald's, which views sponsorship involvement as part of its marketing mix. Promoters once sold McDonald's on simply making contributions to youth organizations and other similar groups since McDonald's prime audience is youth. Today, however, selling fast food is a highly competitive business. McDonald's now uses its money wisely at events that traditionally attract a majority of younger people (such as numerous gymnastic and swim meets). McDonald's presence is felt at every one of these events through banners, discount coupons, and a host of other displayed merchandise. It reaches out to youngsters at an age when they are most impressionable.

THE LOCAL LEVEL IMPACT

All sponsorships, regardless of the event, must have an impact at the local level. That's critical. Promoters will have a tough time selling any event that cannot provide a measure of local benefit.

Promoters of the Conejo Valley Days, for instance, which can draw upwards of 100,000 people during its run, tie local sponsors together with service clubs. Many of these local sponsors have national ties. For example, promoters of the event collect a sponsorship fee from the local beer distributor. In turn, the organizers bring the distributor together with a service club. The sponsor supplies his beer to a Kiwanis club, for instance, for resale. The sponsor also supplies both a beer booth and refrigeration, as well as selling to the service club at a discount. In turn, the service club flies a banner with the beer distributor's (and beer's) name. Typically, the service club raises upwards of $50,000 during the event for charity, and the beer distributor (who gets paid for his beer) generates goodwill from among the club members as well as promotion to the attendees. Thus, the sponsor (the beer distributor) has two goals:

1. better relationships with the leaders in the community (the Kiwanis people); and
2. the marketing of its beer.

Both are accomplished during the event.

Where alcohol is served sponsors have to be especially careful because the "points" they may garner as a participant can be erased by an unruly, alcoholic crowd. The Conejo Valley Days organizers, aware of the image they have to protect, go out of their way to maintain law and order—and sobriety. Each of the four beer sponsors has a booth where two off-duty police officers are stationed. Never has there been a problem, and the organizers don't expect one. Raising $500,000 for charity through the event is a significant accomplishment and the sponsors want to make sure that their investment is protected. Rowdiness is not tolerated.

Southwest Airlines, which is far from being a local sponsor, recently became a sponsor of the Dallas Shakespeare Festival. How did it decide to measure local impact? Southwest provided the promoters of the Festival with $80,000 worth of $20 certificates. The festival can sell the certificates for whatever it chooses. Southwest has a measure of the local impact by the number of coupons that are redeemed.

SPONSORS CAN HELP AN EVENT'S SUCCESS

Proceeds from the International Chili Cookoff were earmarked for a charity, however, expenses coupled with a low admission price, threatened to turn an event that previously generated money into one that ran a deficit.

In 1975, when the cookoff moved to its ghost-town home, the promoters/managers invested $40,000 in a grandstand and thousands more in fencing, contests ("Mr. Hot Sauce" and "Miss Chili Pepper"), entertainment, security, and insurance. Even though the event drew a one-day crowd in excess of 14,000, the organizers came out with just over $1,000 to donate to charity. Obviously, there would be no ceremonial photographs showing the promoters/organizers presenting a check to the children's hospital. The near deficit convinced the organizers to go after sponsors.

Fitting Local and National Sponsors to the Event

Successful promoters/managers, of course, search for sponsors that fit the event and its image. It does not take sophisticated research to determine what chili goes with—beer, soft drinks, and tomato sauce. To generate sponsors in those categories, the chili promoters/managers developed an entire marketing program to go along with it.

The cookoff's bi-monthly, 60-page magazine, which goes to previous attendees of cookoffs and those expressing an interest in the event, carries full-page ads for the sponsors at no additional cost. So, companies get year-round exposure to the same crowd for the one sponsorship fee. (Costs of the sponsorship run from the $10,000 to the low six-figure range for national sponsors.)

Beer sponsors—who provide the bulk of funds for the cookoff as well as for hundreds of other special events staged annually—are particularly sensitive about the event they are sponsoring and how their product is handled. Criticism of alcohol and alcohol abuse, has made beer companies cautious about their involvement.

At the chili cookoff, there is a beer-drinking contest, featuring, of course, the sponsor's beer. But the event bears no resemblance to the traditional beer drinking competition. Contestants do not chug down steins of ale. Instead, the contest has become an event in which competitors sip beer from a nipple attached to a baby bottle.

Beer differs from most other products because it is one of the few industries that has a local distributor (with an advertising/promotion budget) in each market. For promoters of local events, beer distributors are ideal prospects for sponsorship. The distributor's entire business is based upon the local community. Events that draw locals interest them.

There is, however, a catch when it comes to beer distributors. In many states, a promoter/manager cannot give an "exclusive" to a distributor. If the promoter is putting on a fair, rodeo, or chili cookoff, he must provide each of the beer distributors with an equal opportunity to participate. In other words, they can all sell their product at the event. But, the promoter can offer the beer distributor one additional incentive—*signage*. Promoters may not be able to exclude a distributor's competition, but they can display one distributor's signage much more prominently than anyone else's. And prominent signage usually winds up as a TV spot, if the event is televised or covered by the news media.

The Local Tie

Regardless of the product brands featured, sponsors of local events want tie-ins and promoters have to be ready to suggest many of them. If Coca-Cola is the official drink, local supermarkets will be running Coke promotions (tied to the chili cookoff) before, during, and after the event. Coke supplies a portion of the promotional funds, coupons, and perhaps even a display plugging its product at the chili cookoff. At the cookoff, Coke is the only soft drink served and it also has signage on-stage where the entertainers perform.

EVENTS AS TEST MARKETS

Smaller, local events have an additional advantage: They are ready-to-use test markets. Last year, promoters convinced Pillsbury to utilize the chili cookoff to introduce its new "twist cornbread," an ideal fit for chili. It would be the official "cornbread twist of the world championship." Pillsbury was able to use nearly 20,000 people to test market the product before it rolled it out nationally. The 20,000 provided an ideal test group because nearly all are at the event for the chili—for which Pillsbury's product is the perfect fit.

Pillsbury was also in a position to deal with the local supermarkets, thanks to the sponsorship and test. The fact that a company is getting involved locally means they will be spending money (in-store) to promote the product. For a relatively small cost and in a short time frame, Pillsbury will be able to tell much about its product.

The same is true for other manufacturers who want to test new products or a specialized acceptance. But, promoters have to make sure that the sponsor fits the event. The eight-day "Taste of Chicago" food festival is promoted as an ideal venue for sponsors to introduce and test new products. What better place to test the willingness of buyers to purchase a new barbecue sauce or seasoning! Sponsors who buy in can have their own booth, use their product on food, get instant consumer reaction and feedback, use coupons as giveaways (to determine post-test acceptance), and tie-in local chains and displays.

IMPROVING CORPORATE IMAGES THROUGH SPONSORSHIPS

Sponsorships can be tools to change a company's image. Grundig Electronics, looking for a more contemporary image, decided to put money in a number of contemporary sports' sponsorships. It carefully selected events that would help it slide into a new niche. Among the special events it is sponsoring are mountain biking, snowboarding, and freestyle skiing. The plan was to reposition the company as a firm with state-of-the-art products. The seven-figure investment that Grundig made in the sponsorships is designed to appeal to a younger crowd (all of the sports involved are those participated in by younger people).

Not all companies buy into sponsorships for an image change. Irish Spring, the soap from Colgate Palmolive, decided that the best way to keep its young, fresh image was to get involved as a sponsor of a youthful sport. It has become an official sponsor of the U.S. Ski Team and will keep the title through the 1992 Winter Olympic Games. To back the sponsorship, Colgate Palmolive did what many companies are doing—a complete campaign ranging from internal sales and merchandising contests to a consumer sweepstakes. TV spots were tagged with a special offer that tied into skiing, promotional copy that appeared on the Irish Spring wrappers, and a trade incentive was introduced to generate case sales. The expected bottom line: more case sales, which Colgate Palmolive will be able to measure.

Perhaps one of the most interesting recent sponsorships was *The National Enquirer's* involvement in the "Enchanted Kingdom," a special event that is held yearly in West Palm Beach, Florida. The nine-day Christmas display and show event will draw nearly 250,000 people with *The National Enquirer's* name tied into many of the event's displays. Promoters of the event have *The National Enquirer* as a sponsor for the next 10 years.

SELLING LOCAL SPONSORSHIPS TO MAJOR COMPANIES

Major corporations are fast becoming aware of the benefits of local as well as national sponsorships. The increased exposure for their products are only one reason this type of sponsorship is on the rise. As we briefly discussed earlier, promoters now have an opportunity to sell Fortune 500 companies on the value of special events as a test market. Suppose a computer company is anxious to introduce its new line of computers to the growing Latin market. Few events would offer a more cost-effective introduction than the giant Cuban festival that is held in Miami each year. A sponsorship, booth, retail tie-in (where local computer stores have displays and discount coupons for the event), and follow-up sales study could be an ideal investment for the computer manufacturer.

Using the Event as Advertising

Testing by sponsors at special events is a throwback to advertising techniques of the early 1900s. Claude Hopkins, author of *My Life in Advertising*, and one of the men credited with the development of the profession and the marketing techniques used in selling new products, often used this same targeting and sampling technique when he worked on accounts in the early 1900s. Hopkins measured results by actual sales. He usually "primed the sales pump" by having the audience he was trying to reach sample his products (much as sponsors do).

Some major sponsors are not interested in moving products. Rather, they want to establish a presence with and influence an audience. A Burger King may be a sponsor at an Asian-American street fair where the company supplies free discount coupons and/or the fair promoters/managers display signage thanking Burger King for its participation.

WHAT SPONSORS GET

There was a time when sponsorships meant the company supplying the money would be given a couple of tickets to the event. Today, it goes much further. Promoters and managers should be prepared to offer sponsors packages that include:

- *Preferred ticket packages*—often with reserved parking, special entertainment, and souvenir items.
- *Private hospitality spaces* (individual or corporate)—carrying with them the preferred ticket package elements.
- *Visibility packages*—offering opportunities for site signage, product sampling and/or advertising in whatever program-type vehicles are being used for the event.

Creative sponsor packages for specific events (i.e., playoff games, tournaments, and championships) should not only be enticing to the sponsor, but they should afford him/her the opportunity to impress prime customers and specific targeted markets. (The America's Cup package includes tickets aboard the exclusive viewing boat that will be trailing the race.)

Preferred Ticket Packages

Providing private boxes within a stadium is not just for viewing benefits, but for setting the buyer (sponsor) apart from the competition—and it does. Virtually every event in which a sponsor is sought has something special that can be given to the sponsor as an inducement. It may be a special box overlooking a race course, or a private party in a special area during a ballgame. Hospitality villages, like those set up for the Super Bowl, provide the opportunity for special treatment of sponsors and their guests.

Private Hospitality Spaces

If the sponsor is anxious to impress customers, would it be better to have a post-event party (especially if traffic is tied up) or a pre-game celebration? An invitation to a special event from the sponsor to a "targeted" group can mean as much as attending.

At sporting events, the enjoyment of being on the field and/or grounds during a major event is enhanced by the creation of a private "oasis" (i.e., tent) for a specific group. Sponsors—and the promoters who arrange them—can generate thousands of dollars in goodwill on these premises via private entertaining, away from the public. Hence, the value of some of the pre-Super Bowl parties.

Visibility Packages

Multi-day events offer additional sponsor opportunities with increased visibility. Whether they are held at the competition venue or at a totally different site, the connection to the event can add a special aura to a program that would otherwise be run of the mill. In 1991, for example, Nissan decided to do something different: Usually, the automobile manufacturer invited customers to a sumptuous dinner prior to the opening of its golf tournament. In 1991, however, the company switched direction and came up with an "Evening at the 'Phantom of the Opera'," the popular Broadway show.

HOW TO LIVEN UP AN EVENT

Audience Participation

Of course, there are only so many things sponsors can do when they are tied into an event. Sooner or later, they may run the gamut and draw a blank. It is at that point that the event runs the risk of a sponsor losing interest—and the promoter/manager losing a prime source of revenue. Promoters/managers can overcome these occasions by making suggestions as to how pre- and post-event affairs can be changed and livened up. Adding a "participatory" element can offer a new experience to a tired program. For instance, sponsors of golf tournaments soon found that a hit was offering a "pro-am" competition prior to the actual tournament. In some cases, golfing superstars tee off with players from the entertainment, political, and business world. It adds an entirely new dimension to the game and enables sponsors to "dangle" an irresistable element in front of a prospect and/or customer.

Celebrity or pro-am events are found in special events ranging from auto racing to rodeos and tennis. A world class basketball tournament may seem as if there is little room for a pro-am tie, however, it would be the ideal event to feature a free throwing contest among customers and prospects. By allowing guests to participate, sponsors enable them to form an attachment that cannot be matched. There's a big difference between someone sitting in a box, high above the basketball floor, drinking a cocktail and waiting for the game, versus that same person being taken down on the floor and encouraged to participate in a free throwing competition before the game.

Race tracks long ago realized the value of "participation" when they came up with a string of events ranging from daily doubles and exactas to pick six and pick nine. Although it may be illegal in many states for sponsors to encourage prospects and guests to bet, it is not illegal for them to organize a sweepstakes program in which the VIPs in attendance are matched against their peers. Once again, it gives people a chance to get involved.

Distribute Gifts or Souvenirs

Whatever the program or event, promoters/managers can help sponsors enhance the event by suggesting a novelty or gift for key guests of the sponsors. This does not mean a piece of merchandise off the rack, but rather one that is:

1. well-received by the guest; and
2. achieves the host's purpose.

It becomes a fond reminder of the sponsor and the experience the guest shared that evening, day, or during the event.

During the 1960s and 1970s, ABC-TV raised this concept to an art form with its identity packages for guests attending the Olympic Summer and Winter Games. The network supplied collector's pins from the Games in Mexico City, Grenoble, Munich, Innsbruck, and Montreal, which have become some of the most prized possessions of those who attended the Games.

It may not be too far in the future until trading and souvenir cards are utilized by sponsors. Gifts of this type, incidentally, should always be given at a time when they will make the greatest impact and cause the least inconvenience. Sponsors do not want to burden prospects down with bulky items the first day of a convention or at the beginning of a meeting. The gift, regardless of its crafting, becomes a burden—and so does the sponsor.

Other Touches

Aside from gifts that make a lasting impression, there are numerous techniques that promoter/managers can suggest to sponsors that are inexpensive, yet memorable:

- A personal telephone call to follow up, shortly after an invitation has been sent to a special event;
- Assistance at the entry and/or parking area by a member of the sponsoring group;
- Special service in the event area where sponsors provide everything from binoculars to cellular telphones and food service.

Get Ideas from Trade Papers

Special gifts along these lines are always being created. Astute promoters/ managers keep abreast of most new developments by reading publications that cater to meeting planners and convention coordinators. It is relatively easy to "lift" a good idea and pass it on to a valued sponsor by keeping up with publications such as:

- *Amusement Business* (Nashville, TN).
- *Corporate Meetings & Incentives* (New York, NY).
- *Meetings & Conventions* (Secaucus, NJ).
- *Special Events* (Culver City, CA).

- *Special Events Report* (Chicago, IL).
- *Successful Meetings* (New York, NY).

Put Creative Ideas to Work

An interesting sponsor-originated event took place at the 1991 Super Bowl. The NFL, cognizant that its prime "sponsor" was the average fan, had become sensitive to criticism that the Super Bowl was increasingly an event for high rollers, offering little for the average fan in the host community. To counteract the charges, a 250,000-square foot "Town Square" was constructed which offered four days of activities for visitors and locals to enjoy. More than 73,000 people visited it during the four days, with 31,000 on Super Sunday. The food court alone grossed more than $100,000 during the event.

As usual, the Super Bowl was a sellout and a TV success. But equally as important, the NFL had discovered a new event; an event that would offer sponsors special perks and fans special treatment. The NFL's prime customers, the fans and corporate sponsors, both came away smiling. And that's what sponsorship is all about.

FOLLOW THROUGH

Whatever the event, program, or involvement, promoter/managers must be sure they deliver what they promise at the event. The surest kiss of death for an event is a broken promise by a promoter. Sponsors do not want to be embarrassed or inconvenienced. Follow through on your promises or assurances.

SUMMARY

In this chapter, we discussed the intricacies of matching sponsors to the event. Here are 10 tips for promoters/managers when marketing sponsorships:

1. Sponsorships should fit into a company's marketing mix.
2. Sponsorships must have an impact at the local level.
3. Society has made many product sponsors sensitive to the event and how their product is presented by the promoter/manager.
4. Sponsors need local tie-ins which promoters should help in suggesting and formulating.
5. Sponsorships can become part of a company's plan to change its image.
6. Sponsors should be able to measure results.
7. Sponsorships should offer sponsors the opportunity to impress clients and/or customers.

8. Participatory events can enhance the value of a sponsorship to a company.
9. New ways for companies to utilize sponsorships and profit from them can be found by promoters in industry trade papers.
10. Creative sponsor packages and perks should be created for every event.

Now that you are aware of sponsorships and how to obtain them, let's move on to generating total revenues.

CHAPTER EIGHT

Profit or Loss: What Goes into the Revenue Picture

Two events took place 30 days apart, in the same city, and at the same convention center. Each charged the same admission price and drew almost the same number of participants. But, that's where the similarities ended. When it was all over, one show made a profit of almost $500,000, while the other lost $60,000.

In this chapter, we will discuss the reasons that one of these events was a winning proposition, while the other showed a significant loss.

If asked why, most promoters/managers will offer a variety of answers. It suffices to say that not all special events are what they may seem to be on the surface. Each event has its own audience, requires different promotional techniques, and requires its own market research. And, every special event can have pitfalls; they are pitfalls, however, that can be avoided with the proper planning.

PLANNING IS KEY

In the case of a successful small business expo versus an exposition featuring unusual sports, several things happened which caught the promoters/managers off-guard. With the business show, promoters underestimated revenues. With the sports expo, they underestimated expenses and failed to take competition into consideration.

Both shows were scheduled for the mammoth, 80,000-square foot center hall of a convention center in one of the country's largest markets. The sports expo, a consumer-oriented event, was designed to showcase unusual sports—everything from "hacky-sack" (a variation of volleyball) to hovercrafts (fast-moving vehicles resembling motorized life rafts kept airborne by a force of air).

In contrast to the sports expo, the business show was filled with traditional franchise and distributorship opportunities as well as two dozen business seminars targeted at anyone interested in starting his or her own business. Aside from the investment opportunities, the show also featured a row of eight consecutive booths in which the promoter/manager sold practical, how-to start-up manuals on a variety of small businesses. The manuals, which covered 200 businesses, detailed everything from how to pick a site for a business to how to market and sell products and services. Most manuals sold for between $39 and $60. The seminars, usually held in rooms off the main exhibit hall, covered topics ranging from financing techniques to marketing strategies. Admission to the seminars was $10 apiece.

To make the sports expo more intriguing, the promoter/manager arranged to have demonstrations of specific sports every half-hour. Inside, there was a space set aside so the hovercraft and other sports could be demonstrated. Hung from the criss-crossed beams at the top of the center, were mountain-climbing ropes. Every half-hour, a climber would scale the ropes and rappel down from the ceiling to the exhibit floor, 40 feet below.

There was even a miniature racetrack set up directly outside the hall's rear door so the finer points of auto racing could be demonstrated. At the rear of the hall, there were exotic automobiles that were surrounded by a hall of 200 exhibitor booths, all with exotic or unusual sports. The show appeared to be a promoter's dream, and the promoter was confident this show would be a financial bonanza.

Proper planning means recognizing the probable revenues and costs for each event. Estimating costs and revenues can be difficult, but if they can be broken out into specific attributes and needs and planned for accordingly, the vision of a profitable event will be realized.

THE SIX ELEMENTS INVOLVED IN COST

Before any show is labeled a success, the promoters/managers have to first examine cost. At times, even shows that appear to have everything going for them turn out to be losing or, at best, marginal events because of unexpected costs.

Without knowing the cost of the arena, advertising, promotion, and other expenses, promoters have no way of determining how to price tickets nor can they estimate how profitable an event can be. Basic items that make up costs for an event are:

1. Rental charges;
2. Security costs;
3. Production costs (building, special staging, and show decorations);
4. Labor costs;
5. Merchandising costs; and
6. Marketing costs.

A closer look at each of these areas revealed some of the problems.

Rental Charges

The sports expo ran five days, with an arena rental fee of $10,000 per day for a total of $50,000. (Multi-day events can usually negotiate a discount with an arena. The sports expo promoters did just that for a $10,000 reduction.)

Security Costs

As part of the rental agreement, most halls provide limited security. That means a guard at the front and maybe the rear of the exhibit hall. For events with valuable displays or merchandise, it is up to the promoter to supply adequate security. This amount of security can become expensive. (When the America's Cup trophy appeared for two days last year in Las Vegas, the promoter's major cost was more than $2,000 for two, 24-hour security guards.) For the sports expo, the promoter estimated additional

By getting involved in local events like the Little League, businesses can foster a great deal of community goodwill at a moderate cost.

Regional sponsors at an event like the Iowa State Fair can get national exposure through electronic and print media coverage.

The Columbus Avenue Festival, sponsored by the West Side Chamber of Commerce in New York City, not only is a crowd-pleaser, but provides a boost for local merchants by bringing extra pedestrian traffic into the neighborhood.

Always consider which public agencies might be involved in the permit process behind an event like "The Taste of Chicago." If food is involved, the local health department will also be; if the venue is a city recreation facility, count on the involvement of the Parks and Recreation Department.

Because of the huge number of people attending "A Jamboree in the Hills," security combines visible and invisible elements—from the county sheriffs department to the Boy Scouts—for the sake of crowd control. Liability insurance is equally important and no event can be staged without it.

Ancillary events like the Torch Relay run in conjunction with the 1984 Olympics in Los Angeles, can make a difference in the success of an event by affecting public attitude toward it.

An event like Hands Across America can only provide support for social causes when it is run in a business-like manner, with good planning and an understanding of budgets.

Olympic merchandise is a good example of how licensing can help generate revenue from special events.

security costs at $2,500. (See Chapter 7 for a more detailed discussion of security.)

Production Costs

The expo promoters also incurred charges for special staging. The auto racetrack built for demonstrations cost $15,000 and a decorator, hired to set up the exhibition booths at $50 to $100 per booth cost $15,000 for 200 booths. Although exhibitors pay for the furniture used and electrical or water fees which they may need for their booths, the show promoter pays the decorator a standard fee (anywhere from $50 to $100, depending upon city and venue) for the construction of each exhibitor booth. Promoters also pay for banners, special signage, or other decorative materials that have to be placed within the show. If they do not order early, they have to pay a premium to the decorator. The cost of every item varies, depending upon the market.

Labor Costs

Heavily unionized cities (e.g., those in the Northeast) are strict about what the promoter can and can't have vendors handle. Obviously, the stricter the union, the higher the costs since the promoter has to leave more of the handling to the union crew. In some states, the union allows the exhibitor to wheel his own cart, stacked high with merchandise while, in others, the exhibitor cannot carry anything other than his briefcase. To violate the rules is to risk a shutdown of the show.

The stronger the union, the less leeway, and the higher the costs. A show at a major venue in Chicago may generate $25,000 in labor charges, whereas the same event in a Southern venue may only be 10 percent of that. (See Figure 8–1 for tips on handling unionized labor.)

The role of the union in venue selection. Through the years, unions have become a potent influence on a promoter's choice of venues. There are two types of shows that have been affected the most—trade and consumer.

Trade shows cater to specific industries and the buyers in those industries. They are typified by houseware and gift shows, and are major events that are held once or twice a year. Many promoters of these shows have given up on staging them in the northern markets because of the high cost of labor. They have taken them to lower cost venues in the South and West. They know that the buyer for a major chain in Chicago will travel wherever the show is held.

The venues for consumer shows (e.g., the sports expo) are more limited. To reach consumers in Chicago, events must be held at the McCormick Center or some other Chicago-area venue. The extra dollars for the labor costs are incorporated into the price of the ticket. Although the venue for the sports expo was a community where union activity was relatively

FIGURE 8–1.   *Guidelines in Dealing With Unions at Venues*

1. Heavily unionized cities generally have strict rules regarding handling of goods within the venue.
2. Promoters should meet union representatives before the event takes place in order to establish rules and guidelines.
3. The stronger the union, the higher the costs. Remember them in your cost estimations.
4. More stringent unions are found in the Northeast and parts of the Midwest. More lenient unions will be encountered in the South and Far West.
5. Promoters will find that "splits" for the sale of merchandise vary from market to market.

mild, the promoter still had a $3,000 bill from the union for hanging decorative materials.

Merchandising Costs

Virtually every major special event entertains bids from promoters when it comes to merchandise. They will ask the promoter to project sales. If the promoter were to estimate that he/she will sell 50,000 pins at $1 each, he/she would be faced with the following arrangement: 50,000 at $1 equal $50,000 in sales which incurs a 10 percent licensing fee for the product. The promoter would have to pay the $5,000, usually in advance of the event, to ensure the license. This is known as a *guarantee*.

Licensing. Licensing can be a serious and costly business. In the Calgary Winter Olympics, the promoter's guarantee for t-shirts and sweatshirts was $400,000. That meant the promoter had to do $4 million in sales to break even. (He did.)

In Barcelona, before the bids went out for the 1992 Olympics, it was estimated that promoters would be paying $1 million, perhaps higher, for the licensing rights to lapel pins, pens, and other items. That means the promoter would have to generate $10 million in sales to match the guarantee.

Licensing is becoming more sophisticated each year. Whereas promoters used to pay a flat 10 percent to obtain a line, that is no longer the case. Categories have been broken into sub-categories, each designed to obtain more dollars from the person who is selling the merchandise. For instance, a promoter may pay 10 percent to obtain exclusive rights in a single category (e.g., pens). However, that particular category may only cover low- (or high-) priced pens. Suddenly, the promoter finds himself selling merchandise and competing with someone else selling the same item at a lower price.

Matching the product to the market. Certain categories of merchandise sell better than others. *Textiles* (t-shirts, sweatshirts, and so on) usually account for 60 percent of the sales at a special event, while *hard goods* (key chains, lapel pins, and the like) generate the other 40 percent. Some categories will sell better at different events than others. For instance, at the Winter Olympics, sweatshirts easily outsell t-shirts for obvious reasons. Promoters should check previous performance and sales to determine what kind of revenue they should be generating. The information is usually on file. In the case of the international sports, international federations would have most of the sales data. Performance research is critical. Otherwise, a promoter may find himself/herself bidding on merchandise that has no market.

The role of the union in merchandise sales. The union also plays a major role for promoters who bring their own souvenir programs and merchandise to the event. In heavily unionized venues, the vendors may ask for as much as 80 percent of the program and/or merchandise sale. The promoter does not *have* to pay this fee, but if he doesn't, his merchandise will not be sold in the arena.

In other cases, the split will be 50/50, or 75/25 in favor of the promoter. In many instances, the arena will allow the promoter to keep 100 percent of the merchandise revenue if the promoter supplies and pays his own salespeople. Typically, a 100 percent arrangement occurs in the South, areas in the Far West, or other communities where unions do not play a major role in the exhibitions.

The promoters of "Jamboree in the Hills," the yearly country and western festival held outside Wheeling, West Virginia, operate exactly that way. All the t-shirts, baseball caps, water bottles, sweatshirts, and jackets are sold by the promoter, who hires local help. Revenue from merchandise has steadily climbed. This year, the promoters even allowed the performing artists to set up their own booths to sell merchandise. It's big business. In return, the promoter gets (approximately) 10 percent of the sales (the usual rate for promoters obtaining a license to sell products).

Determining the merchandise split. How does the promoter tell what the split might be? By asking! In some instances, the splits are negotiable, but the only way to tell is by feeling out arena management and the union. Again, ask and plan ahead of time.

The overlooked costs—booth sales. Promoters have often overlooked a major cost with shows that have exhibitors, namely, booth sale personnel. The promoter/manager has to hire salespeople to sell the booths. Finding them is difficult. The main reason is that the employment is temporary (e.g., selling booths for one show). A good salesperson is not generally attracted to a position that is only going to be for six or seven weeks. The temporary tag not only means that the promoter will probably end up paying a higher commission to attract the right people, but most likely will spend more advertising dollars to find people willing to do short-term work. If a show has a track record, the cost is going to be significantly less than a first-time event. Selling an unknown generally takes time and more than one telephone call, and that costs money.

Salespeople handling exhibit booth sales for the inaugural of any event have quite a marketing challenge because they must convince potential exhibitors that the fledgling event will be a viable marketing outlet for their products and services. In an event's subsequent years, the cost of sales will drop as the expo develops a stable of exhibitors who follow it wherever it goes. But that first show is expensive. For the sports expo, the cost of sales for exhibit booths ran the promoter more than $60,000, plus additional accounting fees that came to just over $2,500.

Marketing Costs

The most expensive item on the cost side of a profit and loss statement is marketing. Which media will best reach the prospective audience? How many ads must be taken? Will the event require a special supplement? Does the promotion require TV, radio, print, or all three? For the sports expo, the promoter budgeted $80,000. Table 8–1 breaks out the revenues and costs for the sports expo. As you can see, actual marketing costs ran $137,000 as opposed to a budgeted figure of $80,000. Notice that these marketing costs required the most funds. This is more of a norm than you would think. Budget accordingly.

HOW TO ENSURE HIGH REVENUES

Match Ticket Prices to the Event

The promoter of the sports expo estimated an attendance of 30,000 with an admission price of $4 for a total of $120,000. When it comes to pricing tickets, promoters have to weigh carefully what they are selling, how it compares to competitive events, what competitors are charging, and what the market will bear. That final caveat is critical. Fans would gladly pay $75 for a Super Bowl or Final Four ticket, but for concerts, one-night events, or other localized special events, the ticket cost is usually "price sensitive." A dollar too much can lead to failure.

For the Jamboree in the Hills, promoters/managers sell an advance, three-day ticket for $65 but charge $75 at the door. For a one-day pass, the cost is $30, and that's for one, two-hour concert. Consumers are willing to pay because they feel the concert is more than a musical event. It's an experience. The Jamboree takes place on 125 acres with camping facilities and a place for motor homes and RVs. People come for more than the two-hour concert so the cost is not high enough to drive them away.

TABLE 8–1   Sports Expo
Statement of Revenues and Expenditures

Revenues	Budget	Actual
Admission	$120,000	$72,000
Booth Sales	120,000	82,000
Goods sold inside	270,000	162,000
Mailing list sales	2,500	N/A
	$512,000	$316,000
Expenditures		
Rental	40,000	40,000
Labor (security)	2,500	2,500
Production	18,000	30,000
Cost of booth sales	62,500	77,500
Cost of selling goods inside	135,000	81,000
Talent	0	8,000
Marketing	80,000	376,000
	$338,000	$364,000
Surplus	$174,500	($60,000)

In New York, $60 tickets for shows are commonplace. But don't try that in Oklahoma City where costs differ along with the cost of living. Will the crowd in a 15,000-seat arena in Minneapolis pay $30 per seat for 4,000 of those seats? It depends upon the event, the perceived value, how other similar events were priced, and how they fared.

Regardless of the event, when a ticket costs $30 people expect good entertainment. Although they expect entertainment at the sports expo, "good" may not apply because the ticket costs are so radically different. At $30, attendees will expect to hear one of the best entertainers in the country. At $4, for the sports expo, consumers expect to see a martial arts demonstration, an indoor moutain climber, and a hovercraft performance. They accept the fact they have to travel to a convention center, pay for parking, wait in line, be jostled about in a huge hall, all so that hopefully they will be entertained by the exhibits and demonstrations.

Like all shows, the sports expo became an impulse item and the promoter/manager did not want to kill those impulses with too high a price tag. He settled for $4 and a projected gate of $120,000.

Questions to ask when pricing tickets. When pricing tickets, promoters/manager have to ask themselves the important question: "Will people come to this event regardless of the price?" Nearly every event has a threshold where the price can be a deterrent to attendance. The question the promoter really must ask is "What is the maximum amount of money I can get based upon the participants' enjoyment?" That's the magic question. If, for instance, the New York Yankees could raise prices and still keep the same number of fans coming through the turnstyle, they would. But, they compare ticket prices with other clubs, and they are careful not to vary prices too much.

Promoters/managers are selling an entertainment commodity. They try to get as much as possible but, at the same time, they remember that a buyer who suffers remorse because of an exhorbitant ticket price, may not be back next year. The challenge to the promoter/manager is to carefully weigh the market, compare similar and competing events, the crowds they draw, and the prospects for his show. The ideal price is one that does not cause the consumer to turn away, but it does not make him smile with glee either.

Of course, there are certain events that (apparently) have no price-resistance (e.g., the Super Bowl, NCAA Final Four, Opening and Closing Ceremonies to the Olympics, certain Bowl games, the World Series, and so on). But most others do have a point where price turns the crowd away.

The impulse buy. Buying tickets for many special events is the result of an impulse. Consumers do not plan weeks, or months in advance for shows of this type. Obviously, for a Super Bowl or for other events where tickets are going to be scarce or not available, the consumer does have to plan ahead of time. For the others, the consumer may decide just a few days, or few hours, beforehand that they will attend the event.

Even the business show, which was targeted at a narrow segment of the market (those consumers who were interested in going into business), was an impulse buy. The promoter did not even place his first ads until five days before the show opened. (A lengthier discussion on marketing and promoting shows follows in the next chapter.)

The $3.95 admission to the business show made little difference. The promoter discovered that his audience was serious. They wanted to learn about business, and they were willing to pay for it. As a result, the average attendee to the business expo spent $35 once inside. (Compare this to an expenditure of under $10 for the sports expo!) Consumers at the business show bought manuals, attended seminars, and purchased seminar tapes. The business group was serious and they came to learn. In doing so, they spent a great deal of money. They viewed the seminars and books as necessities, and were willing to pay the price.

The Advantage of "Back-end Revenue"

Significant additional revenue can be derived from "back-end" or "post-purchase" sales, which are generated by the promoter/manager after the event is over. In other words, the promoter/manager uses the same people who initially came through the show to sell something else. For example, it is safe to assume that most consumers who attended the sports expo are probably sports fans. If the promoter/manager gathers their names, he/she can rent them to other companies interested in marketing sport-oriented products to the same audience.

Specialized mailing lists can generate a rental fee of up to $100 (and more) per thousand names. The more specialized (and responsive) the list, the higher the rental. A list of surgeons, for example, might bring $100 to $150 per thousand, but a list of surgeons who buy by mail (proven buyers) would probably generate $200 per thousand. For the sports expo, the promoter estimated he would generate $60 per thousand names, and would be able to rent the entire list at least twice during the following 12 months.

Capturing names is relatively easy, especially when it comes to shows. Drawings, door prizes, and other lures are use in order to get those walking in the door to drop their name in a barrel, hat, or other collection device. The show that gives a consumer a chance to win $500 through a drawing is not spending $500. It will get that money back when it rents that person's name.

The promoter/manager of the sports expo knew he would not capture every name; few events can. To do so, they must have a gimmick that attendees cannot resist. But the promoter/manager did estimate that he would generate the names of two-thirds of the attendees, or 20,000. If he rented each of those names twice during the following 12 months, he would generate about $2,500.

Some might say that the additional effort is not worth it because of the seemingly insignificant return. But it is! There is no cost to the promoter/manager in renting the names. He/she can house this list with a direct mail rental agency who will handle all the telephone calls and list fulfillment. In return, the agency takes a percentage, but the promoter/manager—the owner of the names—does not have to do anything. He can earn that $2,500 (less commission) every year until the list "burns out." (That commission can run anywhere from 30 percent to 60 percent, depending upon how good the list rental agency is and how poor the list happens to be. For instance, a list that is "hot" [e.g., gets good response when it is mailed] is going to be in demand by companies. That makes the rental agency's selling job easier, so they are willing to cut their commission.)

The focused nature of the business show provided the promoter/manager with an extremely marketable list of names. The business attendee's proved to be enormously responsive to direct mail offers, especially those revolving around small businesses. In fact, one of the most valuable revenue generators that emerged from the business show was the mailing list. Over a four year period—and the 40 other business shows he staged throughout the country—the promoter/manager collected hundreds of thousands of good, responsive names. The mailing list continued to generate an average rental income of more than $100,000 per year for the promoter, long after he had ceased promoting the shows.

In order to consider a list viable for "post-purchase" or "back-end" sales, the names have to be responsive. If attendees enjoyed themselves at the expo, and they are mail order responsive, the promoter/manager may be able to increase revenues by selling additional products and services to them after the event.

This was a concept developed by retail and service companies, and pertains to the reaction customers have when they buy something. If they are pleased, they buy more. If they have been treated poorly, there is no way they will purchase again. That's why astute salespeople send thank you notes, birthday greetings, and other reminders to their customers. The promoter/manager maintains contact with the group by "capturing" their names when they attend his first show. The captured names then become part of a mailing list that the promoter "rents" to other marketers anxious to sell products to a similar audience.

Over the "spending life" of a client, the firms that do a good job of serving the buyer will generate more than 50 percent in additional sales. If the customer spent $500 his first time, he would spend an additional $250 during the following months. Post-purchase/back-end sales can become a substantial revenue source for promoters.

Use the Event as a Test Market

The sports expo also served as a test market. If it went well, the promoters/ managers would duplicate it across the country. They would take the same show, use the same advertising plans, travel with the same exhibitors, and rent similar halls in markets across the country. Wherever possible, they would augment the exhibitor base with local companies wishing to exhibit.

This *cookie cutter approach*, as it is called, is not a new concept nor is it exclusive to the show and exhibit industry. Promoters of concerts do the same thing. If all goes well the first time out, they utilize the same marketing plans in the next venue. Traveling across country, they seldom change anything, unless something goes wrong and the gate sales drop.

The promoter of the business show was able to "cookie cut," and for the next 48 months he traveled from one major city to another presenting the same attraction. His marketing costs consisted of one major display ad that appeared five days before the show opened. Recruiting exhibitors became routine and required little sales follow-up. Most had excellent shows and were anxious to travel with the promoter to whatever markets he selected.

Moving the show from market to market offers an economy of scale and enables the promoter/manager to increase his profit. The expense of selling a booth might be cut in half, giving the promoter an additional $30,000 to $40,000 of profit. The cost is cut because exhibitors who are in one winning show tend to stay with the promoter/manager who did well for them. The promoter/manager no longer has to wine and dine them, nor does he/she have to have a sales force that calls them twice a week in order to get them to sign up. They are sold.

During the four year tenure, the business show established an enviable track record, as well as serving as a valuable revenue generator and market research tool for the promoter's company. Not one of the 40 shows lost money and the promoter/manager never increased the admission price. When the promoter staged his first show, his company had eight employees and did about $500,000 in sales. By the time he was finished four years later, the firm had grown to a $15 million a year enterprise and was known throughout the country for its successful newsstand publication, *Entrepreneur Magazine*. It was, in fact, due to the business shows that the owner of the company managed to generate enough funds to expand the magazine.

With this cookie cutter approach, the promoter/manager has the opportunity to cut other costs as well. If he/she has done the necessary research and surveyed the attendees at the first show, he/she will be able to determine which media worked—which newspapers, magazines, radio or TV stations did the best job of pulling people into the show. Once the profitable mediia are determined, the budget can be cut down to eliminate the costly and wasted media avenues during the next show.

Examine the Pitfalls Up Close

On paper, the cost/revenue ratio for the sports expo looked great, but in actuality the promoter/manager discovered how many things could go wrong. During the five days, more than 25,000 consumers flowed into the hall. Exhibitors did capacity business booking people for white water rafting tours, mountain climbing expeditions, and martial arts training. The hovercraft dealer sold more vehicles in the five days than he had in the previous six months. The merchandise the promoter/manager sold in his booth moved briskly. By the time the expo closed, the show had become one of the most successful in the center's history—but not for the promoter/manager.

How could a special, five-day event draw well, please exhibitors who were able to sell merchandise by the carton, and still turn into a losing proposition? The answer was underestimated expenses. The promoter/ manager did an accurate job of forecasting, but he missed several critical areas. The most costly was in booth sales. Typically, a trade show, that is, an event that caters to a particular industry or trade and not average consumers, can get a higher price per booth than one directed at common consumers. Trade shows are usually designed to attract people who are in a position to buy: the purchasing agent, chief buyer, or key executive who makes the ultimate decision. A computer show in which manufacturers display wares for distributors who may spend hundreds of thousands of dollars, costs the exhibitor (manufacturer) a tidy sum, but it is worth it.

A consumer show, on the other hand, where exhibitors make their money entirely from sales to attendees, is going to generate lower sales volume and fewer dollars for exhibitors. A consumer who purchases an item at a consumer show generally buys only one of that item. A distributor or purchasing agent attending a trade show represents a multitude of stores and buys many items at once. Exhibitors at trade shows take in more revenue simply because they make volume sales. Their consumer show counterparts do not. Invariably, this means that promoters of shows like the sports expo must price booths lower than their trade show counterparts because the return on investment will not be as great.

The promoter/manager sold 200 booths for the sports expo, the cost of sales was high, and the booth revenue was not as expected. Mountain climbing exhibitors occupied two booths because they were demonstrating their sport, but only had to pay for one. The hovercraft people got a discount on five of their six booths, and the exotic car people were given five booths at no cost in order to just get the cars in the show as an attraction.

When these discounts were added to the bounced checks and exhibitors who never paid, the promoter's $120,000 in potential revenue was down to $82,000. In addition, his salespeople had a particularly difficult time selling booth space, but nonetheless ran up costs of $35,000 in commissions and another $25,000 in salaries. Overhead (e.g., telephone costs, express courier services, and word processing services for the salesroom) ran another $15,000. By the time the show was over and the accounting complete, the promoter had made no profits on 120 booths.

The apparent $100,000-plus in gate revenue 25,000 times $4 was misleading as well. There were discount tickets in the promotional ads, plus a number of free tickets supplied to the media for consumer giveaway, and a number of tickets given to exhibitors for their customers. The 25,000-plus attendees turned out to be closer to 18,000 paid ticket sales for a total of $72,000. Inside, the t-shirts and books sold, but no one bought more than one or two items. So instead of averaging $15 per sale, the promoter brought in just over $9.

The promoter/manager also underestimated other costs and revenues as well. He spent an additional $15,000 for spot television ads and another $21,000 on rock radio ads the week of the event. In an effort to get the best attractions possible, the promoter also agreed to pay for the transportation and room and board for the auto racing team. This cost another $8,000. Before he was done, the promoter/manager had racked up another $21,000 in costs for a public relations and advertising agency. When it came time to reconcile the books, the promoter was astounded when he found he had lost more than $60,000 on the show.

The promoter's greatest disappointment was the realization that the sports expo could not be staged profitably anywhere because the cost of sales would not go down. The promoter/manager hoped the exhibitors would be willing to travel with him as he took the show to other markets, but these exhibitors were not typical. Most were "mom & pop" operations, that is, the booth buyers owned a small store or business and only exhibited in this particular expo because it was close to their market. The white water rafters, for instance, were a husband and wife team that concentrated on providing trips on rafts in northern California. More than 90 percent of their business came from California and it made no sense for them to travel to Chicago with the sports expo. Generating Midwesterners for a West Coast white water rafting tour was a long-shot. The promoter/manager, if he took the show to Chicago, would have to find a white water rafting company in the Midwest—and go through the entire costly booth selling process all over again.

The same was true of nearly every exhibitor in the show. The mountain climbers, martial arts, hackey sack, and hovercraft people were all local. They had nothing to gain by travelling to another city. And that was the greatest pitfall in the entire expo—the inability of exhibitors to sell their merchandise in other cities.

Take Advantage of the Sophisticated Exhibitor

The promoter/manager of the business show, on the other hand, had little difficulty along these lines. When a promoter/manager can demonstrate to exhibitors that his audience will be focused and serious, he has an excellent chance of generating a higher booth revenue. This promoter/manager was also dealing with franchisers and distributors who could market their goods in a multi-state area. They were more sophisticated. They understood the value of a show that advertised heavily (which the expo did) and one that offered consumers an abundance of information through seminars and manuals. With any show that tries to sell merchandise or services to consumers, the most valuable feature a promoter/manager can arrange is to have information and education available for those coming through the expo. When prospective buyers get all the information they want, they are more likely to buy. The more information, the greater the chance the show has to become successful.

Although the business expo only sold 100 booths, the promoter generated nearly $900 per booth, for a sale of $90,000. He operated with his salespeople on a straight commission, and paid out 20 percent, or $18,000, to them. At a show where consumers come to purchase goods instead of being entertained, promoters have to be cautious about ticket pricing. The buyer's mood is set at the door. The consumers intend to buy goods inside and if the admission is too high, it can cause many potential buyers to hold back. The ticket priced too low may be perceived by consumers as representative of a show that could not charge more. Certain consumer shows do charge a high admission fee and are able to get away with it despite having a minimum of entertainment. Auto expos are good examples of these types of shows. Although the expos have merchandise (automobiles) they wish to market, and consumers are aware of it, these special expos perform a service. Instead of having to drive around town and use a tank of gas searching for a car, evaluating styles, and pricing merchandise, auto expo attendees can one-stop-shop at the show. They can see every make and model imaginable. They save time and gas. The show is a convenience for which attendees are willing to pay.

In order to ensure increased revenues, the promoter/manager should keep a number of elements in mind. But the single, most important concept is the market, itself. The event must match the audience.

DIFFERENT MARKETS FOR DIFFERENT CULTURES

Each market reveals something else to the promoter/manager. They all differ, and what sells in one market may not do well in the next. Business opportunity shows sell goods primarily to those people interested in going into their own business. That person is entrepreneurial and the largest pockets of risk-takers in the United States reside in certain major markets (e.g., the Seattle, Los Angeles, and New York markets).

The Risk-Taking Markets

Risk-taking markets are usually melting pots containing a mixture of people. Revenues generated at events depend greatly on the mind-set of the people. In Toronto, Canada, a city which has many immigrants, the typical citizen views his own business as the best way to escape mediocrity or an obscure position in a large company. The same is true of Los Angeles and New York. The more conservative markets, however, are symptomatic of those areas where there risk-takers are virtually absent. Parts of the Midwest and the East Coast (New England) have a more conservative bent.

The Value of a Market's Psychographics

One of the best values of doing business in many of these markets is that they enable a promoter to get a better handle on the prospects for a special event, show, or concert by comparing similar markets. Examine the market's *psychographics* (its strengths and weaknesses). Many markets in the Midwest have audiences that are closely akin. A concert by Joe X in Cleveland usually means that the same event in Buffalo or Indianapolis will generate the same revenues. But a performance by Artist Y in Los Angeles offers no clue as to how the same act will do in New Orleans, Atlanta, or Philadelphia. Los Angeles is a melting pot, but the other three cities are not. Los Angeles is more entrepreneurial than the other three are not. Los Angeles is a place where new, innovative ideas are tried and, oftentimes, accepted, but the other three markets have not proven to be similarly inclined.

Test Areas Will Vary

In many ways, because of the openness and acceptance of new ideas, markets such as Los Angeles and New York are not always good test areas for events. Acceptance of a wide range of events is possible. The question should be, "Will it play in Peoria?" Thus, if a promoter/manager is enormously successful with an event in Los Angeles or New York, he/she has to think twice before launching it on a cross-country tour. In these markets, the only way a promoter/manager can get an idea about who is buying and why is to survey the audience. The promoter/manager has to use market research techniques to find out who is buying and where they are from. Once those questions are answered, the promoter/manager can look for other areas that may have people with similar characteristics.

At first, the previously mentioned business show promoter/manager did not grasp the importance of whether a market was noted for its innovative ideas or not. He assumed his entire success was due to a unique concept presented to people in major population centers. He further assumed that the success of the show depended entirely upon the total population in a market. The bigger the market, the more attendees.

Towards the end of his first year on the road with the business show, when he brought it to Washington, D.C., he discovered that other factors came into play. The metropolitan Washington area has more than three million people, which meant the area would likely be a success for the promoter. To top it off, the promoter surmised that because D.C. had so many government employees, his show would be even more successful. In his mind, government employees all retired at a relatively early age and most would be looking for another career or business opportunity so they would want to go to his show.

After three days, however, he discovered his assumptions were off. Attendance was not dependent upon total population of the market. The numbers coming through the turnstile depended entirely upon how homogenous the market happened to be. The more homogenous, the less attendance. Washington, D.C. proved something else. Government employees were not necessarily waiting to retire in order to jump into another occupation. Some were attracted to the show, but only a small percentage. It convinced the promoter that consumers in one occupation are not suddenly going to change and get into another. Markets such as Washington, D.C., with huge numbers of government employees, were not good for business opportunity shows. Nor were they good for any type of event that stressed becoming an entrepreneur and "doing your own thing." The motivation was not there.

Staging the Right Event for the Right Market

The Washington, D.C. example does not mean there is anything wrong with these types of markets. On the contrary, all can be excellent for the right event. The key is finding that event. Business shows are not the only events that will vary from market to market. The same is true of entertainment and cultural activities. The paid gate that many in the entertainment field are able to draw is usually chronicled in publications like *Billboard* and *Amusement Business*. Checking these magazines, for instance, would give a promoter/manager interesting insight into many artists. Following is the story of one of them.

> For many promoters, this artist's name in concert means success and a packed house. Most would love to have the rights to a local concert in which he will perform; however, if they were to check with the agency that handles him, and double-check with some of the trade publications, they would find that he has an interesting pattern. He does not draw well in Florida, but does in Philadelphia.
>
> The last time he made an appearance in Florida, he sold just over half of the tickets. In Philadelphia, it was a different story. Seldom does he fail to sell-out and quickly. The last time he was there, he sold out an arena for six consecutive nights.

Venues where artists are going to generate significant revenue can be determined by previous performances, trying to match similar markets and performances, or record sales. This star performer is not the only artist to have an erratic gate pattern. Most artists have pockets of strength and weakness. Promoters should be checking on these by following the trade journals and the gate figures. They should also be talking to the artist's agency and finding out where the act is strong and where it isn't. Agencies make money (usually around 10 percent of the fee paid to the artist) from the performer's fee, and they are anxious to keep them working. However, if they discover an artist is weak in a community, they will usually steer away from it. They do not want the performer to do badly, which might cause other promoters to back away from more promising dates. And they do not want to mislead promoters, either. They want the promoter to be as successful as the act. The agency may be tough when it comes to negotiating, but the smart representatives make sure that promoters do not buy bad dates.

Judging New Artist Revenues

But, what about new artists? How does a promoter judge potential revenue? One technique is to check album sales. It has been found that there is a correlation between the sale of CDs (compact disks) and concert tickets. Even when a promoter checks past sales, there is still risk, especially when most artists get a guarantee against a percentage. A big star may get $40,000 (guaranteed) against 60 percent of the gross ticket sales—known as the "gate"—whichever is greater. The star walks away with the $40,000 regardless of the outcome.

In the concert business, typical percentages most often mentioned are 85 percent of 60 percent of the gross, or 85 percent of the net. Although the figures sound radically different, in the end the numbers are close. (A promoter can figure that 40 percent of the gross revenues will be eaten up by expenses.) Here are some figures from a recent Madison Square Garden one-night concert to illustrate the point. First, using the 85 percent of 60 percent gross figure:

Gross Revenue	$415,000
(60 Percent of Gross)	$249,000
Artist Percent	x.85
Artist Fee	$211,000
Promoter Profit	$38,000

In the second scenario, the promoter gives the artist 85 percent of the net.

Gross Revenue	$415,000
Rental Fee	170,000
Net	245,000
85 Percent of Net	208,000
Promoter Profit	37,000

With nearly $500,000 at stake for a one-night concert, and more than $200,000 going to the artist, the promoter's risk is significant. Upfront, the promoter may get the venue for a deposit ($5,000) and the artist's fee may run anywhere from 10 percent to 50 percent upfront. That's a total—in the Madison Square Garden date—of just over $100,000. If the promoter can turn a profit of $37,000, that's a significant return on investment.

MEASURING RISK

Risk goes beyond contemporary music events, and is present in virtually any cultural/artistic attraction. With each event, the sales of tickets will vary. Some events do tremendous walkup business, while others do significant advances. It is up to the promoter/manager to investigate the event, look at its history, and determine if it is going to be an attraction that sells quickly or slowly. What is the sales profile of the event? There are different profiles for different markets as well. Some cities are known as "walk-up" towns, while others sell mainly in advance.

For the Super Bowl, NCAA Final Four, or other special event, tickets are sold as fast as they hit the market. For other events, that may not be true. As successful as the 1984 Olympics turned out, all events were not sold out. Yet 300 event sessions were oversold (via mail) a year before the opening.

For promoters/managers who depend upon a gate, it is vital to find a sales history and do some forecasting because, for most of these events, the promoter's fortunes rise and fall strictly on the strength of the box office and cash flow. This was not true for the business expo mentioned earlier in this chapter (which generated most of its revenue from inside sales), nor is it for many non-business-oriented events.

A good example of a special event that brings in more than a million dollars from spending within the show is the "Taste of Chicago," a giant, eight-day festival in which hundreds of thousands of Chicagoans crowd into downtown for entertainment and food. The promoters generate revenue through the sale of "food coupons" that are redeemable at restaurants participating in the festival. Every restaurant can set up a booth and consumers come through (with coupons) which they give to the restaurants for a "taste of food." The coupon may have cost the consumer 80 cents, however, when the restaurant redeems it, they may only receive 50 cents. The promoter keeps the rest. In general, the hotter the attraction, the more the promoter can keep. He can wheel and deal. He may also generate an additional 5 percent to 10 percent of gross sales for booth rental (5 percent if the show is new and untried; 10 percent if it has already proven itself a success.)

In this kind of event, the split between promoter and vendor may differ, but the arrangement where a promoter provides a vendor with tickets that can be redeemed for cash after the show is most commonplace. Cash can be lost, but a vendor is not likely to lose sight of the tickets that can be redeemed later for cash after the show. The tickets are purchased from the promoter's sellers and tight control is maintained on sequencing and numbering.

The "Taste of Chicago" is a classic case study which shows the many different ways a promoter can generate revenue. There is an admission (around $8) to the festival, along with the marketing of booth space, and the sales of food tickets. Just as the promoter of the business expo we looked at generated a multitude of ways in which to raise revenue, so has the promoter of the Chicago festival.

Sponsors and Risk

While every event has an element of risk, the events that carry the least risk are those that produce the most sponsors because revenue is guaranteed. If, for instance, the international federation for cycling awarded its world championship cycling event to a promoter in Knoxville, Tennessee, the promoter might be better off than one of his counterparts who was trying to stage a rock concert with a contemporary act in a major city. The Knoxville promoter might be able to sell one firm (e.g., a bicycle manufacturer) on the value of sponsoring the entire project.

To generate a hefty sponsorship fee, the promoter could assure the manufacturer of numerous benefits: exclusive signage in the arena, top seats for VIPs, and hosts for a post-event gathering and party. The seats and party are ideal for the sponsor to utilize with key distributors and/or other customers.

The lure of television. The promoter might also be able to market TV rights and generate additional funds. The international federation will ask for a percentage (anywhere from 50 percent on up), but the amount is negotiable. TV rights in the United States are worth more than anywhere else in the world. Realizing this, a sharp promoter can offer an international federation a variety of options when it comes to TV promotion. The promoter could offer to give up all non-U.S. TV rights in return for 50/50 split in the U.S. market. Or, the promoter may offer to give up 70 percent of the foreign rights, in return for a higher percentage in America. The key is that the revenue is in U.S. TV rights. Other countries are not significant and it is generally worth giving up revenue overseas for a better chunk of the revenues in the states.

Not every event is saleable to television. If you can, for instance, put cameras on a public street and televise the event, in most cases the television networks or channel do not have to pay anything. A parade usually does not belong to anyone. (There are, of course, some exceptions.) With events that are "made for television," there are several ways to televise and market the attraction. Last year, for instance, Stanford University held a special event in its football stadium to celebrate its centennial. Being in the stadium assured the promoters that the TV rights could be sold. Hosted by ABC-TV's Ted Koppel and featuring Whoopi Goldberg, the Doobie Brothers, Joan Baez, and a host of other internationally known performers, the event was designed to raise scholarship funds and generate notoriety for the university. The tickets were scaled from $100 to $15, with a crowd of close to 50,000 expected.

The TV arrangements can go one of several ways. The TV network and/or production companies could come into the stadium, tape, and edit it for later play. Another approach is where the promoter has his own personnel tape the show, edit it, and give it to the network later. With stadiums that have large video screens, this latter approach makes sense since there is a camera crew handling the video for the stadium's screen already in place.

The TV question: Who is going to buy it? Will it be a network or cable station? Or will everyone decline? At times, the network (i.e., ABC, CBS or NBC) may sponsor it, provide the filming and other production. A promoter/manager does not know, however, until he tries to market the event. Even then it may be difficult to get the TV networks to understand the value of the event. For instance, even though the city fathers were solidly behind Oklahoma City's Olympic Festival in 1989, coverage was limited to the TNN network. Not one major commercial network showed interest. This does not, of course, happen with the Olympics, nor with most other major international events. The networks are there. But for many sports and cultural events that are not commonplace in this country, TV revenue may be hard to generate.

The promoter does not automatically have TV rights to sell, either. When it comes to events like the Olympics, the promoter has no chance of owning the rights. The organizations and federations running these attractions know the appeal is such that they can sell it with little effort. They do not need a promoter with whom to split TV revenues. Promoters are not going to demand a TV split from these events. A promoter does not have any viable bargaining position when it comes to television and the big time events. If a promoter gave one of these organizations a difficult time by demanding TV rights, it would be relatively easy for the organizing committees to find another city and promoter with open arms.

If the promoter is able to generate coverage, it is a definite selling point for sponsors: When the cameras pan the arena in Knoxville during the cycling event, for instance, the only bicycle manufacturing signage in sight is that of the sponsor, which translates to free TV time.

With this arrangement, the manufacturer gets regional (and national, if televised) targeted exposure to an audience that is full of potential customers. The promoter does not have to worry about talent costs (the federation supplies the talent at no cost to him) or selling out. His overhead could be entirely covered by the sponsorship.

Generating sponsor revenues. Of course, revenue from sponsors is not a "given" for every event. There are hundreds, perhaps thousands, of events that have difficulty attracting sponsor dollars. Why? Part of the reason may be television. A live audience at an event provides a sponsor with a target, but if the crowd does not have significant numbers, the sponsor may shy away.

A small sports association found this out first-hand when it failed to sell any sponsorships, despite the fact it was holding its tournaments in busy, downtown Washington, D.C. The venue and potential audience were too small for a sponsor to measure. A TV audience might have enabled the sponsor to multiply that live audience numerous times, but it did not materialize. Television, although fragmented, is still king and can mean critical revenue to special events.

GENERATING FUNDS AND WHERE THEY GO

An illustration using the "Old Style Chicago Marathon," a special event run in the fall each year, shows how revenue funds are generated and where they go.

The Marathon, which has a budget of about $1 million, generates its funding through 10,000 participants who pay $25 apiece to enter. The night before they run, they are invited to a pasta dinner, at a fee of $14. That's $250,000 via entry fees, and if half the runners show for the pasta feast, another $70,000, for a total of $320,000.

However, the entry and dinner fees are anything but profit. Every runner expects more than a place on the starting line for this $25 and the Chicago promoters provide it. For the $25, participants get a t-shirt (a "must" at a running event), a runner's bag with coupons and premium items from sponsors, a finisher's medal, a certificate of completion printed on parchment, and a commemorative results booklet. By the time the promoter fulfills these requirements, there is not much left. The $14 pasta fee is not pure profit, either. The meal has to be paid for by the promoter and the profit may only be around $4 per meal, or $20,000.

Where the real revenue is generated is through sponsors. Without them, there would be no Chicago Marathon. The promoter has attracted a number, and each provides either cash or "in-kind" services. Sponsorships run from a modest $1,000 to a hefty $1 million, with the fee scale dependent upon what the sponsor wants. The $1,000 sponsors can use the event for sampling new products or market testing. It is a relatively inexpensive investment for a company that is anxious to test-market a product with thousands of people.

In the case of the marathon, the promoter did an excellent job of matching sponsors to the event. Major sponsors included Gatorade—a natural choice for a running or athletic event—and a "hair regeneration" medication developed by a major pharmaceutical firm and recognized by the FDA (Food and Drug Administration). The product works primarily with people who are just starting to lose their hair (e.g., people in their 20s and 30s). The product's presence at the Marathon is an example of how some sponsors zero in on a target audience.

Not far from the Marathon's start is another Chicago special event, the Chicago Jazz Festival. This annual event operates with a budget in excess of $500,000, and the promoter/manager counts heavily on sponsorship. The festival is free to the public, has civic support, and attracts huge crowds. The audience is a "mass crowd." It's a good mixture and so are the sponsors—Pepsi, Eastman Kodak, and Gallo. Each of these products is willing to pay significant fees to the promoter for a chance to reach this captive audience.

DISCOUNTS AND THE COST OF THE VENUE

The one fixed item the promoter can count on when it comes to determining costs and revenues for an event is the venue's rent. Almost every arena charges a flat rate and nothing more. And for good reason. In many markets, there is an abundance of venues and the competition among them is intense, because a venue that is not in use does not generate income for its owners. During slow periods, a promoter/manager may be able to generate an excellent rental agreement—much more favorable than if there was high demand for the venue.

But, when it comes to events that last more than a few days, the venues have the edge because the event needs the right venue. If a promoter/ manager is trying to bring a multi-day world gymnastics event into the market, for example, the venue will have to have certain seating requirements, and the athletes involved may require practice space adjacent to the hall where they will be competing. The bigger the event, the greater the requirements, and the more difficult it becomes for a promoter to pit one venue against another. (There may only be one venue in town that can hold the event.) This situation is quite obvious when it comes to a Super Bowl or any multi-day competition that requires several venues simultaneously. In order to get the Super Bowl in town, every venue will cooperate with the promoters, provide floor plans and make the job of preparing the proposal as easy as possible. Hotels will readily set aside rooms and volunteer to help. Airlines add flights and run schedules on a moment's notice.

Despite the overwhelming cooperation, vendors and venues have one thing in common for major events—they will not discount their rates. The venue will be made available, but the promoter is going to pay the full rate, even though they are bringing thousands of people into town and funneling millions of dollars into the local economy. Venues do not bend because they know the promoter (or organizing committee) needs them. It's all a matter of supply and demand.

For instance, New Orleans could not host the Super Bowl without the cooperation of every hotel in the city. The hotels will put aside the rooms, but the visitors are going to pay full rate with discounts nowhere to be found. If a promoter has the responsibility of providing (at his cost) hotel rooms and other facilities for one of these events, he has to keep that in mind and understand that his expenditure may be significant. Regardless of the venue and the terms, the promoter has to fill the arena.

SUMMARY

In this chapter, we discussed the many ways of planning and estimating actual costs and potential revenues. Here are 10 key tips to promoters for generating revenues and reducing costs:

1. Textile (merchandise) generally outsells hard goods (key chains and the like).
2. Promoters must check previous merchandise sales in other venues to determine viability of the product.
3. Most ticket sales are price sensitive and impulse buys.
4. Promoters can derive significant additional revenue from the "back-end."
5. Mailing lists generated from events can generate rental fees of more than $100 per thousand names.
6. Trade shows attract buyers and purchasing agents who purchase quantities, whereas consumer shows attract people who may only buy one or two items.
7. Risk-taking markets are generally melting pots.
8. There is a correlation between the sale of concert tickets and the sale of CDs by the concert artist.
9. TV rights in the United States are worth more than anywhere else in the world, sometimes more than the rest of the world combined.
10. Promoters do not automatically have TV rights to sell.

In the next chapter, we'll take a closer look at how major events are promoted, advertised, and marketed.

CHAPTER NINE

How to Market and Promote Events

The cavernous old center was musty and dimly lit, but it was the only venue that Cleveland had to offer for special events that could hold upwards of 20,000 people during a two-day engagement. More than 200 exhibitors would be part of the show when it opened the following day, but the booth that attracted the most attention was the one with the live chicken.

As the workers put the last of the booths together, the white and yellow bird stared at them in his cage located in a corner of the eight by ten-foot booth. The three-foot high cage rested on top of a four-foot-high pedestal. Above the cage were 13 words, printed in clear, bold-faced type: "Play tic tac toe . . . see if you are as sharp as the chicken!"

The chicken was part of a computerized tic tac toe game. On the front panel facing consumers who walked up to the game were nine, backlit tic tac toe grids, each approximately four inches square. Behind the grids was the chicken who could see out of the combination cage/game by simply looking over the top grid. Consumers would drop a coin in the slot at the side of the machine and hit an X or O. The chicken could instantly tell when a square had been marked, and responded.

The game had become a star attraction for the show. Wherever the promoter took it, he brought the chicken along because of the fascination the media had with the bird and the game. In every town the show played, a horde of TV cameras (and TV newspeople) descended upon the show to match skills against the chicken.

Was the chicken really a better tic tac toe player than anyone the media could offer? In 12 months, in a dozen cities, the promoter never failed to generate TV news coverage of the chicken who played tic tac toe with news reporters. The day after the newscasts aired, the event would be jammed.

To no one's surprise, the chicken knew nothing about tic tac toe. The game was actually run by a computer, and the chicken was prompted by a light. The chicken's motivation was not competition, but a kernel of corn.

WHAT MAKES GOOD TV COVERAGE?

Obviously, none of the newsmen believed that the chicken was actually a skilled tic tac toe player. What they did know, however, was that the film footage that was shot of the bird playing against the newscaster made an excellent, entertaining segment for the 5:00, 6:00, and 11:00 P.M. newscasts. Free TV news coverage is one of the most effective promotional vehicles for any show, but what promoters must understand is what makes good TV coverage and what does not. Why will a camera crew show up to one event and not another?

Bait the Hook

Camera crews, sent to film an event by assignment editors at TV stations, look for the story that can easily be illustrated with a camera. They search for the vignette that can entertain viewers in 30 seconds or less. TV stations rely on promoters to call these events to their attention. While there is no guarantee the station is going to air the footage, if the crew gets to an event and films, there is a good chance it will air.

Special events provide ideal fodder for the evening news. Whether it be an interview with a rock star the night before a concert, an advance look at an art exhibit, or a coach who is about to have his team play in the Final Four, most TV newscasts are likely to be interested. All four of those interviews offer the TV camera crew something they need—a visual element. The rock star might be filmed on-stage, in front of his band; the art exhibit has drawings/paintings; and the coach can be interviewed on the court with his team practicing behind him.

There are few things in the promotional mix for a show that are more important than television because free media exposure offers something to promoters and special events that advertising cannot match—credibility. Television is especially effective when the highlighted event has mass appeal because television specializes in reaching the masses.

This is especially true of newscasts. Who is watching? Men, women, and maybe some children. All ages, occupations, and interests are tuned in. In other words, a mass audience. Any promoter who is relying upon the average consumer to frequent his event should concentrate on trying to develop a "hook" or "angle" to dangle in front of the local TV assignment editors. As said previously, TV news is interested in the visual and newsworthy, and it's what promoters have to provide if they are going to get coverage. For the promoter who takes advantage of this interest, it can mean thousands of dollars worth of free air time, especially in major metropolitan markets where prime time news spots can run up to $1,000 (and more) for a 60-second commercial spot.

Tie into Audiences' Impulses

Since consumers go to most special events on impulse, television is extremely useful as a medium to stimulate those impulses. A 30-second news "bite" on the evening news may reach hundreds of thousands of people in a market. If the segment is intriguing (such as the chicken), the promoter could find thousands of additional people at his door the next day, all generated via that one television spot. Why? Regardless of how cynical some may be of the media, we tend to believe what we see, hear, and read in the news. Thus, a complimentary, positive segment on a special event gives the event an endorsement that may even cause the consumer to change plans and attend the following day.

Present the Unusual

Several years ago, the *Entrepreneur Magazine* business opportunity shows toured the country. When the show opened, all three network affiliates from both Los Angeles and New York turned out with camera crews. The promoter had an idea that few TV stations could resist. Inside, was a model skateboard park complete with curves and dips. Performing on it were a half-dozen skilled skateboarders doing loops, spins, and tricks. Every camera was there. The reporters on the scene talked to the promoter about the various business opportunities that skateboard parks (and the rest of the exhibits) presented to budding entrepreneurs.

Use Well-timed Segments to Enhance Credibility

The promoter always tried to generate coverage on the day (Friday) the expos opened. When the news segment aired Friday night, attendance would nearly double for Saturday and Sunday. Why? Credibility, thanks to the media. Viewers thought that if the stations believed the show was worth covering, perhaps it was worth their time, too.

Let the Event Speak for Itself

Sometimes, promoters/managers don't have to work hard to obtain media coverage. Some events sell themselves. At the Chicago food festival, for example, the sight of thousands of Chicagoans eating a variety of foods from outdoor stands is enough to turn out the cameras. In Seattle, a plane filled with Russian visitors coming to the United States for the first time in order to see the Goodwill Games was an attraction that led to coverage by all three network affiliates (ABC, NBC, and CBS). The event, by its sheer presence, garnered media air time.

WHAT TV STATIONS LOOK FOR IN EVENTS

Every TV station is in heated competition with its rivals for the viewing audience. News directors know that in order to win this contest, a station's news coverage has to be lively and entertaining. Hence, the interest in special events, which can provide fascinating footage of a variety of different types of events.

Events with Automatic TV Interest

There is, of course, little guesswork with an Olympics, because of its mere size and impact. There is also overriding media interest in the Super Bowl. In fact, networks send crews to the venue days in advance in hopes of generating solid, entertaining features that their rivals do not have. Up until 1991, there was a two-week period between the last playoff and the Super Bowl itself. That year, the waiting period was cut to one week. As a result most of the TV footage generated during the seven-day span was not as redundant as in previous years. However, in 1992 the NFL returned to a two-week interval. The Final Four, major tennis and golf events, and other championships generate the same "automatic" TV interest.

Events with a Visual Story

For lesser events, promoters/managers must work hard to develop news hooks and angles that are above and beyond the norm. Most of the time it will be a brief interview with a personality who has become known through his or her event. In most cases, the media is not waiting for them. The event has to be brought to their attention. In other words, the promoter has to develop potential (visual) stories and relay those stories to the proper people at the TV stations if they are going to get the coverage.

THE POWER OF FREE TV COVERAGE

A 25-year-old Peoria, Illinois retailer found out exactly how potent free TV news coverage could be when it came to promoting an event. The company's promotion manager and promoter developed a week-long special event that would take place in the firm's parking lot. Out in the lot, the promoter had the company construct the "world's largest waterbed." When it was finished, the bed stood more than six feet off the ground and measured 20 by 40 feet in length and width.

The promoter scheduled a week's worth of activities "on" the bed, ranging from a dance and beauty contest, to an event that featured kids bouncing up and down on the bed to see which could soar the highest. The event was visually unusual and entertaining. As a result, two local television stations (one a network affiliate) provided such good footage that the affiliate's network ran the same piece on its national evening news program. As a result of the media exposure, the company saw its retail business soar by more than 32 percent during the first week after the coverage. Equally as interesting was a telephone call that the owner received shortly after the network aired the segment from a waterbed retailer in Chicago who saw the film. He asked to rent the giant waterbed for a weekend promotion. The call gave the managers an idea: Why not rent out the enormous bed on a regular basis? They did. The rental fees generated from the bed has paid for it many times over.

Here's another simple yet ingenious idea developed by the owner of a popular restaurant. While it did not generate rental fees for him, it did generate thousands of dollars worth of free publicity and bring in hordes of new customers. In his ongoing attempt to develop new promotions to bring customers into his establishment, the restaurateur came up with a gem. He placed a round card table in the middle of his bar and drew a circle (in white chalk) about four inches from the edge of the table. He then introduced his customers to "Mr. Bones," "Mr. Jones," "Ms. Smith," and "Ms. Brown"—four crabs. He put the four crabs in the center of the table, let go and watched along with the customers. The first crab across the chalk like was the winner of the "official crab race." The races proved to be an instant, Thursday night hit.

Consumers would jam the small bar to see if the champion would be able to defend his title. In less than four weeks, two networks affiliates and two independent stations came in the bar to film the competiton. During the next year, the crab races appeared on "Eyewitness News" no less than four times. And the business in the bar swelled.

WHAT'S THE BEST TIME TO ATTRACT TV COVERAGE?

Promoters/managers know what the media can do. Whenever possible, they try to design activities within special events that will generate coverage.

Choose the Best Time of Day

Attracting cameras involves just as much timing as luck. The best time for events is earlier in the day, no later than one or two o'clock in the afternoon. Remember, that a crew must come out, film, get back to the studio, edit the film, and have the segment ready for the 5:00 or 6:00 P.M. newscast that night.

Plan for the Best Day of the Week

Of all the days, Friday usually is the best day to attract the news crews because it is usually a quieter news day and there may be less competition for coverage. (Of course, Saturday and Sundays would even have fewer distractions, but most stations do not have an abundance of crews working over the weekend. Saturday is the better of the two, but Sunday is considered high risk.)

Give Advance Notice

For a special event like the crab race, waterbed competition, or other strictly visual occasion, promoters/managers should contact TV planning and assignment editors about three days in advance, with an explanation of the event and what is going to happen. The day before, the promoter makes the contact again, reminding the assignment and/or planning editor of the event.

In the case of interviews, promoters should contact TV media about a week in advance. Most television stations have two key people in the newsroom. One is the planning editor, who handles any events that are for the future (e.g., anything that is slated for the following day[s] or weeks). The planning editor also supplies the assignment editor a daily rundown on potential events that are candidates for news coverage. The other key person, the assignment editor, works only one day at a time. On Friday morning, for instance, he or she is given Friday's events, and assigns crews based upon what he or she thinks will make the best news segment. Some stations only have an assignment editor who serves both functions.

A promoter calls a planning editor and outlines the opportunity being offered; the editor then has the option of passing it on to the assignment editor or to a reporter who may be suited for the interview (e.g., many stations have reporters who specialize in sports or finance). Most of the time the planning editor will ask for a written summary of the interview or event and person who will be doing it, prior to passing it on to the assignment editor or giving it to any reporter.

Produce Your Own Coverage

When the promoter attempts to get a film crew out to film a crab (or other) race or a personality interview, there is no guarantee that the filming and interview will ever happen. Even if planning and/or assignment editors decide to cover the event, if there is a major freeway accident, robbery, or sudden press conference by a noted politician, the cameras may very well go there.

Feature coverage almost always can be preempted at any time. Most promoters are cognizant of the value of free TV coverage, and in recent years they have become more astute and developed ways to get TV coverage even if the crew and reporter do not show up. One of the most effective is through "canned" film or a video news release that is supplied by the promoter to TV stations. A word of caution: Many stations accept this kind of material, but they will not air it if it is overly commercial or lacks entertainment value. Thus, when the International Chili Cookoff promoter supplies film, he has a few seconds on the beauty contests, "baby bottle" beer-drinking contests, entertainment, and a brief overview covering the cookoff and what it is all about.

Why would a promoter go to the expense of filming his own event for publicity reasons? The Cookoff promoter films highlights and services it to media because the Cookoff's location is about 65 miles from the studios of the nearest TV station. The promoter knows his chance of attracting cameras is not good. So, for the past five years he has had a professional crew film and edit a 30-second segment that is fed, via satellite, to local TV outlets as well as stations throughout the country.

Glean Additional Benefits

The Cookoff only runs one day, so why does the promoter bother with it? After all, regardless of the exposure, his event is over before the film airs. It cannot help draw additional attendees. But it can help in another way and that is with sponsors. Sponsor signage is always used on-stage and as background for any of the contests or events that are held at the Cookoff. When the camera crew shoots these events, the sponsors' logo and/or message is always in the background. Sponsors know this and that is one of the reasons they are willing to pay six-figure fees to the Cookoff. The time and effort the promoter makes shooting his own footage is considered well worth it.

Here's a list of free TV guidelines:

1. Look for the story that can be easily illustrated with a camera.
2. Television newsrooms and assignment editors rely on the promoter to call these events to their attention.
3. Special events provide ideal subject material for the evening news.
4. There should be a news and visual hook for the station.
5. The location (or distance from the station) impacts the chances of coverage.
6. Promoters have the option of filming their own coverage and servicing it to stations, however, these segments must not be overly commercial.

THE PROMOTIONAL TIE-IN

Another technique used by promoters to generate inexpensive or free media coverage is the promotional tie-in. These tie-ins involve two parties or two companies and benefit both. The tie can be between a special event and sponsor or a special event and a non-sponsoring firm. This is best illustrated by an enormously successful tie-in that was generated by a well-known restaurant.

> A restaurant had just opened on a busy boulevard, and the manager was searching for a way to let everyone know it was around. He thought about how other restaurants promoted themselves but then his mind turned to special events that were held in the area. It did not take long before he came up with an idea that would involve his restaurant with one of the best-known special events in the country—a collegiate football bowl game.
>
> The restaurant's manager approached the group responsible for putting on the football game and presented his relatively simple idea. The game was between the champions of a football conference in the Midwest and one in the West. The two best teams meet in a game on January 1. The game is traditionally a sellout. It is also nationally televised. Still, the restaurant's manager had an idea that he thought the organizing committee would love:

Since both football teams were usually housed in the local area for about two weeks prior to the game to practice, the manager suggested a diversion for them: Why not bring both teams to his restaurant one night and have a "Beef Bowl" contest. The object of the contest was to see which team could eat the most beef. The committee loved the idea and implemented it.

The first year, when both teams arrived at the restaurant for the "Bowl," there were three television cameras waiting, including one from the network. The television coverage mentioned both the game and the restaurant and it showed the players "in action," as they faced off against each other to see who could eat the most beef.

The event was a media success. It made every local newspaper as well as radio and television. The contest has been repeated every year since and the event has become so popular that there are now odds on the Beef Bowl. It seems that the team that can eat the most beef also wins the football game.

THE PROPER PROMOTION ATTRACTS MEDIA COVERAGE

This restaurant promotional tie-in illustrates several points. First, a promotion that is well done can attract media coverage. Second, tie-ins work extremely well for special events (i.e., the Rose Bowl). They are glamorous and the event itself intrigues the media. At times, promoters/managers may hesitate in presenting an idea to another firm because they have the impression that the other company (or event) may not care for it. Or perhaps they may surmise that the other event does not need the exposure because it is a sell-out. Nothing could be farther from the truth. Every special event that becomes successful is that way because the promoter/manager understood the importance of promotion and that they should promote the event in whatever way possible.

Even with events that are normally sellouts, the promoters/managers are interested in working tie-ins because they know the more they can keep their event in the news, the better known it will become, and the more demand there will be for tickets. Major special events are always open to tie-ins.

Take, for instance, major league baseball. Every team has a bat or ball night, that is, where the first 10,000 or so kids through the gate get a free bat or ball. Or, they may have a baseball card, photo, or calendar day. They always have some incentive that may convince people to turn out for the game. They also tie-in with groups; everything from Rotary and Kiwanis clubs to the local chamber of commerce.

Some promoters have developed promotional tie-ins with the media. For instance, in most cities you will find a promotional spot in the newspaper for the circus, an ice skating show, or another similar event. The thrust of the tie-in is that the newspaper gives the special event (e.g., circus, ice capades) free space, and, in turn, the event provides the newspaper with free tickets that can be given to readers.

Typically, the newspaper gives the tickets away via a write-in sweepstakes for readers or they run the name and address of a reader in the classified section of the paper. If the reader sees his/her name, he/she calls the newspaper and wins the tickets or whatever prize is offered. (The free tickets are a gimmick designed to get people to read the classified section.)

Promoters/managers often work similar tie-ins with radio stations. If a promoter is bringing a rock concert to town, they may work with the local rock radio station's management to develop a tie that promotes the show in return for tickets that the station can give away. In some instances, the radio station may even become a co-promoter. The advantage to the station is that if a well-known artist is coming to town and the station is a co-promoter, then identifying the station with the artist will earn it notoriety and enhance its reputation.

The same principle is used with more elaborate tie-ins. For instance, a cruise line may be offering a trip to the Caribbean. The promotion/manager of the trip will visit the local newspaper and propose the following tie-in: We'll give you two tickets, each worth $2,000, and you give us $2,000 worth of free advertising space. It is up to the newspapers sales promotion manager (and department) to decide if the tickets are something they want to utilize. If the newspaper judges its audience to be travel-oriented, they will frequently buy the proposal and give the cruise line the free space.

THE TRUE COST OF PROMOTIONS

Does the free space really cost the newspaper $5,000? No. It would cost an advertiser $5,000 to buy the space, but it does not cost the newspaper anywhere near that amount to print it, just as it does not cost the cruise line $5,000 for the tickets. Thus, both companies have a chance to benefit from the promotion. The cruise line will get free advertising, and the newspaper will get free tickets to give away in a promotion attractive to its readers.

The newspaper usually carries the event one step farther. Once it obtains the tickets, it starts promoting the trip. Most of the time they give the cruise line far more than $5,000 worth of space because they want the promotion to succeed to generate as many entries as possible.

Why? To prove itself a terrific advertising vehicle. When the contest is over and the winners have been selected, the newspaper's sales department can visit local travel agencies and tell them: "We just ran a promotion and gave away a free cruise. Believe it or not, we generated 50,000 entries, which shows how travel-oriented our reading audience happens to be. You should be advertising in our newspaper." Those are not, of course, the exact words, but the message is the same.

This tie-in principle carries over to every business and event, regardless of how big or small the companies involved happen to be. One of the best examples of how potent this type of promotion can be for an event or business is one that started more than 20 years ago.

THE MULTI-MILLION DOLLAR PROMOTION

It began with the opening of a small hamburger stand on a busy intersection in a major city. The owner, like many entrepreneurs and promoters who open businesses or develop special events, had little funds for advertising and/or promotion. The first thing he did was what every smart promoter practices: He defined his market. A hamburger stand has a local market (e.g., its customers do not travel much farther than three or four miles [at most] in order to buy a hamburger). Within that market area were his customers. Who were his customers? Mainly the youth market. They buy the majority of fast-food type hamburgers.

With this information, the promoter began to look at his market and think how he might reach those kids without spending a good deal of money. He had an idea. He went up to the local high school, explained to the principal that he was a local businessperson who had just opened an establishment down the street from the school. He explained that he was interested in the high school and the kids because they were, of course, his customers. He wanted to do something special for them. He proceeded to explain a tie-in to the principal.

It went something like this: Each week, the principal and/or teachers would select five students and submit their names to the hamburger stand owner, who would take a small space ad in the weekly high school newspaper. The five names appeared at the bottom of the ad. All the students had to do was tear out the ad and bring it to his hamburger stand to receive a free hamburger, french fries, and a soft drink.

The principal and teachers liked the idea because it helped the school recognize successful students by building their esteem and morale. They knew the students would love seeing their name in print. The hamburger stand owner saw other benefits: The promotion would enable him to "network" with his prime customers. He also assumed that the school would be rewarding leading students, both academically and athletically, who would likely bring in other students (customers). That is exactly what happened.

Within weeks of the start of the promotion, the hamburger stand owner began to pull business away from his competitors. Within months, no one could compete with him. Even today, no one can compete with his 14 hamburger stands which still carry on this promotion revolving around small space ads in high school newspapers and recognition for students. How about the owner? Well, he's a retired millionaire.

HOW TO RECOGNIZE PROMOTIONAL OPPORTUNITIES

The lesson on how a promoter must recognize promotional opportunities extends much further than the hamburger business. For example, Hunt's Tomato Sauce, a sponsor of the International Chili Cookoff, recognizes the chance it has to reach distributors as well as consumers through its promotional tie-in with the Cookoff. Hunt's runs coupons, point-of-purchase displays, and contests just prior to the Cookoff, especially in the market where the Cookoff takes place.

There are opportunities for beneficial tie-ins with every event, but they are not always obvious. They may call for the promoter to use his imagination. For example, radio stations are always looking for tie-in opportunities. Promoters of the "Jamboree in the Hills" in West Virginia, for example, tie-into a country music station. An oldies station may join with a promoter to back a one-night concert with artists from the 1950s and/or 1960s. A cultural event might want to tie-in the talk radio station. Each station and promoter finds its own niche, and in doing so they can generate a great deal of exposure. The exposure not only will be virtually free, but can be 10 times more effective than any advertisement because of its direct relationship with the media.

SUMMARY

In this chapter, we discussed techniques for promoting your event. Without the proper promotion, your event may never get off the ground. The following are 10 key tips on promotion for special events:

1. Promotional tie-ins generate inexpensive or free media coverage. Use it to your advantage.
2. Special events have an edge when it comes to attracting media attention because many are glamorous and may feature well-known performers or activities that have a broad interest among consumers.
3. Involving the media in a promotion generates credibility in the eyes of the consumer for the event.
4. Events in smaller markets may have a greater chance of TV exposure via a promotion because there are usually fewer events and activities that compete for the free media time.
5. In most cases, the media are not standing in line to cover a special event—the promoter has to bring it to their attention and sell them on its value.

6. Tie-ins can be between a special event and sponsor or a special event and non-sponsor.
7. Tie-ins can also be between the event and the media.
8. Radio stations and newspapers provide excellent tie-in opportunities for special event promoters.
9. The key selling point of a promotional tie-in is that it benefits both parties (e.g., the media and the event).
10. The more successful an enterprise, the more open its managers are to a promotional tie-in, and the more aware they are of its value.

Remember, promotion is a powerful tool that is a critical ingredient for every special event. In the next chapter, we will look at another potent vehicle for an event—advertising.

CHAPTER TEN

The Role of Advertising

In the promotional and marketing mix for a special event, the importance of advertising should never be underestimated. In the long run, almost every event has to utilize funds to advertise. The question promoters have to answer before spending any funds is "which media reaches what market?" Today, there are more choices than ever before:

- commercial TV;
- cable TV;
- radio; and
- print.

Of course, there are others—from skywriting to commercial blimps—but these four are the best choices for most events.

COMMERCIAL TV—THE MEDIUM FOR THE MASSES

Commercial TV is, of course, the medium for the masses. Most commercial channels draw a variety of viewers and it is difficult to discern who is watching and when. Some surveys have gone so far as to determine demographics of viewers. During the 1990–91 TV season, for instance, a survey determined that viewers of NBC-TV's "Matlock" were older adults. Advertisers, who are sometimes obsessed with reaching a younger market because of its heavy buying power, backed off the show. NBC canceled one of its highest-rated productions (although it did return as a replacement series in the 1991–92 season). Saner heads prevailed and the show was brought back on the air later in the season.

CABLE TV HITS SPECIFIC MARKETS

Commercial TV is difficult to pinpoint when it comes to viewers. Determining the demographics of many cable stations may not be as difficult. For instance, stations that program financial news 24-hours a day obviously appeal to the businessperson. ESPN (all-sports) appeals to the sports fan, and the HSC (Home Shopping Club) has a heavy female audience. This segmentation takes a lot of the guesswork out of buying time. It gives a promoter/manager a definite picture as to who will be watching.

The problem, however, with TV advertising is the numbers. As more TV stations compete for viewership, there is no dominance by any one delivery method. Cable has cut into commercial TV and viewership is down. Monday Night Football is still around, but now consumers can frequently find Sunday Night Football, as well. In some instances, the game airs on a national cable network, but because of the cable's lack of penetration in some markets, a local independent channel may air it instead.

THE IMPACT AND VALUE OF RADIO

As with most media, buying time on radio can be confusing because the radio time salesperson wants his station to be attractive to the gamut of advertisers. In other words, statistics a promoter receives can prove inconclusive or misleading.

Promoters can target audiences via radio much more efficiently than with television. Radio stations, by their format, attract certain demographics. For instance, talk and all-news radio is skewed to an older audience. Although the promoters can reach a portion of the younger audience on talk/news radio, the audience is dominated mainly by those 40 years of age and over.

On the other hand, all-music stations can be segmented. The classical music outlet is going to reach an older, more affluent audience. In most markets, the rock music station reaches a younger, less affluent crowd. This usually means that classical music stations may be great for advertising Cadillacs and Mercedes, while all-music rock stations are the ideal outlets for rock music concerts.

One of the best methods of evaluating radio and its effectiveness is through the use of something every promoter has—common sense. All the promoter has to do is sit down and think about radio and the listening habits of its listeners. When it comes to rock radio, kids and younger adults listen. But, they also do something that upsets advertisers—as soon as a song is finished and a commercial comes on, the listener flips the dial to another station because they do not want to be bothered by commercials. But if promoters/managers use the correct campaign to advertise rock music special events through the use of the right musical spot, listeners will not turn off the promo until after they have heard the message. Getting and keeping the listener's attention is key.

WHERE PRINT ADVERTISING FITS

Can print ads do the job for special events? Yes, depending upon the vehicle and how the audience is targeted. Print would not be suitable for a promoter trying to reach a teenage audience, however. Print is not an attractive option for youth-targeted products because the audience does not read much. This has long been a problem for the print media. Readership is getting older and most publications have not been able to attract younger audiences.

There are exceptions, however. Some newspapers have created special entertainment or similar sections that are geared to a younger audience. Some have weekly entertainment guides, while others have even developed "ethnic supplements," that is, a section that may come out once or twice a week and is written in Spanish, Vietnamese, or whatever is the language of the target audience.

With print, it is up to the promoter to determine what publication and/ or section may reach his market. For example, when *Entrepreneur Magazine* began to stage its small business expos across the country, the promoters decided that the only type of TV coverage to use was TV news. The promoter's rationale was that anyone interested in going into business (or anyone running a business) is both busy and serious and was unlikely to watch any television other than the news. The promoter did not have any factual data to back his assumptions but relied purely on his own instincts (frequently one of the best indicators a promoter can use). Instead of buying TV time, the promoter concentrated his entire media budget on print advertisements.

WHEN TO BEGIN AN ADVERTISING CAMPAIGN

Once a medium or media are selected, the promoter has to decide when to advertise. With a few exceptions, special events are impulse buys. People who attend most cultural, music, and sporting events do not plan months in advance. They usually purchase tickets no sooner than a week beforehand.

At one time, promoters/managers of such events as concerts believed that the best way to sell the event was to build ticket sales momentum. A month or so before the event, they would begin by running small space ads in entertainment sections. As the event drew closer, the size of the ads grew larger. The promoter/manager would place his biggest ads the week before the event.

At the same time, many promoters/managers were able to get radio stations to co-sponsor concerts. Program directors of these stations often refused to promote the event if there were more than seven to 10 days left before the performance. The promoters/managers argued that the "last-minute" push was not a great benefit, while the program directors pointed out that consumers made last-minute decisions that were not usually finalized until the week of the event.

Eventually, some promoters began to experiment with this impulse buy or "radio theory." One promoter, who was responsible for filling a 10,000-seat arena for the introduction of the Bee Gees to the United States, held all advertising until the Sunday before the Friday night introductory concert. On that Sunday, he ran the first full-page ad ever placed for a rock music concert. The same week, the local radio station, a co-promoter of the event, began spots on behalf of the event. By the time Thursday night came, the concert was sold out.

THE ADVENT OF ADVERTORIALS

The last-minute, impulse-buy theory held true for *Entrepreneur's* business shows as well. The promoter/manager looked upon the event as an impulse item; a show that people would only commit to during the week prior to its opening.

The promoter/manager held all advertising until the Sunday prior to the opening of the three-day event scheduled for the following weekend. On that day, the promoter used his entire advertising budget to place an ad in the largest newspaper in town—a six-page, full-sized insert. Inside were telephone numbers for consumers to make advance reservations for seminars, along with an order blank for cassette tapes of the seminars for those who could not attend. The six-pager, which cost more than $50,000 in the local newspaper, generated nearly $20,000 in advance orders for tapes and seminars via the mail and telephone.

Most important, it introduced a new concept to the promotion of special events. It was the first advertisement to be placed in a newspaper designed to look exactly like the publication itself. It had the appearance of being an editorial, not an advertisement. An editorial has a distinct advantage over an advertisement because it implies media endorsement. When a newspaper writes a story featuring an act, artist, or upcoming special event, consumers assume that the publication picked the subject because it was worthy of the exposure. The fact that someone (i.e., a public relations representative) probably sold the idea for the story to the newspaper never occurs to most readers.

With an ad, every consumer, however, is well aware that the company or individual behind an event paid for space. But when the advertisement looks like editorial coverage, consumers often do not realize it is a paid ad. These are known as *advertorials*. In the case of the business expo, the show broke the attendance record at the convention center and the promoter/manager made a return on his investment many times over, partially due to the success of the special ad section. The value of advertorials and the knowledge that attendance at some special events is not decided by the consumer until the last minute, are key elements that promoters should keep in mind when promoting shows.

Keep in mind, though that there are special events that are not entirely last-minute decisions. Take the West Virginia three-day "Jamboree in the Hills." The event has become more than a music festival. Many people who come solely for the event arrive days early and stay on afterwards. In other words, it has become a vacation, complete with families in motor homes and RVs. Since vacations are often planned months ahead of time, the Jamboree promoters now begin their campaign long before the actual concert. By the time the show arrives, most of the motor home and RV spaces are filled. An advertorial would be wasted on this audience.

Advertorials and Television

Recently, advertorials have taken on new meaning. Many cable, and more recently, network TV stations have instituted special half-hour "talk/

interview/demonstration" shows. These programs have become potent marketing tools for selling special events as well as products. These shows, which are a throwback to the three-to-five minute "Ginsu knife" commercials which aired years ago on TV, are entertainment-oriented. They sell as they entertain. Although audiences today are more sophisticated than ever, many viewers do not perceive the subtle differences between one of these paid specials and regular programming. Tapping into such audiences could prove extremely productive for the promoter/manager promoting a special event.

THE POWER OF THE NEWSSTAND

For promoters/managers, there is one other print media phenomenon that can have a large impact on special events promotions. This is known as the *motivational difference* between home delivered and newsstand publications. When consumers subscribe to a newspaper or magazine, receiving it at home, they are oftentimes too busy to read every issue. The Tuesday edition may simply sit there for days and never be read because no one has time. But, if a consumer purchases a newspaper or magazine from a supermarket, newsstand, or at the drugstore, it usually means that they bought it to read.

This purchasing pattern is important in planning the marketing of a special event. The publication that sells more copies via a newsstand may be a better advertising vehicle than its home-delivered counterpart because the consumer "wants" to read it. There can, for instance, be a significant difference between the readership of the two publications. One has a circulation of 100,000 circulation (all sold via newsstands) and another has a 150,000 circulation of 100,000 with 90 percent (135,000) delivered to the home. In comparing the two, the lower circulation publication demonstrates something that cannot be measured with its rival—the consumer's desire to read it.

WHICH IS THE BEST DAY TO ADVERTISE?

Regardless of the medium, there are certain days that offer advertisers more readers or viewers than others. For special events, the best day to advertise is a Sunday. Traditionally, Sunday is the day of the week that has the highest circulation and the largest viewing audience. Sunday is also the day of the week when the head of the household usually spends time at home, reading the newspaper or watching television.

This pattern of Sunday reading and viewing has not escaped advertisers. Most Sunday publications are twice as thick as the daily publication. Advertisers have surveyed and studied the market and they know that Sunday is a heavy readership day. If you want to hit the largest audience with a specific ad, run it on a Sunday.

USING OUTDOOR ADVERTISING

Outdoor advertising encompasses billboards, bus and bench placards, cab sideboards, and the like. Don't overlook their possibilities. There is no guarantee that consumers will read outdoor advertising, but if the copy is well-structured and the message brief, there is a good chance it will catch their eye. The most common mistake in outdoor ads is the tendency to use too much copy. Studies show that consumers have approximately three to five seconds to read a billboard ad. To get the message across, promoters should keep their messages short and to the point.

The same goes for bus, cab, and other similar placards. The boards are small and reading space is limited. Although a bus may not speed by, it is difficult to read clutter. Keep it simple. With outdoor advertising, promoters should also keep their audience in mind. Placards inside a bus reach an audience that is entirely different from outside signage. The audience on the bus is limited; a promoter/manager can research a bus rider's demographics. The outdoor signage is attempting to reach a much broader spectrum of consumers. (The audience is only limited to the route of the bus.) The same is true of billboards. Reaching a common denominator is key for outside signage.

HOW TO BEST USE DIRECT MAIL

For the promoter/manager who uses direct mail to sell a special event, there are several proven ways of reaching and attracting an audience.

Select the Right List

First, select the right mailing list. As basic as it may sound, renting the right list is not the easiest thing to accomplish. Promoters/managers should use a broker to help find and screen lists. They can also look through the *Standard Rate & Data Service (SRDS)* book on direct mail lists. This book contains the names of virtually every company offering a mailing list. The lists are broken into categories and promoters can generate anything ranging from a business and sport's list to art and cultural enthusiasts. The SRDS book also provides information on the number of names per list, price per thousand, and also indicates the list's source (where names were obtained). For instance, were the list of buyers generated from a space ad (advertisement in a newspaper and/or magazine) or are they a list composed of people who have already purchased through the mail? (The list of buyers who purchased through the mail is better.) A list of sports fans, for instance, who bought sporting goods through the mail can be extremely valuable.

Some companies merge these two buyer categories. If they do, the SRDS listing should break out the percentage of buyers who purchased through space and the percentage through the mail. The list source may say

"90 percent space, 10 percent direct mail." The list still may be good for mail order, but is less reliable.

Determine the Buyer's Price Threshold

When using lists, promoters should also be careful to try to determine the price threshold of the average buyer on the list. If a promoter is marketing a $90 event (e.g., the "Jamboree in the Hills"), and the list averages $14 per sale, the promoter is probably renting the wrong list. Promoters should try to obtain through the list broker the last mailing piece that used the list. Do this to get an idea of the type of offer and if the offer (and buyers) fit the promoter's event.

Three Keys to Buying Lists

The most important thing for a promoter to request when buying a list is an RFP—Recency, Frequency, and Price. *Recency* indicates how long has it been since the list was last used and the number of buyers who purchased an item. *Frequency* indicates how often the buyers purchase. *Price* indicates the amount they spend when they do buy. All three types give a promoter clues as to how the list will fit his event.

Ensure List Quality

Even if the list appears to make a good product fit, promoters/managers should "walk through the list," that is, buy it a piece at a time to test it. If a list has 100,000 names, purchase 5,000, mail to them and wait. If the response is good, take another 5,000.

Despite the fact that the direct mail business is strictly policed, there are still companies and list brokers who will fill the first 5,000 names with people they know to be great respondents. The remaining 95,000, however, may only be so-so. The promoter/manager renting such a list finds himself with poor response.

Another way to ensure list quality is ask for the "*n*th" name selection. This requires that the company renting the list provide the promoter/list renter with a wider selection of names. For example, if a list has 100,000 names and the promoter orders 5,000, the promoter will get every 20th name. The total number of names ordered is divided into the total number of names on the list. Without any additional effort, the promoter can sample an entire list with his or her first test. Nth name selection can be used on any size list. If the list is national, the *n*th name will provide a profile of the entire country for the promoter. And with computers, selection of mailing lists has become more scientific. If a promoter knows his product (special event sales) works better in certain sections or states, he can pick the *n*th name selection according to geographic region or state.

Choose the Right Broker

The best list brokers have knowledge about every list. They know which ones pull best, and oftentimes why. They are not anxious to merely sell a list but to provide the client (promoter) with a good list so he/she will become a repeat customer. For help in choosing a local list broker, promoters should consult the general merchandise section of the SRDS. (The SRDS can be found at most major libraries.) If a broker is handling a number of different lists, they must be doing a good job. They would not be handling many lists if they did not generate sufficient rental monies for their clients. Here, the main criterion for success is whether they have steered mail order promoters down the right path.

Use One-Step, Two-step Direct Mail Ads

Space ads can be approached in two ways—as one-step or two-step ads. In a *one-step ad*, you present your entire sales message and "close" in the same ad. There may be a coupon, address, or telephone number at the bottom of the ad so customers can respond and place an order for tickets to the special event.

Obviously, a one-step ad requires more ad space and capital. The ad has to be packed with information and answers designed to overcome the buyer's objections. It is the promoter's one shot at the prospect and he must answer everything on the customer's mind.

Two-step ads are cheaper and certainly less risky. They are called two-steps because they involve two distinct operations (or steps). The initial step is placing a small ad that, hopefully, generates inquiries. Step two is answering and selling to those who made the inquiries. Usually this is done with a mailing piece which answers all the questions a prospect may pose. The 1984 Summer Olympics in Los Angeles did a superb job in this category. Inquiries were answered with an elaborate, effective mailing piece. Not only were the in-demand events sold (e.g., opening and closing ceremonies plus gymnastics), but the response was such that 300 sessions were oversold.

In the long run, promoters may spend the same amount on a two-step ads, because of the cost of the follow-up mailing piece and the postage. However, they can market products with a lower cost since the two-step (or "inquiry") ad is smaller and it does not have to provide all the information the prospective customer needs to know before the purchase.

All the inquiry ad has to do is generate prospects. It may generate those prospects even if the sales approach is not quite right. The mail order follow-up piece must, however, contain all the key things about the event. With a two-step ad, the promoter can reach, and possibly sell, the same event at a fraction of the cost. A two-column, one-inch ad designed to get people to send for more information (e.g., a brochure about the event), may run $100 or less in a publication that charges $10,000 for a half- or full-page ad. The key is the follow-up material. Does it sell and answer all the questions the potential customer may pose?

Sell Sizzle, Not Steak

Whatever kind of mailing piece the promoter sends, it should be one that sells the "sizzle" and not the "steak." When a store markets a winter coat (steak) it does not sell a coat, but it markets "warmth." That's the sizzle. When a salesman sells a life insurance policy, he does not do so by telling the customer he needs "life insurance," but rather he tells the prospect he needs "protection." Protection is the sizzle, the thing that excites the buyer, not the policy (steak) itself.

Equally as important when it comes to direct mail is the headline or cover copy for a brochure for an event. To generate maximum interest, a general headline (or brochure coverline) works better than a specific one. For example, the "greatest athletic event of the year" will interest many more sport fans than the "greatest track meet of the year." Using a specific headline can limit the brochure's appeal to a segment of the audience. The object is to get as many people as possible to open the piece and read it. Even non-track fans may be turned on by an event if the copy inside is provocative and paints a vivid picture. On the other hand, if the non-track fan sees a headline that is specific, he may just throw the piece away and never read it.

Ultimately, people buy for emotional reasons (e.g., to gain status, to earn more money). Later, they rationalize those reasons with logic. Someone who pays a broker twice the face amount for a ticket to the NCAA Final Four does so for emotional reasons. He or she wants to be part of the crowd. Later they may say they did it because:

1. There will never be a better game between two, more evenly matched teams; or
2. we are going to see two of the best senior forwards in the country on the same court at the same time.

Good direct mail advertising plays upon those emotions.

How Mail Order Customers Differ

Another important mail order research tool is the *Editor & Publisher's Annual Market Survey*. For promoters/managers this book is a must. The book helps promoters to pinpoint the differences in different markets. *Editor & Publisher* contains information on every market. It describes prime industries, where people are employed, and dozens of other useful facts that would help a promoter analyze buyers in his city or any other market. It dissects markets, tells who lives there, what they do, and how much they make. For example, the two key industries in Bakersfield, California, are agriculture and oil. That information tells the promoter Bakersfield is a blue collar market, as opposed to a community of white collar service businesses. That gives the promoter a clue as to what events might sell in a particular market. Traditionally, for instance, blue collar workers are not overwhelming fans of art shows. On the other hand, they might be enthusiastic supporters of a football or basketball special event.

Comparing Bakersfield to Houston, Texas may seem applicable because Houston is a prime oil-producing area as well. But the *Editor & Publisher* yearbook indicates there are 1.1 million wage earners in Houston with 187,000 employed in manufacturing, possibly oil or oil-related businesses. But there are nearly 950,000 in non-manufacturing or white collar occupations. So, Houston's demographics are much more varied than Bakersfield's.

Editor & Publisher does not relate the psychological attitudes of buyers in a market. If it did, there would probably be no risk involved in the direct mail response and special events field. But common sense and sensitivity can give a promoter an excellent insight into each market and the potential customer, once they know the demographics of the community.

The Importance of Personalization

Whether a consumer is white collar or blue, they all share one desire when it comes to direct mail—to be treated as individuals or personalized. The more personal the envelope in a mail order campaign, the better the chance it will be examined and opened by the prospective customer.

The least personalized piece is the printed label on the envelope. The label is a giveaway that there is junk mail inside and dramatically decreases chances of getting the envelope opened. The most effective piece is the one in which the recipient's address is typed directly on the envelope.

Figure 10–1 is a list of some of the important factors you should keep in mind when using a direct mail campaign. Study them and use them.

USING P.I. OR P.O. TIME

Of course, direct mail can be expensive. However, there are other ways to generate exposure and sales (in other media) with minimal expenditure. One important technique is called *P.I.* (Per Inquiry) or *P.O.* (Per Order) *time*.

Using P.O. time is simple and cost-effective. There are many independent TV (network and cable) stations that do not sell all of the available commercial time they have. Obviously, if they cannot sell it, it goes to waste and they lose revenue. Many stations are open to suggestions from promoters for a P.O. arrangement in which the promoter supplies a spot, the station airs it at no cost, and the station is compensated through a percentage of the ticket sales.

P.I. time works in a similar manner, except the station is compensated on the basis of inquiries. The spot may allude to a brochure that consumers

---

FIGURE 10–1. *Key Elements When Using Direct Mail*

1. List source should be examined before purchasing any group of prospective buyer names.
2. Names generated through space advertisement differ dramatically from those obtained through a previous mail order offer.
3. Recency, Frequency, and Price (RFP) are the measurements used in evaluating lists.
4. "Nth" name selection helps protect a promoter when renting a list.
5. A one-step ad generally requires more capital than a two-step. Two-steps are cheaper and less risky.
6. People buy for emotional reasons and defend their selections later with logic.

---

can request via the mail or telephone. The station is paid for every request. The basis of both these programs is that the promoter does not risk cash. He can maintain cash flow, generate an additional marketing channel, and increase sales without paying for the time.

What works for TV time also works for radio time. The promoter can work a similar tradeout which can be especially effective if the promoter targets the right radio station and program. That is, if he can generate a P.O. spot on the station's sports broadcast or talk show, and he is promoting a special sporting event, he has successfully targeted his buyers.

With print advertising, however, the promoter has less of a chance of working a deal. Newspapers and magazines never "waste" space. That is, if a hole develops they can always put in a house advertisement. Thus, working deals with the print media is tougher than with television or radio.

But does it work? In today's environment, P.O. and P.I. time is becoming commonplace. This is particularly true when it comes to cable TV. Most cable channels are short of revenue and the P.O. or P.I. approach is more than welcome.

Using P.I. and P.O. time requires creativity and imagination on the part of the promoter. A classic example of how well P.O. time can work is that of K-Tel Records. A few years ago, this company set a precedent with massive tradeouts that were so successful that the firm was transformed into a multi-million-dollar company in just a few short months. Special event promoters are not, of course, selling records but they are marketing products (e.g., tickets), and products can be sold in this manner.

Most stations also welcome "video advertorials." These programs, as mentioned previously, usually run 30 minutes and are visual versions of print advertorials. They contain interviews, testimonials, and other product and/or ticket prices that come across initially as editorials. Once again, although today's consumer is more sophisticated than ever, there are not many who can tell the difference between a well-done video advertorial and a commercial. It also requires limited funding. The promoter does not have to pay for the commercial time, but with most arrangements, he has to pay for the production of the commercial.

Production costs are not exhorbitant. With the abundance of television studios (e.g., all the cable outfits), an independent promoter/manager can probably get a spot filmed in-studio and a master copy made for under $2,000. Cable stations, in particular, have "dead time," that is, the studios are not being utilized. Rental of the studio at such times is extremely reasonable. They also have the capability to supply the announcer and help with the scripting.

GETTING PUBLICITY FOR EVENTS

Radio, TV, and print advertising require funds. Even P.I. or P.O time requires cash because of the commercial production cost. But one area where the promoter (and event) can benefit with hardly any expenditure is *publicity*. With publicity, the promoter can target the media to reach his or her (potential) market.

There are different publicity vehicles which promoters/managers can use in order to obtain free media exposure. The most basic is the *news release*. These are factual documents that usually run no more than a page to a page and a half. They are used for general news about the special event. For instance, news releases could be used in the following circumstances:

1. The announcement of the event. When it will take place. Where. Who will be participating. (For example, with the International Gymnastics World Championships, the release would contain the countries participating, the city, venue, times, and dates).
2. Ticket prices and where to obtain tickets.
3. Names of participants as they become available. (If someone well-known is going to participate, this could generate a separate release).
4. Facts and figures on the event. (A release can detail how often the event is held, what the events are, and how they are scored).

The promoter/manager would send each release to the media that last reaches his/her market. If the event were a world championship boxing match, the promoter/manager would send the initial release to sports pages throughout the community. If the promoter felt that attendance would be coming from outside the area, he/she would also send the release to key newspapers in other cities.

The promoter could also take the release and try to get it on the "wire." The news wire service is a valuable tool for special event exposure. It is similar to a teletype machine and most major newsrooms (radio/TV/

print) have these machines in their news departments. By sending a release over the wire, it reaches media throughout the country. (The cost is actually less than it would run to mail the release to the media throughout the country.)

Whether the promoter services the release to all markets depends upon the event. A local concert is not going to appeal to a potential audience 1,500 miles away. But the world weightlifting championships, the gymnastics championships, the Final Four, or the NCAA track and field championship may. The promoter has to make the judgment. It should be based upon the promoter's belief (or non-belief) that attendance will (or will not) consist of all locals, or if attendees will come from thousands of miles away. In the case of a Super Bowl or other similar event, attendees will certainly come from thousands of miles away.

What goes into a release? Everything from ticket prices to who, what, where, and when are included. It's all factual. For a closer look at news releases and how they are structured, promoters should visit a local library. Most have volumes of research material and information on press releases and how they should be structured.

THE IMPORTANCE OF RECOGNIZING THE FEATURE

The most important aspect of getting PR is the *feature* story. The story is sold (or "pitched") to media in advance of the event. For instance, before a heavyweight championship fight, the newspapers are loaded with interviews on the two competitors. It's human interest, and human interest stories sell tickets. No one buys a ticket to a fight; they purchase tickets to a contest between two individuals—and they may identify with one of them because of a feature story which ran in the newspaper.

A good example of the value of features is the Super Bowl. For days before the event, reporters and writers are trying to drum up feature stories about those who will be involved in the event. They do not just write about the event, but about the people involved. Once again, it is the human interest that draws consumers to special events.

This same principle applies to non-athletic events. What makes an art show fascinating to consumers is something about the painter/artist. Potential attendees like to get some kind of insight that enables them to feel as if they know something about the artist. They would like to see, for example, how the artist's personality had an impact on his or her work.

SUMMARY

It all boils down to human interest. When an event has it, there can be a tremendous following and enormous sales. When it lacks it, the event suffers. If there's no pizzaz, there's no draw. The following list provides 10 keys to the effective advertisement of an event. Use them when you plan your special event's advertising campaign.

1. Television is the medium for the masses.
2. Radio can target market segments more effectively than television.
3. Advertorials, a relatively new way to generate credibility for an event, are proven sellers.
4. Sunday is the best day of the week for print advertising.
5. Billboard messages must be readable in three to five seconds.
6. Per Order (P.O.) and Per Inquiry (P.I.) time offer promoters/ managers the opportunity to advertise without paying money up front.
7. Publicity is an area that allows promoters/managers to target the media that best reaches their potential market.
8. *Standard Rate & Data Service* should be used by promoters/managers to find and screen mailing lists.
9. Promoters should "walk through" a list and never buy all the names at one time.
10. As in all advertisements, promoters/managers should be selling the "sizzle" and not the "steak."

CHAPTER ELEVEN

Shutdown: It's *Not* Over When It's Over

"It's not over 'til it's over" goes the old adage. That wasn't exactly the case, though, for the 1984 Olympic Game and many other special events. Even when the doors are shut, some events continue to have a life of their own. In fact, the books on the 1984 Games could not be officially closed for seven years. Why? Frivolous lawsuits, which seem to multiply geometrically when an event is as successful as the Los Angeles games were with its $230 million surplus, are partly the reason. Among the many lawsuits it attacted was one from a convict who complained that the television transmission from the Games interfered with his "karma." Another came from a motorcycle gang member who was irate because the organizing committee would not let him carry the torch (he was eventually permitted to take part in the torch run).

In the case of special events, the term "over" means shutdown. The shutdown process for any event is no minor task. In fact, the shutdown procedure is really misleading in name because it consists of dozens of activities ranging from dealing with legal actions to the final accounting. These activities actually do not begin in the final hours of an event, but start with the initial planning stages of an event.

Generally, shutdown involves:

1. Venue closedown;
2. Insurance settlement/claims;
3. Legal claims;
4. Human resources and outplacement activities;
5. Contract finalization;
6. Debriefings;
7. Final accounting; and
8. Final media communications
9. Closing celebrations and follow-on events. (See Figure 11–1 for a timeline for shutdown procedures.)

Although every event will have its own scenario, they do have one trait in common: They must come to an end. Shutdown usually encompasses a number of steps, ranging from the close for each day of a multi-day event, to the shutdown of a venue at the finale of the event. In either case, similar procedures need to be followed.

THE NINE STEPS TO SHUTDOWN

Once the spectators are ready to leave, there are nine closedown steps the promoter/manager must handle:

1. Exterior and interior security to facilitate departure of spectators. Special attention to security should be paid in regards to the participants in the event.

FIGURE 11–1.   *Special Events Timetable*

Although the following timeline allows for almost two years of planning, it can be condensed for any length of time and any event. "Construction" does not necessarily mean the building of a facility. It can refer to remodeling of a venue or the actual building of a stage, and the like. The order of the steps is key in the proper use of the chart.

Month 1	Planning	Month 22	Venue Closedown
Month 5	Coordination		Human resources outplacement begins
Month 10	Construction		Insurance issues identification
Month 21			Legal claims coordination
Month 22			Debriefings
	Shutdown	Month 23	Primary human resource outplacement
			Contract finalizations
Month 24			
			Final Media communications
			Closing celebration
		Month 24	Final outplacement

2. Parking and transportation staff should expedite the flow of traffic away from the venue. There should be consideration as to towing capabilities and police traffic control.
3. Venue personnel should undergo a briefing to determine the need for follow-up and ascertain their recommendations for the next event.
4. Payments should be processed for various workers (e.g., ushers, cleaning crew, and the cash that might be needed for them).
5. Clean-up crews are needed to remove trash and clean the venue. This includes seating and restrooms.
6. Tear-down of construction assets and/or equipment (e.g., speakers, amplifier, video displays, and sporting equipment) that were put in place. This may also require reconstruction for the next event that is going to occupy the venue.
7. Final accounting processing with various parties, including "shared revenue" contracts (concessionaires, licensees, ticket brokers, if applicable).
8. Contract sign-off by the landlord or venue management as to the satisfactory completion of each party's obligations.
9. Accountability and custody of all the equipment that does not belong to the venue—telephones, PCs, and so on must be returned to

their rightful owners. This should be part of the planning and carried out as soon as possible after the event has finished, before anything can disappear.

Each of these closedown steps will vary depending upon the venue and the elaborate nature of the event. At the 1984 Olympics Games, for example, hundreds of telephones, televisions, and computers "walked away" because security and accountability procedures were difficult to enforce with the vast number of people and diverse venues in the place.

DEALING WITH INSURANCE AND LIABILITY ISSUES

Insurance claims, of course, can go on for months or years, especially if a liability issue is involved due to injuries. Liability issues arise more commonly at a rock concert than at more sedate events. The promoter/manager will be wise to put money in a trust if this kind of issue is at stake.

Although the settlement period for matters relating to the 1984 Olympics was inordinately long, it is not uncommon to see insurance and liability issues drag on for at least a number of months. Unfortunately, the length of the dispute can have a negative effect on the profitability of the event. Legal disputes can be almost unlimited in scope. Disputes may involve damage to an object being exhibited at the event or even to the venue itself. There are, at the same time, many unusual claims which promoters can encounter:

1. Interruption of the event for whatever reason.
2. Performer interruption (illness, cancellation, or injury).
3. Injury of spectators inside or outside of the venue. This may have been caused by slipping on wet surfaces, falling down stairs, fireworks, or injury inflicted by another spectator.
4. Theft by venue personnel and/or spectators.
5. Auto accidents in parking facilities.
6. Construction failure, such as falling displays, decorations, or collapsed seating which can result in injuries.
7. Fire and/or water damage.
8. Hearing damage (e.g., rock concerts produce high decibel level).
9. Alcohol and drug afflictions causing harm.

THE DEBRIEFING

A venue debriefing is more than a look back at what did or did not happen at the event. It enables the promoter to focus on what issues may be coming up (e.g., pending insurance problems, litigation, and other claims). It also provides a guide for future, similar events. Written debriefing reports

---

FIGURE 11–2.   *Venue Debriefing Questionnaire*

VENUE LOCATION:

NAME OF EVENT:

DATE:

TIMING OF EVENT (FROM OPENING TO WRAP UP):

PROVIDE DESCRIPTIVE DETAILS OF ANY OF THE FOLLOWING OCCURRENCES.

ACCIDENTS:

INJURIES:

SECURITY PROBLEMS:

EVENT INTERRUPTIONS:

THEFTS:

CONSTRUCTION FAILURES:

THREATENED CLAIMS OR LITIGATION:

OTHER ACCIDENTS:

SUGGESTIONS FOR IMPROVEMENTS OF ANY ASPECT OF THE EVENT (SUGGEST BY YOU OR HEARD BY YOU FROM OTHERS, INCLUDING SPECTATOR COMMENTS):

---

are usually available from most national federations and are valuable guides for promoters/managers who are about to stage a special event.

The debriefing process can be handled in two separate different ways or the two can be combined. It can be a questionniare that is filled out in an interview session with employees (or given to individual employees to fill out themselves) or in a debriefing session in which a group gives a kind of oral history of what occurred during the event. (See Figure 11–2 for a sample debriefing questionnaire.)

The larger the event the better it is to provide all employees with their own individual questionnaire. Everyone associated with the event is asked to explain—in his or her own words—what happened. This is extremely valuable in determining liability issues as well as providing other pertinent information. Debriefing allows the promoter to plan for problems based upon employee recall. It is critical that these sessions be held immediately after the event closes, because it gives workers the chance to reconstruct problems while they are freshest in their minds. It also gives them a chance to remember any unfortunate or similar incidents that could result in a lawsuit.

The promoter/manager can learn a lot from these sessions. He or she has a chance to learn what went wrong (and right) and how to plan a better event the next time. International committees are anxious for these debriefings as well, since the final report, prepared by the promoter following shutdown, contains debriefing information that can be used future events. A well-run debriefing should take no longer than 10 to 20 minutes, a half-hour at most.

To facilitate effective debriefings, input from varied sources is essential. They include:

1. Participants in the event.
2. The press.
3. Volunteers.
4. A varied cross-section of staff and key management.
5. The attendees.
6. Selected personnel from key vendors (e.g., security).

The debriefings should also assess any suggestions for improvement, problems encountered, the sense of success or failure of the event, and the willingness of the various participants during the debriefing to participate in a similar event at some point in the future.

OUTPLACEMENT FOR EVENT PERSONNEL

One of the most difficult processes provided by the promoter's human resource area is outplacement services. Obviously, the extent of these services is going to vary with the size and duration of the event. For an event the size of the Olympic games, some employees may work five or six years, while at an Olympic festival, they may be employed for more than a year, and for some cultural or other similar events a matter of weeks. As the end of the event approaches, employees begin to realize they will soon be out of work. Their minds turn to finding a new job and, unfortunately, some may go off on interviews at critical times during the closing days of the event.

The original plan should have included a procedure to deal with the departure of all personnel. This can include everything from outplacement services to referring employees to outside employment agencies for assistance such as resume writing, mock interviews, and career counseling. It may be necessary to provide incentive bonuses for performance near the end of the employment period, because there is always the problem of the employee losing interest as the time for shutdown (and unemployment) approaches.

FINALIZING THE EVENT'S CONTRACTS

One of the most critical aspects in shutdown is the finalization and sign-off of the numerous contracts to which the promoter/manager may be a party. Today, almost everything is put in writing. Some contracts may be with the venue, while others may deal with such matters as the follow-up and split of parking revenues, ticket sales, and merchandise. Contracts play an astoundingly important part in the event. Before the 1984 Olympic Games, 4,400 contracts were signed. An Olympic Festival frequently can have close to 500 agreements; and a simple, one-night rock concert can have dozens.

Contract finalization may culminate in lengthy settlement negotiations or in simple sign-offs. The complexity of various contracts, such as those generating revenue, may require the gathering of data to determine the final outcome. Events that occur between the initial signing and the final sign-off may alter the original contract or cause unforeseen or opposing interpretations of the language in the contract. Figure 11–3 illustrates a sample contract extract.

SENDING FINAL MEDIA COMMUNICATIONS

As the final stages of shutdown approach, some final communication with the media should be considered, particularly if the event was successful and the promoter is thinking of staging another in the future. Once again, the 1984 Games were a model for dealing with the media, generating enormous attention via dozens of press releases and positive financial reports. This interest, of course, is not usually as prevalent when it comes to smaller events (in fact, the media seldom show more than a passing interest in the more modest event), but the promoter has nothing to lose and everything to gain by making one last effort at publicity.

Media communications can take many forms:

1. "Canned" articles or press releases on certain portions of the event (e.g., ticketing, new technology, and the like).
2. Write-ups/interviews on certain key people or special interest stories on volunteers.
3. Interviews on radio/TV programs.
4. Information about the final financial results.
5. Press conferences.
6. The video press release, which can be distributed to a variety of cable and broadcast media.
7. Books/articles on "behind the scenes" of the event.

FIGURE 11–3.   *Sample Contract Extract*

The following "Contract Extract" is a sample document that can be used for most events. It is simplified and lists the key elements that would be found in most agreements. This can be used as a model for a contract, an addendum to the contract, or as a guide for the promoter/manager so he can instantly refer to the key provisions within the contract.

CONTRACT EXTRACT

DATE OF EXECUTION OF CONTRACT:

CONTRACT WITH (ENTITY NAME, ADDRESS, AND PHONE):

PRIMARY CONTACT AT ENTITY CONRACTED WITH (NAME, POSITION TITLE, ADDRESS, AND PHONE):

RESPONSIBLE PRIMARY CONTACT WITHIN OUR COMPANY (NAME, PHONE):

CONTRACT DESCRIPTION (PURPOSE):

LENGTH OF CONTRACT (TERM):

EXTRACT OF SIGNIFICANT PROVISIONS OF CONTRACT, INCLUDING MILESTONES, DUE DATES, RESPONSIBILITIES, AND ULTIMATE CONCLUSION:

AUTHORIZATION OF CONTRACT

NAME   DATE

FINAL SIGN-OFF OF SATISFACTORY COMPLETION OF CONTRACT:

NAME   DATE

THE FINAL ACCOUNTING

Most times, the final accounting takes the form of a financial statement. The statement may be geared to an international federation or even a bank that helped finance the event. The accounting not only includes completing the books and records, but also may include:

1. Comparing actual financial results to original (or revised) budgetary amounts.

2. Preparing tailored reports for various parties (e.g., governmental entities, economic assessment reports, contract resolutions, and licensee/concessionaire finally payments).
3. Final tax returns, including final release from federal and state taxing authorities if the entity is to be shutdown.
4. Processing dissolution legal papers if the entity is to be disbanded.
5. Payoff of any debts (or possible resolution through bankruptcy process).
6. Asset disposition—What to sell, give away, or destroy. This also includes resolution of in-kind contributions to the entity which possibly might require return to the person or organization that provided them (e.g., donated computers which require return). Hopefully, the resolution of in-kind assets will not result in payment for lost items.
7. Decision as to whether and when a final audit by outside accountants might occur. This might also entail royalty audits for various licensees. This final audit must be started ahead of the final days of the event to enable interaction with the remaining accounting personnel and records.

Planning for this final process not only enables the promoter/manager to see where he/she stands, but it can help him/her reach a conclusion as to whether the event should be staged in the community again.

A CELEBRATION—IS IT WARRANTED?

Naturally, if the event has been an enormous success, the promoter/manager may want to celebrate with those who helped make a go of it. Aside from being a way to say "thank you," the final party/celebration allows for networking between those in the group. If the promoter/manager is contemplating another similar event, it would be wise to maintain contact with as many of those who were involved as possible.

Some promoters, such as those who staged the 1984 Olympics, establish an "alumni" organization and group in an effort to keep the experienced workers together. Of course, celebrations and alumni groups only make sense when the promoter has carefully evaluated the event. Only then can he or she determine if the event was worthwhile; only then can he or she determine if the shutdown is temporary or permanent.

SUMMARY

An event is not truly over until everything pertaining to the event is wrapped up. This shutdown process involves:

1. Venue closing.
2. Settlement of insurance and liability claims.
3. Placement of employees through outplacement activities.
4. Contract finalization.
5. Debriefings.
6. Final accounting.
7. Final media communications.
8. Closing celebrations.
9. Follow-up events.

Once every aspect of the event has been finalized, the promoter/manger can then start to glean the important lessons learned from staging the event—namely, the *do's* and *don't's*. Chapter 12, the Epilogue, lists most of the *don't's* that any promoter/manager should keep in mind before the initial planning stages.

CHAPTER TWELVE

Epilogue

There are 10 DON'Ts that every smart team involved in putting on a special event will never forget:

- DON'T ever overlook details.
- DON'T ever count on the availability or participation of an act or venue until everything is in writing.
- DON'T ever try to promote an event in a market that you don't know.
- DON'T ever try to promote an event in a market that doesn't have a solid infrastructure in place.
- DON'T ever underestimate the importance of security and how the requirements change with each event or venue.
- DON'T ever forget that each community, politican, and organization has its own agenda—and it is very likely that it will not coincide with your own.
- DON'T ever forget the importance of cash flow. Without it, the best event in the world can't be a success.
- DON'T ever underestimate the value of volunteers and how much their enthusiasm means to an event's success.
- DON'T ever underestimate the potential for a community to stage a major event when its has the infrastructure in place and the backing of its citizens.
- DON'T ever forget the radical differences between the public and private sector—and how fast one (the private sector) usually moves in comparison to the other (public).

  And, of course, as we have mentioned many times, there is the most important DON'T of all:

- DON'T ever underestimate the importance of planning.

As we have already said, when a special event is successful, the benefits can be much more than a healthy bottom line. Certainly, there can be economic impact, especially if the event is on the scale of a Super Bowl, Final Four basketball tournament, or an international gymnastics championship in one of the largest communities in the United States. But it can mean just as much—or more—in a smaller context, whether it is the Pan Am Games in Indianapolis, a concert in Enid, Oklahoma, or a fund-raiser for a local ballet company or the Little League. A well-staged event can put a community "on the map." It can provide a community with a reputation outside its region or country and foster a sense of confidence and pride that money itself can't buy.

A P P E N D I X   A *

Expand Your Resource Library: Helpful Publications to Have
Compiled by Frank Zang
Information Specialist/Publications Manager
USOC Public Information and Media Relations

Taking advantage of your resources is a key factor in your productivity. It's critical to get your information into the right hands or it gets lost in a trash recycling bin. It is also important to have a complete reference book so you can reach the right people at the right time. The following publications can help your organization's public relations by identifying the key contacts.

Editor & Publisher International Yearbook
11 West 19th Street
New York, N.Y., 10011
(212) 675-4380

This periodical provides a listing of all the daily, weekly and special newspapers published in the United States (state-by-state), newspapers published in Canada and other foreign countries (Europe, South America, Central America, etc.), news and syndicate services (AP, UPI, Gannett, Agence France-Presse, Reuters, etc.) and other newspaper organizations and industry services.

Sports Market Place
P.O. Box 1417
Princeton, N.J. 08542
(609) 921-8599

This directory covers the following areas—sport-by-sport listing of professional, amateur and international organizations and publications; professional and trade associations; college athletic organizations; multisport publications (magazines, journals, newsletters); TV/radio broadcasters and syndicators; promotion, event and athlete management services; market data; trade shows; suppliers and sales agents; and executive, geographic and master indexes.

---

*Permission from the United States Olympic Committee.

Bacon's PR and Media Information Systems
332 S. Michigan Avenue
Chicago, Ill. 60604
Toll Free 1-800-621-0561
In Illinois (312) 922-2400

A series of complete reference books covers the following areas:
Clipping Bureau—Comprehensive coverage of the top 600 daily newspapers in the U.S. and Canada and all the important business, trade and consumer magazines, plus the major news wire services.

Publicity Checker—Two volumes (magazines and newspapers) that include more than 17,000 publications listings and more than 110,000 editorial contacts for the U.S. and Canada. A separate international publicity checker is also available, with information on 12,000 magazines and 1,000 national and regional newspapers in Western European countries.

Radio/TV Directory—Geographical listing of 9,000 radio and 1,300 television stations with programming information, format, staff contact names and network affiliations.

Media Alerts—Marketing tool with editorial calendars, profiles and lead times for 1,900 magazines and 200 major dailies to help plan publicity campaigns.

New York Publicity Outlets
P.O. Box 1197
New Milford, Conn. 06776
(203) 354-9361

Alphabetical index in the New York metropolitan area of contacts for newspapers, news services, out-of-town correspondents, radio stations, syndicated newspaper magazines, television stations, trade publications, magazines, black press and feature syndicates.

Hudson's Washington Directory
44 W. Market Street
P.O. Box 331
Rhinebeck, N.Y. 12572
(914) 876-2081

Directory for Washington, D.C., of the news services, newspapers, foreign newspapers, radio and TV stations, magazines, newsletters and freelance writers.

O'Dwyer's Directory of Public Relations Executives
J.R. O'Dwyer Co. Inc.
271 Madison Avenue
New York, N.Y. 10016
(212) 679-2471

Biographical material from all established, business-related public relations executives, whether they are employed at corporations, associations or public relations firms.

CoSIDA Membership
Dave Wohlhueter
Cornell University
P.O. Box 729
Ithaca, N.Y. 14851
(607) 255-3752

Even if you aren't a Sports Information Director, you can become an associate member of the organization with an annual fee of $25. Some of the benefits of the membership include receiving the CoSIDA Digest and phone directory (see descriptions below).

CoSIDA Digest (College Sports Information Directors of America)
Fred Nuesch
Campus Box 114
Texas A&I University
Kingsville, Texas 78363
(512) 595-3908

The digest is published 11 times a year (September through July). In addition to general news about the profession, it contains ideas, opinions, contest information, information on job openings and articles on top people in the profession. The CoSIDA Digest is one of the membership benefits of the organization and is an excellent avenue for keeping up-to-date on other public relations and sports information professionals at the collegiate level.

CoSIDA Phone Directory
(same address as CoSIDA Digest)

The annual directory contains the names, addresses and phone numbers of Sports Information Directors and assistants at virtually all U.S. four-year schools and many U.S. junior colleges and Canadian senior colleges. There is also a long listing of major conferences, national organizations and magazines, and athletic associations. One section is a complete listing of the National Governing Bodies. The phone directory is another CoSIDA membership benefit.

NCAA News
National Collegiate Athletic Association
6201 College Boulevard
Overland Park, Kan. 66211
(913) 339-1906

A weekly newspaper with complete coverage of all divisions of the
NCAA, featuring coverage of championship events, legislative news,
opinions, job announcements, statistics, notes and features.

Yearbook of Expert Authorities & Spokespersons
Broadcast Interview Source
2233 Wisconsin Ave., N.W.
Washington, D.C. 20007
(202) 333-4904

Listing of 1,400 groups that wish to be available for media contact as a
source on a variety of subjects. Entries include a contact name, phone
number and brief description of the group.

Facsimile Users' Directory
Monitor Publishing Company
104 Fifth Avenue
2nd Floor
New York, N.Y. 10011

Key FAX numbers in the U.S. and affiliated offices in Canada, Europe and
the Far East for organizations in different fields, including advertising and
public relations firms, federal government, media and publishing firms,
trade and professional associations and universities.

A P P E N D I X   B *

Questions Asked by International Olympic Committee to the Atlanta Organization Committee

1. Are there any laws, regulations or customs that would limit, restrict or interfere with the staging of the Games in any way? Note: this should address such matters as quarantine, import of equipment and materials, including foodstuffs, ammunition, medical supplies, competition weapons, animals, etc., and the removal of the same following the Games.

2. Provide general information on the city: geographic position, climate, size, population, altitude and all reasons why it should be considered an appropriate site for the Games.

3. Describe the air, rail and other transportation facilities and infrastructures.

4. Can you guarantee that the local transportation facilities, including the provision of cars and buses for the Olympic Family and for transportation of the public at large will be sufficient?

5. What accommodation facilities are available for the Olympic family, media and visitors?

6. What security provisions do you envision?

7. What experience has your city had with respect to the hosting of important international events and to what extent are you familiar with the organization of previous Games?

8. What are the proposed dates for the Games?

9. Can you guarantee that no political meeting or demonstration will take place in the stadium or on any other sports ground or in or near the Olympic Village(s) during the Games?

10. Will you be able to organize all sports on the Olympic programme?

11. What technical facilities and venues now exist, what facilities exist but require alterations and what facilities are planned?

12. Have the International Federations (IFs) been consulted and have they approved your proposed facilities?

*Permission from the International Olympic Committee.

14. Provide details of the Olympic Village(s) including their location, the nature of the facilities and services available and the costs (if any) to be charged to participants.
15. What cultural programme is proposed?
16. Please provide details on any Olympic coin programme you plan to undertake.
17. Give detailed information regarding the financing of the Games, including financial support from the central or federal government, the state or provincial governments, the municipality and private sources.
18. Can you provide assurances that the IOC will not be subject to any taxes, duties, levies or similar charges in respect of any of its activities relating to the Games, including, without limitation, matters related to television and sponsorship?
19. Provide any other information which you believe will assist the IOC in reaching its decision regarding your candidature.

A P P E N D I X   C *

SUPER BOWL REQUIREMENTS

Super Bowl XXVI	Minneapolis (CBS)	January 26, 1992 Sunday
Super Bowl XXVII	Los Angeles (NBC)	January 31, 1993 Sunday
Super Bowl XXVIII	Atlanta	January 30, 1994 Sunday
Super Bowl XXIX	Miami	January 29, 1995 Sunday
Super Bowl XXX	Phoenix (tentative)	January 28, 1996 Sunday

REQUIREMENTS

1. Firm and binding (no tentative) advance commitments, including statement on maximum room (rack) rates and minimum length of stay required from area hotels (three or four days recommended).
2. Firm and binding commitments, including guarantees on rates and total number available from transportation companies, including availability in numbers of buses, limousines (limited guarantees), taxis and rental cars (NFL reeds 425 buses, 65 limos, exclusively signed agreements on these should be noted). A detail of access and cost of up to 100 additional "school" buses for use by the pre-game and half-time shows.
3. Appointment of a local coordinator or minimum-membership Super Bowl Task Force with whom the NFL's Super Bowl staff can maintain regular contact in pre-game planning. Must have direct access to hotel industry and transportation industry. Small committee to evaluate price and packaging policies with power to prevent rate gouging in all areas including hotels, limousines, buses, etc.
4. Statement of cooperation from game-related services, especially police agencies.
5. Establishment on single telephone contact who can coordinate all needs of NFL office, media, television network and at the stadium.
6. Provide detailed map showing distances and locations of main hotel space, stadium, airports and practice fields.

HOTELS

1. Need for 15,000 top quality rooms for NFL-related groups. Commitments should include number of rooms and suites at each

---

*Permission from the National Football League.

property. Cutoff date for release of rooms as of September 1 of the year preceding game.

2. Community must have 35% as many "quality" hotel rooms within a sixty (60) minute drive of the stadium as there are seats in the stadium (i.e., 75,000 seat stadium needs 27,000 rooms.) No properties of less than 50 rooms should be included in total.

3. Binding rates and length of stay requirements must be posted with respective Convention Bureau at least six months prior to game from all hotels in area.

4. NFL/Media headquarters hotel with minimum committable allotment of 650 rooms and all suites, arrival starting Monday prior to game. Rate should be established at a percentage below existing rack (preferably conforming to less than $125). Indicate type of phone system and its capabilities.

   Meeting space needs are as follows: ballroom must be able to accommodate media work space for 50 typing positions and 100 more work positions, separate communications areas (telecopiers, Telerams, Western Union and telephones) and adjacent area for hospitality lounge, registration and information section. Media area-15,000 square feet is minimal. In addition, another area needed for major press conferences and parties, an additional 15,000 square feet. All meeting space for media areas blocked for nine days prior to gameday. Need for office space for NFL staff of approximately 60 people (25 to 30 separate offices starting two weeks prior to game).

5. Adjacent or nearby hotels (total rooms needed 900) to media headquarters for spillover of related groups—200 to 400 rooms each, indicate meeting space. Press rate needed the same or lower than headquarters.

   All spillover hotel recommendations must be accompanied by a signed letter, from that hotel, confirming: block, rate, deposit, cancellation, cut-off date and guarantee policies.

6. Accommodations including 60 to 70 suites and 600 rooms for NFL official family in top quality hotels—club owners, top club personnel and their parties.

7. Top facilities for network covering game (750 rooms including numerous suites, over what is placed at the headquarters hotel) ideally in three hotels—sales, production and technicians. Also top quality rooms for the networks not covering (75 to 100 rooms each, including suites).

8. Team Hotels:
   A. 275 to 300 rooms needed at Grade AAA facility for each team arriving Sunday and departing following Monday. Good meeting, office and banquet space (17,500 to 20,000 square foot ballroom). Close to workout sites; good security. Team rate in $90's or rate

should be established at a percentage below existing rack. A hold should be placed on all meeting space for entire week (as many as 15 meeting rooms needed); no deposits; suburban location is ideal. Letter from general manager should accompany proposal.

B. Spillover hotels for each team's ancillary groups, arriving Friday and departing Monday, accommodating 200-250 each.

9. Other hotel space to fill out 16,000-room block as required by the NFL and related groups including NFL Properties (1,700 including suites from two or three properties primary hotel should have 900 rooms), NFL films, sponsors, associates and 4,000 rooms for the NFL travel package companies. All should be no more than three or four night minimum stay.

10. Arrangements for half-time show production staff, field preparation crews, etc. at a property near stadium or rehearsal site (property similar to Residence Inn) at a reduced rate for 10 day to three week stay.

11. Organized plan for the handling of 20,000 potential additional hotel roms needed by general public.

12. Complimentary accommodations for up to 60 rooms for three night stay for NFL Players Clinic (traditionally held the weekend before Super Bowl).

PRACTICE SITES

1. Workout site for each participating team from Monday through Saturday which has:

—Class AAA field, ideally having both artificial and grass fields.

—Good locker rooms, exclusive use.

—Coaches' facilities.

—Meeting facilities.

—Pro-type training quarters, including weight room (nautilus and free standing).

—Two fields are preferred.

—Practice equipment.

—Security and privacy.

—Tarpaulin.

—Film towers.

—Blocking sleds.

—Professional goal posts.

—Laundry facilities on site.

The workout site should be no more than 20 minutes travel time from the team hotel and no more than 30 minutes maximum travel time from the other team hotel and practice site; closer proximity preferable; sites should not be adjacent.

2. If January mean temperature is less than 50 degrees the practice fields need to be covered. If the stadium is an option it must be reserved exclusivity for the NFL for two weeks prior to the game.
3. Practice site and cost of upgrading to NFL status should be offered free of charge. If a charge is expected please note. NFL will assume the cost of field preparation.

STADIUM FACILITY

1. Exclusivity of stadium for minimum of one week prior to game if artificial turf, two weeks if natural grass surface and two weeks for site with average January temperature less than 50 degrees. An understanding that the NFL has approval of *everything* relating to stadium operation on game day including assignment of meeting rooms, tent space, parking lots etc. NFL is to be consulted on all activities in the stadium during the week prior to game, including tours, security, etc.
2. If the mean January temperature is below 50 degrees, the stadium must be domed.
3. Minimal salable size of stadium is to be approximately 70,000. If temporary seating is proposed, detail exact nature, cost to install and funding of this cost. Salable is defined as capacity less seats needed from extra media, obstructed, trade out for suite holders, etc. Architectual renderings should be included on all temporary needs.
4. Details on chairback or special section seating. Note total seats between goal lines. Include any obligation or right to retain seats for existing ticket holders.
5. Box suites or other suite exclusive access, for NFL. Indicate any obligation to existing suite holders for tickets. A minimum of fifty (50) percent or no less than 45 total of all box suites must be allotted to the NFL. It is recommended that at least 75% be between the goal lines including 50 yard line locations for broadcasting network, competing team and commissioner. Detail any obligations necessary to provide existing box suite holders or for resale of boxes by Task Force or municipality. Include sample lease and renewal dates.

   The NFL insists that any box suite contracts that would be in effect for the Super Bowl that a clause be inserted in the contract that allows the NFL to void an agreement to sell tickets to those individuals that resell their boxes or a portion of their boxes at a cost per ticket higher than the face value on the ticket. The league reserves the right to void the issuance of the tickets if it discovers such a resale.

6. The NFL wants to retain the rights to all novelty sales in the stadium. This includes the right to negotiate with a vendor other than existing concessionaires.

   Included in the above novelty rights should be: the right to prohibit the sale of any related merchandise on stadium grounds or surrounding areas without prior NFL approval. All temporary vendor licensing, within a half mile radius of the stadium property boundaries, should be subject to NFL consultation.

7. Lease details, including ceiling on game day expenses or flat fee to cover all if preferred. (Detail normal staffing including all related areas, such as traffic control, ushering, special police patrols, parking, attendants, ticket takers, etc.). Super Bowl will require levels at least 150% above normal sellout.

8. Maximum security personnel, including extra police on game day. Indicate status of contracts with outside groups—including no strike clause. Note individual who has direct responsibility on security. Security level planned should be at least 150% of largest event.

   Plans and cost should be detailed for securing stadium a week prior to the game. Stadium will be closed, except for planned tours, to public media and all others for week prior to game.

9. Quality field illumination subject to network survey; normal lighting may need to be bolstered or supplemented. Note ability of lights to be brought back to full power after being turned off and time to re-light to full intensity, 150-foot candle for entire field minimum.

10. Quality sound system, including sound to concourses, concession stands, restrooms outside stadium perimeter (capable of separate feeds). Recommended contractor to supplement existing system and public address in stadium and press box. Stadium must have full range, undistorted and uniform coverage capable of 105 decibels (DB's). Audio cable pairs to each side of stadium to and from press box.

11. Quality field condition, including tarpaulin.

12. Locker room details—space should be large enough for 55 players, separate training area, separate locker rooms for head coach and up to twelve assistants.

13. Special spacious interview areas with close proximity to locker rooms (20,000 square feet total or 10,000 for each of two areas). If not available in stadium should detail alternative and cost.

14. Maximum media work space plus areas that can be converted to auxiliary sections without dramatic loss of seating for sale. (750 working spaces, with access to power supply.) Maximum number of booths for radio, TV, networks, coaches, team officials, foreign

broadcasts, etc. (28 minimum). Indicate status of wiring each position for telephone and power. Detail number of seats in existing press box (275 minimum) and booths. Plans for accommodating additional space and total loss of seats. Architectual renderings should be included for all temporary plans. Location for holding media from TV crews who attend any post-game press conferences (7,500 square feet).

15. If average January temperature is less than 50 degrees then compound for networks should be enclosed. Otherwise area should be designated.

16. Description of photographer locations (deck) on sidelines and endzones, plus location for team film/NFL Films locations.

17. Ancillary meeting and dressing room availability for cheerleaders, groundscrew, officials, chain crew, staff office, pre-game and half-time production teams, etc. Also areas to serve as dressing rooms for celebrities in pre-game and half-time shows, coin tosser(s) and anthem singer.

18. Available space for 20,000 square foot media workroom for post-game, space for photographers darkroom (AP, UPI, USA Today, participating team home town newspapers, etc.). If not available on premises note alternative and cost, plus access to power and water.

19. Maximum electrical output for networks, television (team city's stations, ESPN, CNN, etc.), media, etc. Note existing maximum level and ability to add. Stadium must have available 8,000 amps for use by the NFL, networks, media, etc. Power should be provided cost free to these entities.

20. Access and availability of photographer dark rooms on field level.

21. Location to park television satellite units with access to power and phones, present needs are 45/50 uplink trucks and unobstructed access to Southern sky.

22. Complete stadium club utilization by NFL, including required NFL approval of any use of other stadium meeting facilities.

23. Cooperation of concessionaire, including statement to sell only NFL Properties merchandise. Detail status of contract (length, percentage payable to authority, exterior stadium rights, etc.).
    A. NFL wants approval if the concessionaire will change from existing contractor or subcontract a portion of their rights.
    B. Approval by NFL of final pricing list for food, beverage and merchandise. Guarantee that prices will not exceed those charged for regular season game.

24. Release for NFL to have exclusive authority to sell programs.

25. Recommended contractor for construction at stadium for NFL and television needs. Note any available minority vendors.

26. Waiver by city to allow construction done in stadium for auxiliary press and additional announce booths to be treated as temporary

structure, i.e. use wood instead of pressure treated fire retardent lumber, electrical structures, etc.

27. Wheelchair seating availability, (field level is unacceptable) note total seating available and location. Ideal minimum is 100 handicap seats plus attendants.

28. Status of union contracts in existence, expiation dates, "no-strike" clauses, etc.

29. Restriction on tours in stadium week of game. Times to be determined in consultation with NFL. Responsibility over security, pricing of tours, etc. to be negotiated.

30. Release on existing scoreboard obligations for use of temporary Diamond Vision system. NFL insists that use of existing boards be exempt from use of *any* advertising responsibilities. If existing scoreboard, detail any costs for use and rental if applicable. Note any exclusive agreements in stadium.

31. Designate space in immediate proximity available for hospitality tents (700,000 plus sq. ft.). NFL wants exclusive control over the entire compound including any contracts issued to set up compound and approval of pricing structure. There should be a release to allow any NFL designated food vendor. Exceptions for any compound must be made for NFL, NFL Properties and televising network. Ideally, space should be given to NFL for their deposition.

32. Special locations, perhaps in conjunction with the hospitality village, for use for activities such as card show, Hall of Fame exhibit, merchandise mart, etc. (up to 250,000 square feet).

33. Site for helipad which may need to accommodate up to 350 landings on game day.

34. Note availability of space to serve brunch/lunch for media (2,500 people) in proximity to stadium, free of rental obligation or rights percentage.

35. Insurance liability coverage. The NFL requires that the stadium provide a certificate of insurance evidencing comprehensive general liability coverage with a limit of no less than $10 million, indemnifying and naming the NFL as an additional insured. Responsibility for security and fire/fan safety plans should be with hosting agency(s).

36. All fixed signage, and length of contracts, must be documented to the NFL. The NFL insists on no signage advertising lotteries of any kind.

STADIUM PARKING

1. Exclusive use of 700 car parking spaces—cost free, more if there is not a special area for television trucks and technicians.

2. Parking areas for 400 buses, cost free, including 35 for media, 25 for each team, up to 50 for half-time personnel, 75 for NFL Properties, occasional member club buses, 200 for NFL travel package etc. Well-lighted area for post-game departures up to five or six hours after game.
3. Transportation plan for stadium ingress and egress, special attention for up to 800 buses needed for the general public.
4. Cost free parking for NFL teams and network during week preceding game.
5. Parking for network trucks and technicians on game day, possibly 20/25 trailers, 150 cars for technicians (also free if normally charged for during week).
6. Space for team city television uplinks (trailers), newspaper darkrooms, cable TV remote studios, etc. (will need access to substantial power and phone lines). Present needs call for 40,000 sq. ft. See inquiries in stadium category.
7. Available space for handicap parking in close proximity to seat assignments.
8. Guarantee that prices charged for parking will not exceed those charged for regular season games.
9. Location to host game day function for bus and limousine drivers, parking lot attendants, police, etc. Facility should be provided rent free and allow sponsor to provide own caterer.

FRIDAY NIGHT PARTY

Facility, or an optional facility, for Super Bowl party to accommodate 3,500 guests (75,000 to 125,000 square feet, unobstructed) with adequate parking and traffic flow. This facility, or an optional facility, should be offered free of charge including a release by existing concessionaire and a fee if unable to meet food service requirement, subject to NFL evaluation. If NFL brings in own caterer, must have use of kitchens three days prior to event. Detail any obligations to union contractors or exclusive vendors such as technical facilities, security, lighting, sound, staging, etc. The facility should provide a certificate of insurance evidencing comprehensive general liability coverage with a limit of no less than $10 million, indemnifying and naming the NFL as an additional insured. Need facilities starting Tuesday night prior through Saturday (for removal).

MISCELLANEOUS

1. If a host committee is planned, a detailed description of its purpose, staffing, budget and source of funding. If the city plans to raise money for task force, stadium expenses or renovation, or for

social commitments, the method of raising the funds should be detailed. NFL must retain veto over any sponsorship activity.

2. Letters of cooperation of all municipalities or counties involved in proposal.

3. Indication of agencies responsible for traffic plan to stadium on game day and statements of cooperation.

4. High management airport contact for cooperation with those needing special services, including arrival-departure team charters, private planes, special fan charters, etc.

5. Weather surveys dating back 15 to 20 years for two-week period prior to game date and week thereafter. Special note on mean January temperature, total January rainfall (snowfall) and average number of rain days (snow days).

5. Anti ticket scalping ordinance on stadium grounds, in community and preferably, in state. Complete description of existing laws and penalties.

7. Status on all state and city tax arrangements, including city hotel occupancy taxes, noting percentages.

8. NFL Properties exclusivity on licensing of trademarks—cooperation in other areas, including plan for prevention of trademark infringements.

9. Merchandising rights of the Super Bowl logo and commercial use of the term Super Bowl exclusively belong to NFL Properties. No host committee shall use the same without permission of NFL Properties.

10. Ability of NFL to have own security organization, release on state/ city licensing requirements.

11. Recommendations on office furniture and other suppliers, special equipment installers and supervisors, including duplicating equipment, etc. Note any minority vendors available.

12. Special tickets for the media to other events—racetrack, jai alai, dog track, concerts, other sporting events (college and professional), etc.

13. Assistance in obtaining special licensing for up to 450 courtesy cars.

14. Need to provide golf course for NFL Charities Golf Classic Thursday prior to Super Bowl. Waiver of green fees if possible.

15. Need two practice fields, cost free, for use by the pre-game and half-time shows for rehearsals for two weeks preceding game. Also need additional sites for tryouts for the performers in October and November preceding games. Should also have storage area for props. Facilities should be rental free.

16. Detail total airline lift into this area in one day. Please note daily flights and number of seats available arriving from major cities (New York, Las Angeles, Chicago, etc.) and hub cities (Nashville,

Raleigh-Durham, Pittsburgh, Dallas, etc.). Note areas to park private aircraft.
17. Hold on all arenas and potential concert sites for consultation with the NFL on events to be held in area.

ENTICEMENTS

The NFL prefers the following be provided:

—NFL control over hospitality village.
—NFL assignment of novelty rights at stadium.
—Free rental of the stadium.
—Free rental of practice sites.
—Free rental of pre-game and half-time rehearsal sites.
—NFL assignment of program vendor.
—Release on all scoreboard/videoboard advertising.
—Free use of party site, release of rights existing food vendor.
—Free use of golf course for charity golf classic.
—Free rooms for NFL Players clinic.

The NFL will accept enticements in the following areas:

—Free stadium rental and game day expenses.
—Sharing in concession and novelty revenue.
—Sharing in parking revenue.
—Sharing in hospitality tent revenue.
—Free limousine or bus service for teams and/or media.
—Free rooms for individuals, participating teams or NFL staff.
—Box suite access to enable sales to sponsors

As of 10/1/91

A P P E N D I X   D

SAMPLE BUDGET

NAME: _____

WORLD TOUR BUDGET STATEMENT OF BUDGETED CASH RECEIPTS AND
DISBURSEMENTS FOR THE PERIOD _____ THROUGH _____

	BUDGET
TOUR RECEIPTS:	
GROSS GUARANTEES	$5,250,000
OVERAGES	500,000
OTHER	250,000
TOTAL TOUR RECEIPTS	$6,000,000
TOUR DISBURSEMENTS:	
ARTIST WAGES SCHEDULE A	$491,607
CREW WAGES SCHEDULE A	175,200
PER DIEMS	95,040
COMMISSIONS:	
PERSONAL MGMT.	900,000
ACCOUNTING/BUSINESS MGMT.	300,000
AGENT	575,000
PRODUCTION COSTS SCHEDULE B	600,000
HOTELS SCHEDULE B	151,920
TRANSPORTATION SCHEDULE B	523,181
GROUND TRANSPORTATION:	
TAXIS	5,000
LIMOUSINES	20,000
PARKING	0
CAR RENTALS	0
GRATUITIES	21,600
OTHER TOUR EXPENSES SCHEDULE C	129,125
SUBTOTAL TOUR EXPENSES	$3,987,674
TOUR EXPENSE CONTINGENCY (5%)	199,384
TOTAL TOUR EXPENSES	$4,187,058
LESS: REIMBURSED EXPENSES SCHEDULE 1	200,000
NET REVENUE (DISBURSEMENTS)	
BEFORE ARTISTS TOUR BONUS	$2,012,942
ARTISTS TOUR BONUS:	
NAME _____	
NAME _____	
NAME _____	
NAME _____	
NAME _____	
NAME _____	
NET TOUR REVENUE (DISBURSEMENTS)	$2,012,942

NAME: _____

WORLD TOUR BUDGET STATEMENT OF BUDGETED CASH RECEIPTS AND
DISBURSEMENTS FOR THE PERIOD _____ THROUGH _____

ARTIST & CREW WAGES
SCHEDULE A

	PER WEEK	BUDGET
ARTIST WAGES:		
NAME _____	$5,000	$77,500
NAME _____	5,000	77,500
NAME _____	5,000	77,500
NAME _____	5,000	77,500
NAME _____	5,000	77,500
NAME _____	5,000	77,500
TOTAL	30,000	$465,000
PAYROLL TAXES (MEDICARE)		6,743
PAYROLL TAXES (SOC SEC)		19,865
TOTAL ARTIST WAGES		$491,607

	PER WEEK	
CREW WAGES		
ROAD MANAGER _____		0
NAME _____	$1,000	$15,500
NAME _____	1,000	15,500
NAME _____	1,000	15,500
NAME _____	1,000	15,500
NAME _____	750	11,625
NAME _____	750	11,625
NAME _____	750	11,625
NAME _____	750	11,625
NAME _____	750	11,625
NAME _____	550	8,525
NAME _____	550	8,525
NAME _____	550	8,525
NAME _____	550	8,525
NAME _____	550	8,525
TOTAL	$10,500	$162,750
PAYROLL TAXES (MEDICARE)		2,360
PAYROLL TAXES (SOC SEC)		10,091
TOTAL CREW WAGES		$175,200

NAME: _____
WORLD TOUR BUDGET STATEMENT OF BUDGETED CASH RECEIPTS AND
DISBURSEMENTS FOR THE PERIOD _____ THROUGH _____

SCHEDULE B

	PER WEEK	BUDGET
PRODUCTION COSTS:		
REHEARSAL HALL	n/a	$15,000
SOUND	$18,500	286,750
LIGHTS	7,500	116,250
MONITORS	5,000	77,500
RISERS	0	0
SPARES	0	0
PASSES & BADGES	161	2,500
CARNET (LEGAL DOCUMENTS & FEES)	129	2,000
EQUIPMENT RENTAL	0	0
EQUIPMENT SUPPLIES & MAINTENANCE	0	0
OUTSIDE PRODUCTION FEE	6,452	100,000
TOTAL PRODUCTION COSTS	$37,742	$600,000
HOTELS:		
ARTIST	6,271	97,200
CREW	2,746	42,560
DRIVERS	785	12,160
TOTAL HOTEL COSTS	$9,801	$151,920
TRANSPORTATION COSTS:		
AIRFARES	$20,968	$325,000
BUS RENTAL - BAND	0	0
BUS RENTAL - CREW	2,506	38,850
BUS DRIVER(S)	967	14,985
PAYROLL TAX re: BUS DRIVER(S)	74	1,146
BUS FLOAT (fuel, etc.)	1,200	19,200
TRUCKING	8,000	124,000
TOTAL TRANSPORTATION COSTS	$33,715	$523,181

NAME: _____

WORLD TOUR BUDGET STATEMENT OF BUDGETED CASH RECEIPTS AND
DISBURSEMENTS FOR THE PERIOD _____ THROUGH _____

SCHEDULE C

	PER WEEK	BUDGET
OTHER TOUR EXPENSES:		
CARTAGE	$645	$10,000
INSURANCE - TOUR	750	11,625
INSURANCE - MEDICAL	645	10,000
WARDROBE & MAINTENANCE	968	15,000
SHIPPING & POSTAGE	484	7,500
SUPPLIES	0	0
UNION DUES	323	5,000
STATE, LOCAL, FOREIGN TAXES WITHHELD	2,903	45,000
TELEPHONE	645	10,000
OTHER MEALS	968	15,000
PRINTING	0	0
TOTAL OTHER TOUR EXPENSES	$8,331	$129,125

A P P E N D I X E

SAMPLE CONTRACT

Rider to Agreement dated _____ between _____ hereinafter called "Artist" furnishing the services of _____ and _____ hereinafter referred to as "Purchaser".

The following provisions shall be deemed incorporated in and part of the Agreement for the performance of _____ at _____ in _____ on _____. In the event of any inconsistency between the provisions of the rider and the Agreement to which this is a rider, the provisions of this rider shall control.

I. BILLING/ADVERTISING

A. _____ shall be afforded 100% sole star billing in all advertising or publicity disseminated or displayed by Purchaser for or in connection with the engagement.

B. Tickets for this engagement will display _____ in the largest possible type. Neither Purchaser's name, nor the name of the building may appear larger than ten percent (10%) of the size print used for _____.

C. No other act may appear on the same program without the prior written approval of Artist.

D. No advertising may be issued in any form, prior to receipt of a single contract from Artist.

E. If the facility has a marquee then _____ must appear on the marquee on each night of the performance.

F. Purchaser agrees to use only the official photographs of _____ available in press kits from _____.

G. Piggyback or dual talent spots are unacceptable and will not be allowed for payment.

H. All invoicing presented at settlement for payment must be original and must contain the following:

1. Gross, net and commissionable or discountable amounts.

2. A notarized affidavit of performance (through two (2) days prior to event) starting: dates run, times run and contract rates.

3. Co-presents packages must be detailed in letter form by a station official and notarized.

4. An invoice number, date and _____ listed as client.

I. Promoter/Agency orders are not acceptable for payment approval.

J. Radio station ticket giveaways or trades can only be done with Artist's written approval. In the event this approval is granted, the tickets can only be given in exchange for spots on a one to one basis, ie: 100 × $10.00 tickets in exchange for $1000.00 in radio time invoiced. In this eventuality, an original invoice from participating station must be presented during settlement along with the written approval confirmation and the comp sheet from the box office.

K. Original tear sheets must accompany all invoicing for print advertising.

L. _____ has been selected by _____ to service their 1990 fall/winter tour. Call _____ for service.

M. Any sponsors, co-promotions, tie-ins with radio stations or other entities having a commercial interest must be approved in writing by _____ Management, before start of any campaign.

II.   GENERAL STIPULATIONS

A. No cameras will be allowed without authorization. No portion of the performance rendered hereunder may be photographed, recorded, filmed, taped or embodied in any form for the purpose of reproducing such performance and Purchaser agrees that he will not authorize any such recording, and to exert maximum effort to prevent any such recording by audience and employees.

III.   ANCILLARY RIGHTS

A. Artist and its designee(s) or licensee(s) shall have the exclusive right to advertise, promote, disseminate and sell in and about the facility of the engagement and elsewhere, items including but not limited to souvenir program books, pictures, articles of clothing, jewelry, posters, stickers, recordings, _____ or other articles or merchandise whether or not related to the engagement, and to collect and retain for its (or their) account(s) all proceeds thereof, or, at Artist's option, to refrain therefrom. Purchaser will provide adequate space for Artist or its designee(s) or licensee(s) to vend such material, and Purchaser agrees that Artist and its designee(s) and licensee(s) will, as they may reasonably require, have access to any hall facilities and all areas adjacent to the facility. Purchaser further agrees to use its best efforts to prevent and stop the sale or distribution by any person other than Artist and its designee(s) and licensee(s), whether inside or outside the facility, of any merchandise at the Engagement. It is understood that no person or entity other than Artist or its designee(s) or licensee(s) will have the right to sell or distribute any non-food and non-beverage items at the Engagement without the express written consent of Artist.

B. Purchaser agrees that he will not commit _____ to any personal appearance, interviews or any other type of promotional appearance.

IV. PERFORMANCE

A. Opening acts may not place equipment on stage before _____ equipment and road crew arrive, without prior notification to _____ production manager.

B. Purchaser agrees that Artist has the right to control all aspects of the performance, including, but not limited to, the production elements of any other acts on the bill. The right shall include set times and length, house lights, sound, lights, doors opening, sound level, security in the stage area and back stage areas and stage position.

C. If an unusual situation exists in which all arena or dome lights cannot be turned off for performance for any reason, (e.g.: fire regulations, safety, etc.) Purchaser will advise _____ production manager prior to show day.

D. If, for any reason, _____ should choose not to be the final act on the show, they may perform in any slot during the show at the discretion of the Artist.

V. SETTLEMENT, BOX OFFICE, PAYMENT

A. Fifty percent (50%) of the total guaranteed price in cash or cashier's check shall be deposited with _____, simultaneously with the signing of this contract.

B. The balance of payment shall be made in cash, prior to the show on the date of the engagement, to a representative of the Artist.

In cases where the Artist is being paid on a percentage basis, Purchaser agrees to deliver to the Artist, at least three (3) weeks prior to the date of the performance, a full-house seating plan and stage to scale and a printer's manifest of the house (notarized, signed statement from the printer of tickets, listing amount of the tickets printed at each price). No monies should be deleted from the original ticket price other than stated city taxes, no additions made.

C. Purchaser agrees that if contract price herein includes a percentage payment to Artist, Purchaser will provide Artist, on the night of the engagement, proper invoices and bills corresponding to the show's expenses. Purchaser agrees that any expenses not documented by proper invoices can, at the Artist's discretion, be excluded from computation of show's expenses.

D. Purchaser understands and agrees that the contract is computed on the basis of estimates for total expenses. A list of these estimated expenses is expressed in writing on the AF of M contract included herein. Both parties agree that during the process of settlement, the above expense statement will be compared against corresponding invoices made available by Purchaser. Should the sum of invoiced expenses exceed the estimated cost, the Artist shall not be liable to accept such increased expenses and may receive payment based on the deal incorporated in the above stated AF of M contract. In the event that the sum of available invoices is less than the estimated show cost, both parties agree to re-compute the "split point," utilizing the exact formula employed in computing the original "split point."

E. Purchaser agrees to provide the Tour Manager or Artist Representative with a copy of the certified ticket manifest and original copies of all show expenses actually incurred immediately prior to opening the box office on the day of the engagement. In the case where ticket prices vary according to whether they are purchased on the day of the engagement or before, Purchaser will obtain different colored tickets for each type and price of sale.

F. Both parties agree that any discrepancies or disputes occurring in the settlement process will be settled according to the principles set forth in this rider.

G. Purchaser will present to the representatives of Artist a signed statement of the number and price of all tickets sold in advance, (prior to the opening of the box office on the day of the engagement) together with all of the unsold pre-show-day tickets.

H. Artist shall have the unrestricted right to designate one or more of its employees to enter the box office at any time before, during, or after the engagement to examine and extract Purchaser's box office records to verify compliance by Purchaser with its obligations set forth in this Agreement. Purchaser shall have all unsold tickets on hand at the engagement for counting and verification by a representative of Artist. Artist shall be compensated for all seats for which there is not an unsold ticket on hand with the exception only of the complimentary tickets permitted under heading VIII below.

I. If there is assessment of tax by any taxing authority on Artist for monies earned during the engagement, said tax is to be paid by Purchaser. It must be understood and agreed that no deductions whatsoever are to be taken from the contract price contained herein or from any percentages earned hereunder.

J. Ticket prices and the number of tickets available in each price category must appear on the face of this contract. All tickets shall be printed by a bonded ticket printer (example: Globe Tickets, National, Quick Tick, etc.) or if the performance is at a college or university, the official printing department of the college or university.

K. Purchaser further agrees to furnish Artist, at the place of engagement on the night of the show, all unsold tickets. If the Purchaser violates any of the preceding provisions, it shall be deemed that Purchaser HAS SOLD A TICKET FOR EACH SEAT IN THE HOUSE (and permitted standing room) at the highest ticket price for which the house is scaled, and that Artist shall receive from Purchaser compensation based on 100% sell-out.

L. Purchaser may not sell tickets to the performance herein as part of a series of other concerts without prior written consent of the Artist. All tickets printed under the manifest shall be of the one-stub, one-price variety. There shall be no multiple-price tickets printed. Examples of tickets prohibited under this agreement are:

One price for students and a different price for general admission under the same ticket, or;

One price for tickets bought in advance and a different price for tickets bought at the gate on the same ticket.

M. Ticket counts shall be available daily.

N. All tickets in the first 25 rows must be sold on a first come, first served basis. None of these tickets are to be given to any ticket agency or held back by the box office for any reason.

O. Except where specified, all performances hereunder shall be held indoors and shall not be subject to cancellation due to weather conditions.

P. Purchaser agrees to provide Artist's agent, _____, with a written, certified attendance count and statement of Artist's earnings for the performance no later than seven (7) days after completion of the engagement.

Q. All advertising costs are to be settled at the actual net "out-of-pocket" costs to the Artist for purchasing such advertising, it being expressly understood and agreed that any advertising agency fees charged by any so-called "in-house," "captive" or otherwise affiliated or associated advertising agencies shall not be counted in making the settlement.

VI. CANCELLATION: ILLNESS, FORCE MAJEURE

A. _____ may terminate this agreement if:

1. Any individual member of _____ or the sound engineer or lighting director contracted for the show shall die become ill or incapacitated for any reason.

2. In Artist's judgment, performance of the engagement may directly or indirectly expose _____, any employee of _____, any employee of any company contracted by _____ or of Purchaser or any portion of the audience to danger of death or injury by any outbreak of violence or civil strife of any kind.

3. Performance of any of Producer's obligations shall be rendered impossible or impracticable by any reason of strikes, civil unrest, gasoline rationing, unforseeable act or order of any contractor or subcontractor or of any public authority, epidemic, dangerous weather conditions, national or local state of emergency, fire, or other event or condition of any kind or character.

4. Performance of any of Artist's obligations shall expose any member of _____ INC., or Purchasers employees, agents or independant contractors to civil or criminal proceedings of any kind.

B. It is Purchaser's sole responsibility to ensure that it is safe for _____ to perform. If missiles such as bottles, explosive fireworks or other objects should hit the stage before or during the performance, and such missiles endanger the persons or property performing thereon, then _____ may refuse to perform, or quit the stage and Purchaser shall still be liable to pay the full amount due hereunder.

VII. HALL CONTRACT

A. Purchaser shall provide Artist with a copy of Purchaser's Agreement with hall and any additional documents relating to this engagement prior to tickets being put on sale.

B. Purchaser may withdraw only the number of tickets set forth in the hall contract for use by the hall. Said number of tickets must be stated in the hall contract that is sent to _____.

VIII. COMPLIMENTARY TICKETS

A. Purchaser will hold one hundred (100) top price tickets for use by Artist. These top price tickets should be taken from the preferred seating areas (e.g., loge or riser sections) not the arena floor. Purchaser shall also hold ten (10) additional tickets for the opening act to be in a better than average location. This is a total of one hundred-ten (110) complimentary tickets.

B. Purchaser may distribute twenty-five (25) complimentary tickets.

C. No complimentary tickets may be taken from the first twenty (20) rows.

D. Except as specifically provided above, Purchaser shall not distribute complimentary tickets or permit the same to be distributed. Purchaser shall not, in any event, discount tickets as a premium, package or series of concerts or performances or impose or permit to be imposed any service or handling charge on or in connection with the sale of tickets, except and unless Artist grants prior written express permission, which it may refuse to do at its sole and absolute discretion.

E. There shall be no "guest list" for free admission.

F. Purchaser is liable for any and all counterfeit tickets and under no circumstances will Artist assume a loss on any such ticket.

IX. MERCHANDISING

_____ will provide their own merchandising personnel, _____. Purchaser will ensure they are welcomed and are put in contact with the proper people and coordinate their sales of _____ merchandise during the performance. No other sales of _____ will be permitted.

Any other act on the show must contact _____ no later than ten (10) days prior to performance concerning sales to their own merchandise. Be advised that _____ and the Artist strictly enforce their exclusive merchandising arrangement.

X. INSURANCE

A. Purchaser agrees to provide Public Liability Insurance coverage to protect against injuries to persons and/or property as a consequence of the installation and/or operation of the equipment provided by Artist, and will name Artist.

B. Purchaser shall maintain in effect a policy of Workman's Compensation Insurance covering all of its employees and/or maintenance of the equipment provided by Artist.

C. Purchaser shall further idemnify and hold Artist, its contractors, employees, licensees and designees harmless from and against any loss, damage, cost or expense, including reasonable attorney's fees, incurred or suffered by or threatened against Artist in connection with or as a result of any claim for personal injury or property damage, or otherwise brought by or on behalf of any third party person, firm or corporation as a result of or in connection with the engagement, which claim does not result directly from the willful acts of Artist, its employees, contractors, or agents. To this end, Purchaser will obtain at its sole cost and expense, a policy of insurance therefore naming Artist and the individual members thereof as additional insureds, in an amount as required by the venue contract, but in no event less than one million dollars ($1,000,000.00). As proof of such insurance, a fully paid certificate of insurance will be submitted to Artist by Purchaser for Artist's prior approval at least four (4) weeks prior to the engagement hereunder. Such policy shall contain a provision requiring the insurance company to give Artist at least ten (10) days written notice prior to any revision, modification, or cancellation thereof. Any proposed change in certificates of insurance shall be submitted to Artist for its prior approval. Artist shall be entitled to a copy of then prevailing certificate of insurance, which shall be furnished to Artist by Purchaser.

D. Purchaser shall also name Artist as additional insureds on the public liability insurance policy/policies carried at the facility at which Artist shall appear hereunder, such coverage to be to the fullest extent applicable to any other party named in such insurance policy/policies.

As proof of such insurance, a fully paid certificate of insurance naming each of such parties as additional insureds shall be submitted to Artist by Purchaser for Artist's prior approval at least four (4) weeks prior to the engagement hereunder. Such policy shall contain a provision requiring the insurance company to give Artist at least ten (10) days written notice prior to any revision, modification, or cancellation thereof. Any proposed change in certificates of insurance shall be submitted to Artist for its prior approval. Artist shall be entitled to a copy of the facility's then prevailing certificate of insurance, which shall be furnished to Artist by Purchaser or the facility itself.

It is specifically understood that failure of Purchaser or the facility to provide either policies or certificates required above, or the failure of Artist to approve the same, shall not be deemed a waiver of Purchaser's obligations herein; Purchaser shall still be solely responsible for providing or causing to be provided all of such insurance, and Purchaser shall be fully liable for its failure to provide or cause to be provided the same.

E. All references to Artist in this insurance section shall be deemed to mean _____ and members thereof namely, _____.

XI. DAMAGES

_____ will not be held responsible for any damages, nor will there be any monies held back at settlement for a damages contingency, if any kind of beer or other alcoholic beverage is served or consumed inside the facility by the patrons. In addition, _____ will not be held responsible for any damages if a proper search of all patrons is not conducted prior to entry into the facility.

XII. MISC.

A. TOWELS: Artist requires that Purchaser provide twenty-four (24) towels to _____, on the day of the show. Artist will not allow any expenses for towels beyond said twenty-four (24) as requested above in the settle-up.

B. WARDROBE: Provisions are to be made in advance for a same day dry cleaning and laundry service, plus a responsible person to carry out this chore, pending instructions of Artist's Representative.

TECHNICAL RIDER

SCOPE

Technical conditions necessary for the performance of _____ shall be adhered to without exception. If, for any reason, any of the requirements in this rider cannot be met, Purchaser must send a written notification to _____ (Production Manager) at least twenty-one (21) days prior to the first scheduled performance.

If the Purchaser is unable to meet a requirement due to his inability to arrange for a service or item, or for any other reason, and that service or item can be provided by efforts made by _____ or their staff, the Purchaser shall be liable for any and all reasonable fees, charges or other renumerations required to provide said service or item.

_____ shall have the first right of set-up for all instruments, property, scenery, and other equipment used in the presentation of the production, and the aforesaid instruments, property, scenery and other equipment shall not be moved, relocated and/or used by any person without the express permission of the Tour Manager or Production Manager of _____.

Purchaser agrees to furnish, at his/her sole cost and expense, all of the electrical and physical equipment which is part of the permanent equipment of the place of performance, including any other staging, risers, sound and/or lighting equipment, and other items or services required by _____ that is not part of the permanent equipment of the facility at least eighteen (18) hours prior to the scheduled starting time of the performance. Purchaser further agrees to furnish and/or pay for all other items including, without limitation, electricians, stage hands, riggers, fork lift operators, truck loaders, maintainance personnel, ticket sellers and other box office personnel required for advance and day of show sales, ticket takers, ushers, police, all licenses and fees thereof, and other materials and services as per this agreement and the Technical Rider made a part thereof.

Purchaser shall comply with all regulations and requirements of any union or unions that may have jurisdiction over any of said materials, facilities and personnel to be furnished by Purchaser.

_____ shall have the sole and exclusive control over the production, presentation and performance of the entertainment unit in connection with the engagement, including but not limited to, details, means and methods of the performance of the entertainment unit and each member thereof, and personnel to be provided by Purchaser in performing the provisions hereof on the part of _____.

PRODUCTION CONTROLS

_____will supply the necessary sound system and stage lighting, for a fee to Purchaser for each performance which is stated on the face of the contract. _____ reserves the right to withhold any portion of the sound and lighting systems for their exclusive use and retain all rights in the use of all of the production equipment provided by them, at the sole discretion of the tour/production manager and lighting/sound engineers.

In the event that _____ is not carrying their own production, Purchaser agrees to provide, at his own expense, the necessary staging, sound and light systems to the Artist's specifications.

It must be specifically understood and agreed that a representative of _____ shall have the sole and absolute authority in mixing and controlling all sound equipment during rehearsal and each performance scheduled herein. It shall be at his sole discretion whether or not the house sound system shall be used in combination with, or in lieu of, the system provided by _____. The Purchaser must inform the Production Manager immediately if there are any volume restrictions in force at the venue. If these are found to be unacceptable, _____ has the right to cancel this agreement forthwith.

The lighting director shall give all light cues and shall have the option of using any or all house lighting systems by him in conjunction with the lighting system provided by _____. Purchaser's lighting director/stage manager shall have absolute control of the house lights.

CURFEWS

The Purchaser must inform the Artist's management and Production Manager at the earliest possible opportunity of any curfew in effect at the venue, in order that running times, sound check, meal times, load-in, etc. can be adjusted accordingly.

NOTE: Artist's set length is approximately two (2) hours.

The Purchaser must make every effort to have the curfew waived. In the event that the Tour or Production Manager discovers that a "curfew" is simply a financial one, and assuming that this has not been made clear to the Artist's management well in advance, it will be held the Purchaser's sole responsibility to discharge any cost incurred by running over said "curfew."

PERMITS

The Purchaser agrees to secure and furnish all necessary permits and licenses to insure that _____ can properly stage the production.

PURCHASER'S ATTENDANCE

Purchaser agrees to furnish his personal representative capable of making any decision pertaining to the engagement from the time of arrival of the production equipment (including any outside staging materials) through to the time of departure. The representative must have copies of this entire contract, together with any riders, copies of all fax's and mailgrams, letters and other correspondence pertaining to the engagement, and copies of support act(s) contracts and rider on hand.

Purchaser's representative will remain in the immediate backstage area and must be in constant contact with the Producer's stage manager. Producer's stage manager will make all decisions relative to the staging of the Artist's show. Purchaser's failure to comply with reasonable requests may require that the show be cancelled.

The Purchaser will provide the Production Manager of _____ with telephone numbers (business and residence) where he/she can be contacted during the twenty-eight (28) days prior to the engagement.

POWER REQUIREMENTS

Purchaser agrees to supply adequate electrical service and electrical facilities, installed by licensed electricians and professional personnel in accordance with the standards of the community for the installation and operation in a safe manner of electrical appliances, facilities and wiring. All power sources are to be run and/or installed at Purchaser's sole expense and ready for use at the time the production arrives at the place of performance. All licenses, permits or fees necessary for the installation and/or use of this power will be obtained by the Purchaser at his sole expense.

LIGHTING SERVICE

The Purchaser must provide the following service:

One (1) house service, with a minimum of 800 amps 3 phase, 4 wire plus mechanical ground, 120/208 volts "wye" configuration, for a total of 2,400 amps. Or, two (2) services of 400 amps 3 phase, 4 wire plus mechanical ground. Each distribution box must have double lugs to accommodate a parallel tie in of two (2) sets of 3 hot, 5 wire 4/0 cable per box.

The ground for the lighting service must be separate from the sound service, with an absolute zero potential ground tap. The service must be stable: i.e., when full current is drawn, voltage must not vary more than five percent (5%) from voltage with no current drawn. The lighting service is to be located no more than fifty feet (50') from upstage left.

SOUND AND STAGE EQUIPMENT SERVICE

The sound and stage equipment service must be totally separate from the sound service. Ideally, the service must be from a separate transformer used solely for the sound and stage equipment supplied by

_____

One (1) house service, with a minimum of 200 amps 3 phase 4 wire plus a cold water pipe ground, 120/208 volts "wye" configuration, for a total of 600 amps.

Again, a zero potential ground tap is required. The service must also be stable within five percent (5%) when current is drawn. The sound and stage equipment service is to be located no more than fifty feet (50') from upstage right.

BUS SHORE POWER

Two (2) house services, with a minimum of 60 amps single phase each: located within fifty feet (50') of the bus parking area.

GENERATORS

If a generator or other alternative power source is to be utilized, the Artist's Production Manager must be notified immediately. The Artist's production Manager must be given the name and telephone number of the supplier of the alternative power source so that he can determine if the service(s) will be acceptable. When generators are to be used, Purchaser must ensure that adequate fuel is available for each show and that said generators should be well baffled, have a stabilizer unit, and be placed well away from the dressing room areas. The generators must be supplied with a competent service person and operator to maintain and protect the equipment through the set-up, sound check, and performance.

All services will be used at the discretion of the Artist's Production Manager.

All services must be installed and available to Artist's electrician no later than load-in and kept available until the end of load-out.

ELECTRICIAN

A qualified, licensed house electrician familiar with all power sources, transformers, etc. at the venue, equipped with all necessary tools including spare fuses and circuit breakers, must be available from load-in throughout the day until the end of load-out, or until released by Artist's Production Manager.

RIGGING

It is imperative that the show fly all sound and lights. This will be done from twenty (20) rigging points, each capable of supporting between 500 and 2,000 lbs. The total weight of the hanging production is approximately 16,000 lbs. Please notify the Production Manager immediately if there is any problem hanging this show.

For the sound and lights to be flown, the minimum necessary clearance from the stage to the lowest beam or obstruction is forty-two feet (42') over the entire stage area.

If the access to overhead beams is not normally available, a cherry picker or bucket truck with experienced operator must be provided by the Purchaser at no cost to the Artist.

Notification must be made at least twenty-eight (28) days in advance to the Artist of any local rules pertaining to weight limitations, safety inspections, building codes or permits. Any such permits, inspections, licenses, etc. will be the sole responsibility and cost of Purchaser.

Any removable obstructions (flags, banners, false ceiling tiles, etc.) must be removed prior to the rigging call. Arena scoreboards must be raised to their maximum height. The Artist must be advised as soon as possible of inaccessibility to normal flying areas. Examples of such are a site with no beams, permanent obstructions, etc.

All house riggers must be experienced at their trade and must be able to climb to all accessible rigging points. If the house riggers will only climb on the catwalk or go only to the easily accessible points, the Purchaser must hire competent outside riggers.

If the Artist's equipment is available, the Artist's Production Manager will determine with the Purchaser whether it is feasible to rig the night prior to the first engagement.

FORKLIFTS

From the beginning of load-in until the end of load-out, two (2) forklifts are required. The forklifts must have a load capacity of 5,000 lbs. and a minimum lift height of twelve feet (12'). The forklifts should be of a known make, be in good repair, and have an experienced operator. The forklifts must be fueled before load-in and have plenty of extra fuel within easy access. The forks must be five feet (5') long with extensions available to eight feet (8').

STAGE CALL/PERSONNEL

Purchaser must provide the following personnel at the times indicated. All personnel must be able-bodied, proficient in their profession, and be at least eighteen (18) years of age.

The number of personnel indicated for all calls are for working personnel. If there are any non-working personnel, these are to be in addition to the requested calls.

The exact times and number of personnel for the stage calls indicated may change due to travel schedules, hall availability, or other reasons. Final crew calls will be arranged by the Artist's Production Manager well in advance of the scheduled date.

STAGE CALL

9:00 AM	One (1)	Steward
	Two (2)	Riggers (climbing required)
	One (1)	Ground Man
	Four (4)	Truckloaders
	Twelve (12)	Stagehands
	Two (2)	Forklift and Operator
	One (1)	Electrician
	One (1)	Promoter Rep
	Two (2)	Runners

SHOW CALL

7:30 PM	Ten (10)	Spot Operators
	Five (5)	Deck hands (for support acts)
	One (1)	Houselight Operator
	One (1)	Forklift and Operator
	One (1)	Electrician

LOAD-OUT

11:00 PM	One (1)	Steward
	Sixteen (16)	Stagehands
	Two (2)	Riggers (climbing required)
	One (1)	Ground Man
	Two (2)	Forklifts and Operators
	One (1)	Electrician
	One (1)	Promoter Rep
	Four (4)	Truckloaders (8 may be needed at some venues)

SEATING

No seats are to be sold to the sides or the rear of the stage without the express written permission of _____. If permission to sell these seats is granted, no seats are to be put on sale until the Artist's Production Manager is consulted as to production kills.

There must be no seats erected on the arena floor until instructed by the Artist's Production manager. Immediately after the show all seats on the arena floor must be removed. Purchaser must ensure that there is enough personnel available to complete this task in the shortest possible time. No forklifts, stagehands or other personnel allocated to the production are to assist in this task.

Two hundred (200) seats are to be held from sale in the center rear area of the arena floor to accommodate the mixing position.

The first row of seats must start one (1) foot from the barricade. In cases where that is impossible or impractical, security must insure that there is no traffic in front of the stage during a song. During the breaks between songs security must allow only people seated in the front row access to their seats. This stipulation is not valid in a general admission situation or when all patrons are allowed up to the barricade at all times.

STAGE/BARRICADE

The stage must be placed a minimum of six feet (6') from the rear wall to allow for enough space for equipment four feet (4') wide to be maneuvered around the stage. The stage must be extremely sturdy and strong, capable of supporting nine hundred (900) lbs. per square foot. In some cases the stage must be crossed decked with ½ inch plywood to distribute the load. The stage must be perfectly level with no holes, cracks or ridges.

STAGE

Fifty-six feet (56') from left to right, forty feet (40') from front to back, and four and a half (4-1/2') feet high.

NONE OF ARTIST'S EQUIPMENT WILL BE UNLOADED OR PLACED ON THE STAGE UNTIL THE STAGE HAS BEEN INSPECTED AND DEEMED SAFE BY THE ARTIST'S PRODUCTION MANAGER.

SIDE STAGE WINGS

There are no side stage wings (wound wings) if the stage is 4-1/2 feet high. If the stage is higher than 4-1/2 feet then risers must be provided to compensate for the difference in height.

Stage right: Twelve feet (12') wide by twenty-four feet (24') deep

Stage left: Twelve feet (12') wide by sixteen feet (16') deep

Both wings set back four feet (4') from the front of the stage.

STAIRS

Two (2) well constructed and adequately lit stairways must be provided, one (1) stage left and one (1) stage right. The stairs must be securely fastened to the stage.

BARRICADE

A barricade four feet (4') high and four feet (4') from the stage must be erected at a time designated by the Production Manager. This barricade must be extremely strong and braced properly so that the stage and barricade will remain rigid at all times.

MIXER

Due to the extremely specialized technical aspects of the show, a large mixing control area is needed. Please ensure that enough seats are held back from sale to accommodate this area.

The mix area must be located in the CENTER OF THE HOUSE, one hundred feet (100') from the front of the stage. A mixing platform must be constructed prior to load-in with dimensions of sixteen feet (16') wide by twelve feet (12') deep by eighteen inches (18") high. Immediately behind this riser an additional platform is to be constructed sixteen feet (16') wide by eight feet (8') deep by twenty-four inches (24") high. Please provide one (1) eight foot (8') table and six (6) chairs at the mix riser.

In a hall where there is no seating on the floor, a barricade must be constructed around the mix area.

OUTDOOR SHOWS

Roof: Sixty feet (60') wide by forty feet (40') deep and be capable of supporting 12,000 lbs.

Tarps: Twenty feet (20') by twenty feet (20') over each wing. The house mix area and the spotlights must be covered.

Visquene: Six (6) rolls of 100' by 20" 4 mil plastic

Misc.: Two squeegees, two mops, and 36 extra towels

SPOTLIGHTS

Purchaser agrees to provide, for the use of _____ six (6) Strong Co. "Super Trouper" followspots. Positions for these spotlights must be in the rear half of the arena, at no less than two hundred feet (200') from the stage. In some cases, if existing positions are adequate, it may be necessary to remove seats at the Production Manager's discretion, so that temporary followspot platforms can be installed. These platforms and spotlights must be installed prior to stage call. Under no circumstances will any labor from the stage call be used to set up or remove these positions or spotlights. Each spotlight must have a separately fused thirty (30) amp circuit.

The spotlights must be in good condition, each with a minimum of five (5) sets of carbons and good working irises and dausers, all cleaned and tested prior to the performance. Spare parts must be readily available.

Operators for these six (6) spotlights and four (4) truss spots (for a total of ten (10)) must be provided. Operators must be made aware of the importance that followspots play during the performance. It is of the utmost importance that the spotlight operators be fully competent. Operators must be available thirty (30) minutes prior to the performance for a pre-show briefing: they should report to the lighting crew chief.

Purchaser will ensure that the operators are at their positions no less than twenty (20) minutes prior to the commencement of the performance of _____ for final instructions from the Artist's lighting designer and for a headset check. Any overtime incurred due to the tardiness of the spotlight operators will be the direct responsibility of the Purchaser and will not be a show expense.

HOUSELIGHTS

The houselight operator(s) must be on headsets from at least twenty (20) minutes prior to show time until the end of the performance. Houselights are to be the complete control of the Artist's stage manager at all times.

The Purchaser will make arrangements for all lights not specifically required by local safety ordinances to be turned off during the performance. This especially applies to clocks, scoreboards, advertising billboards and concessions in the hall. All doorways to lighted hallways must be curtained off as a total house blackout is required for the entire performance.

SOUND CHECK/DOOR OPENING

The show requires a technical rehearsal to commence approximately between 4:00 P.M. and 6:00 P.M. every performance day for a minimum of two (2) hours. There is no time allowed for sound check for support acts. Purchaser must agree to make all parties aware of this fact. Set-up time and any time allowed, if any, for support acts sound checks are totally at the discretion of the Artist's Production Manager.

Purchaser must understand that the complexity of the production necessitates a complete check before each show. The check may be performed by _____ or by road crew members at the Production Manager's option. No audience shall be allowed to enter the place of performance until the sound check has been completed to the Producer's satisfaction. No other equipment, i.e., support act's equipment, shall be placed on the stage until the sound check and full focus of the lights have been completed to the satisfaction of the Artist's Production Manager. THE DOORS WILL NOT BE OPENED WITHOUT THE PERMISSION OF THE ARTIST'S PRODUCTION MANAGER.

BACKSTAGE PASSES

All Artist's personnel will have laminated tour passes. The passes will allow these people to have total facility access, including the stage. Producer's stage manager will provide all dated passes to working crews, promoter personnel, caterers, guests, etc. A representative of _____ will inform the hall security chief of the access allowed with these dated stick-on passes. No other passes will be honored.

HALL TEMPERATURE/CLIMATE

The hall, dressing rooms, and tuning rooms must be maintained at a constant 72 degrees Fahrenheit plus or minus two (2) degrees.

There must be no drafts from open doors or from air conditioning during the performance of _____

If the climate of the hall warrants, the Artist's stage manager may require that air conditioning and/or heating to be operational or continued during load-in and until the end of load-out. Artist's stage manager is also to have complete control of the amount of house lighting necessary during load-in and load-out.

RUBBER MATTING

Purchaser must provide, at his sole expense, matting to cover the sound and lighting control cables on the facility floor.

FIRE EXTINGUISHERS

One (1) twenty pound (20 lb.) CO_2 and one (1) dry chemical fire extinguisher must be available at load-in for safety purposes.

DOCTOR

Purchaser agrees to arrange for the services of one (1) physician qualified in internal medicine and having privileges of admission to a first-rate hospital in the vicinity. The physician must be on a twenty-four (24) hour call to come to either the venue or the hotel for the duration of the Artist's stay in your city. In addition, _____ must have immediate access to a qualified Dentist and a qualified Ear, Nose and Throat Specialist.

GARBAGE

In order to keep the backstage area completely clean and safe, the Purchaser must provide two (2) 36-gallon leak-proof trash containers, one (1) on each side of the stage on the floor. Additional trash containers must be placed in each dressing room and the food service area. These containers must be in place at the start of load-in and emptied periodically up until showtime. In addition to the above, Purchaser should provide separate trash containers marked for recycling of cans and bottles, and Purchaser should make arrangements for appropriate disposal of these bottles and cans. Thank you.

BLOWER/HALL CLEAN-UP

The use of blowers (electric or gas) to clean the hall will not be tolerated while _____ or the Artist's crew is in the building: i.e., until the end of load-out.

The arena floor must be swept immediately after the performance.

RUNNER

Two (2) intelligent, reliable runners with good knowledge of the area and the stores that provide the items necessary for a touring production is needed. One (1) runner with a van or other large vehicle in good operating condition is to be available at 9:00 A.M. The second runner with a reliable car is to be available at 10:00 A.M.

PARKING/VEHICLE ACCESS

The production is carried in three (3) forty-eight foot (48') air ride trailers (total length sixty-two feet (62'). The immediate load-in area must be clear of all vehicles in order to enable speedy and efficient maneuvering, load-in and load-out of these trucks.

Purchaser may make all necessary arrangements regarding local parking and/or police permits if loading is from the street into the venue. Parking must be made available within close proximity to the loading door.

The show also travels with two (2) buses. Please arrange for parking throughout the day and night of the show as near to the backstage door as possible. Purchaser must also supply, within fifty feet (50') of each bus, a 60 amp electrical supply.

The Purchaser must provide, regardless of where the truck/buses are parked, armed uniformed security guards to stay and guard the vehicles from the arrival of the vehicles until their departure, or until released by Artist's Production Manager.

FUEL EMERGENCY

Purchaser must understand that there may be transportation problems caused by fuel allocations which are entirely outside Producer's control. However, if these fuel problems should occur, a local supplier of diesel fuel must be located within twenty-five (25) miles of the engagement and one thousand (1000).

MINIMUM SECURITY

Purchaser shall warrant and guarantee security at all times to ensure the safety of _____ and their property before, during, and after the performance. Therefore the following must be adhered to and shall be included in the show cost.

REQUIRED SECURITY

Mixing Area   Three (3) men

Dressing Rooms	One (1) on each room
Vehicles	One (1) or more armed guards
Stage Stairs	One (1) on each
Backstage Door	One (1) (to commence at load-in)
Barricade	Two (2) each side and six (6) inside
Backstage	One (1) supervisor for special problems

GENERAL RULES AND ALLOCATIONS

The hall shall be closed to the public during set-up, sound check and break-down, and only those people directly involved with the show shall be allowed on the premises. The Purchaser agrees to be held responsible for any theft or damage caused by his staff, the patrons or any third party. _____ shall have absolute control of the security personnel, stage access during Artist's set, as well as during any performance by a support act.

One (1) T-shirt security to report to stage manager at load-in to commence internal security.

An armed guard must be positioned at the parking area from the arrival of the first vehicle to the departure of the last vehicle. If the positioning of the guard does not allow a clear view of all vehicles, then more than one (1) guard may be needed.

It will be necessary for the promoter's security chief to meet with the tour manager or security director at 5:00 P.M. to outline the security arrangements for the evening. All security personnel must be of at least eighteen (18) years of age, all of whom should have flashlights and identical T-shirts or blazers for purposes of identification. None of these security personnel shall carry or possess any firearms, clubs or dangerous weapons. All manager and/or security director from a time commencing not later than two (2) hours prior to showtime and ending not sooner than the time at which the last member of _____ or _____ Artist's employees leave the venue.

No uniformed guards are to patrol or be in front of the stage at any time.

_____ retains the right to demand substitution of any security guards who, in the Artist's sole judgement, are not physically capable of performing their duties. Any security guard who uses excess violence in pursuance of his/her duties may be ejected from the building upon demand by the Artist's tour manager, stage manager and/or security director. In addition, _____ reserves the right to cancel or terminate the show immediately, and _____ entitled to the full _____ contracted fee.

Three (3) security guards (including one (1) supervisor) must be available for use solely at the house mixing area and must be in position before the doors open.

Should the public have access to the spotlight positions, there should be a platform plus one (1) security guard per platform.

In the event that _____ plays two (2) or more shows on successive nights, Purchaser must supply adequate security overnight: i.e., at least three (3) men.

Additional adequate external house security must be provided to ensure safe direction and supervision of any audience build-up outside the venue prior to doors opening, as well as safe and orderly admission of the audience. The Artist's tour manager, stage manager and/or security director must be informed of any substantial build-up audience prior to doors opening.

PRODUCTION OFFICE/TELEPHONES

Purchaser must provide a production office for the sole use of _____. The office must be located no more than two hundred feet (200') from the backstage area on the same floor as the stage, be air conditioned and must have dimensions no less than twelve feet (12') by eight feet (8').

   One (1) sturdy eight foot (8') table and four (4) chairs
   Two (2) electric outlets
   One (1) telephone for incoming calls
   One (1) telephone for outgoing calls. Please note that this telephone cannot go through a switchboard and must have a standard AT&T plug adaptable to the computer and fax systems carried by _____.

CREW ROOM

Purchaser must provide a large (team-size) room, located away from the dressing rooms, for the use of Artist's crew. This room should be well-lit, heated and have private toilets and showers with hot and cold running water.

Please provide forty-eight (48) large bath-size towels and twelve (12) bars of soap at load-in.

DRESSING ROOMS

Purchaser must supply four (4) dressing rooms for the sole use of _____ and their guests. All of these rooms must have private bathroom facilities, adjustable heating/air conditioning, electrical outlets, proper lighting and be clean.

The dressing rooms must be in the same building as the concert hall with easy access to the stage. Each room must have fresh bars of soap, twelve (12) towels, non-leaking garbage cans, ashtrays and comfortable seating. Dressing rooms must be easily accessible to the stage without passing through the audience area.

TUNING ROOM

The room must be at least twelve feet (12') by eight feet (8') with a private toilet and a minimum of two (2) electrical outlets. The room must contain two (2) six foot by three foot (6' × 3") tables and two (2) chairs. This room must be the same temperature as the stage area, plus or minus four (4) degrees Fahrenheit.

HOSPITALITY ROOM

This room must be of large size with private toilets and electrical outlets, and contain a minimum of one (1) couch, six (6) comfortable chairs and two (2) six foot by three foot (6' × 3') tables. All of the drinks for the guests after the show are to be put in this room.

BAND ROOM 1

This room must be a large team-sized room with a private toilet and electrical outlets, and contain a minimum of one (1) couch, six (6) comfortable chairs, one (1) six foot by three foot (6' × 3') table, two (2) full length mirrors, one (1) clothing rack, and a total of thirty-six (36) towels.

BAND ROOM 2

The room should be medium sized with a private toilet, electrical outlets, three (3) comfortable chairs, one (1) six foot by three foot (6' × 3') table and one full length mirror.

Each of these rooms should be locked, with a set of keys made available to the Artist's tour manager or Production Manager: any deposits for keys must be paid by the Purchaser. These rooms should be clean and available no later than 8:00 A.M.

CATERING RIDER

CATERING

Purchaser agrees to supply the following food and beverage items for each performance. All items are to be considered a show expense and may be modified by the Artist's Production/tour manager. Any food and drink for union personnel or other personnel not connected with _____ in addition to that mentioned below should be provided accordingly. Meals for guests and other persons not necessary to the production of the show will not be accepted as a show expense. Support bands and crew will be fed an evening meal only, as it is not necessary for them to be in the building until 4:00 P.M.

All Artist and crew food and beverages, including liquor, shall be set aside for the band/crew to take after the show.

ROAD CREW FOOD AND BEVERAGE REQUIREMENTS

1. Drinks must be available not only during meals, but at all times during the engagement.

2. All beverages are to be served in coolers/ice chests or shallow bus trays. AT NO TIME will garbage cans be allowed. SHALLOW CONTAINERS ONLY.

3. Fresh ice is to be provided at all meals and in the dressing rooms in a clean cooler or bus tray with a serving scoop.

4. Two (2) large ice chests are to be on the stage all day. All leftover drinks from meals are to be delivered to the stage coolers after the meal.

5. _____ laminated passes are to be used in lieu of meal tickets for _____ personnel.

6. Two (2) cardboard boxes are to be delivered to Artist's dressing room before show time.

CREW BREAKFAST

A. Breakfast starts 1/2 hour prior to stage call and is served until 12:00 noon: food and drinks for eighteen (18) persons plus local crew.

    1. BEVERAGES
        Coffee—freshly brewed—cream, sugar, and Equal
        Hot water, tea and instant cocoa, lemon and honey
        Juices—orange, grapefruit, V-8, cranberry and apple
        Milk—homogenized and 2%
        Spring water
        Sodas—Classic Coke, Pepsi, 7-UP, Mountain Dew

2. FOOD DISHES

Fresh fruit—oranges, bananas, melons, strawberries, and grapefruit

Assorted sweet rolls and Danish

Instant oatmeal

Toaster items—Thomas' English muffins, white, wheat and multi-grain breads

Peanut butter, jam, butter, margarine

HOT ENTREE: Either a prepared hot breakfast to order or provide three (3) electric skillets, utensils, and the following:

Fresh eggs, cheeses, chopped onion, tomatoes, green peppers, bacon or sausage, potatoes (sliced or hash browned)

Optional: French toast or Pancakes

CREW LUNCH

Lunch is to be served from 12:30 P.M. to 3:00 P.M.: food and drinks sufficient for twenty (20) persons plus local crew.

1. BEVERAGES

Three (3) gallons milk—two (2) homogenized, one (1) low-fat

One (1) gallon iced tea with lemon and sugar

One (1) gallon orange juice

Two (2) gallons spring water

One (1) case Classic Coke—12oz. cans

Two (2) six (6) packs each of the following:

    7-UP, Dr. Pepper, Rootbeer, Mountain Dew

Two (2) six (6) packs—Vernors or Squirt

One (1) six (6) pack Pepsi

★★REMEMBER-FRESH ICE—SHALLOW CONTAINERS★★

2. FOOD DISHES

DELI TRAY consisting of fresh deli (no packaged)

    Meats—sliced turkey, roast beef, ham

    Cheese—sliced American, Swiss, Cheddar

    Vegetables—sliced tomatoes, onion, lettuce

TUNA SALAD—White albacore in spring water

    Mayonnaise

    No eggs

    Celery and/or onions

EGG SALAD

PEANUT BUTTER and JELLY

BREAD—whole wheat, white, multi-grain

CONDIMENTS—Frenches mustard, dijon mustard, mayo, ketchup, sweet relish

HOT DOGS AND HAMBURGERS (OPTIONAL)
HOT ENTREES—Two (2) from the following:
SOUP (meatless) vegetable, minestrone, noodles in chicken broth
CHILI
SOUP with either beef or chicken

★LOCAL SPECIALTIES ACCEPTED AFTER CONSULTATION
WITH PRODUCTION MANAGER★

CREW DINNER

Dinner will be served from 5:00 P.M. to 7:30 P.M. Food and drinks sufficient for twenty-eight (28) people.

1. BEVERAGES
    Three (3) gallons milk—two (2) homogenized, one (1) low-fat
    One (1) case Classic Coke—12oz. cans
    Two (2) six (6) packs 7-UP—12oz. cans
    One (1) case Pepsi—12oz. cans
    Two (2) six (6) packs Dr. Pepper—12oz. cans
    One (1) six (6) pack Pepsi—12oz. cans
    Two (2) six (6) packs Mountain Dew—12oz. cans
    Two (2) gallons iced tea—lemon and sugar
    Hot coffee and tea

★FRESH ICE AND SHALLOW CONTAINERS★

2. FOOD DISHES
    All meals to include the following:
    Two (2) main dishes
    Two (2) vegetables
    One (1) potato dish
    Garden salad with choice of four (4) dressings
    Condiment and seasonings
    Dessert

    Monday—Turkey and Fish
    Tuesday—BBQ Ribs, Chicken, and Fish
    Wednesday—Pork Chops and Fish
    Thursday—Italian with meatballs and Fish
    Friday—Oriental Food and Fish
    Saturday—Prime rib and Fish
    Sunday—Steak and Fish

NOTE: There are seven (7) vegetarians in the band and crew. The fish dinners are for them. The main course selections are examples only, please discuss exact meal arrangements with the Production Manager when the show is advanced.

FOR CREW BUS

Please have the following delivered 1/2 hour after the show to the _____ wardrobe and catering specialist.

Twelve (12) sandwiches or pizza for twelve (12) persons
One (1) case Budweiser
One (1) case Corona
One (1) six (6) pack Classic Coke
One (1) six (6) pack assorted sodas
One (1) six (6) pack Perrier in small bottles
One (1) gallon spring water

STAGE DRINKS

One (1) bus tray containing one (1) gallon spring water, six (6) Perrier, one (1) six (6) pack Coke, one (1) six (6) pack Pepsi, ice and twelve (12) 16oz. cups.

One (1) iced tray of six (6) Cokes, six (6) Perrier, six (6) assorted sodas to monitor mix position during intermission.

One (1) iced tray of six (6) Cokes, six (6) Perrier, six (6) assorted sodas to house mix position during intermission.

ARTIST DRESSING ROOM REQUIREMENTS

1. BEVERAGES
   A. One (1) gallon fresh squeezed orange juice
   B. One (1) large bottle no sugar apple juice
   C. One (1) quart 2% low-fat milk
   D. Two (2) 6-packs Diet Coke (caffeine free)
   E. Two (2) 6-packs Diet Cherry Coke
   F. Two (2) 6-packs Diet Coke
   G. Two (2) 6-packs of 6oz. bottles of Classic Coke (no twist off cap)
   H. One (1) case of Evian spring water (no gas)
   I. Two (2) six (6) packs of Sundance Cranberry
   J. One (1) case beer—Michelob Dry (long neck bottles) or Kirin Dry
   K. Two (2) six (6) packs non-alcoholic beer—O'Dooles
   L. One (1) bottle of chardonnay white wine (a good Calif.)
   M. One (1) bottle of cabernet red wine
   N. Coffee maker and fresh brewed regular and decaffeinated coffee-served with half and half, coffee mate, Equal, honey, and sugar
   O. Set up for hot tea—regular and herbal tea
   P. One (1) 6-pack IBC root beer
   Q. One (1) 6-pack Yoohoo (chocolate soda)

2. FOOD
A. A deli tray only with fresh Turkey breast, lettuce, tomatoes and a loaf of whole wheat bread
B. A box of unopened Honey Maid Graham crackers
C. Two (2) boxes of cereal (large), choices are:
Honey Nut Cheerios
Kelloggs Nutragrain
Shredded Wheat and Bran
Common Sense
D. One (1) large uncut fruit tray with bananas, apples, pears, seedless grapes and strawberries
E. Raw vegetable tray for six (6)
F. Six (6) bagels and cream cheese
G. Bavarian pretzels
H. One (1) jar dry roasted peanuts
I. Two (2) boxes Pop Secret natural and butter flavor microwave popcorn
J. M&M's chocolate (not peanuts) and carob raisins
K. Peanut butter natural style and jelly (any kind)
L. Condiments—lemons (fresh), Butter Buds, mustard, ketchup, mayonnaise and soy sauce

BAND AFTERSHOW MEALS

The items listed below are suggestions for the band's aftershow meal. NOTE: IT IS LIKELY THAT THE SPECIFIC MEAL WILL VARY, SO IT IS IMPORTANT TO CONFIRM THE EXACT DESIRED MEAL

A. Angel hair pasta with marinara sauce
B. Pasta with ground Turkey, onions, mushroom, green pepper
C. Chicken burritos—white meat only/vegetarian beans made with no lard
D. Bean burritos—vegetarian beans made with no lard
E. BBQ Chicken—1/3 legs, 1/3 thighs, 1/3 breast with rice or baked potato and broccoli
F. Turkey dogs/Turkey burgers
G. Fish (broiled), BBQ or baked Swordfish, Halibut, Sole, Salmon, and Sea Bass
H. Cheese pizzas and garden salad
I. Chicken Chow Mein/Chop Suey—white meat only
J. Side dishes—garden salad—no oil dressings (e.g., Catalina/no-oil Italian), baked potatoes, rice—white and brown, low-sodium soy sauce
NOTE: Dressing rooms should be set up one (1) hour before showtime, except for the hot food, which should be set up during the show. ★★★ALL FOOD TO FEED TEN (10) PEOPLE★★★

ALL CHANGES MUST BE APPROVED IN WRITING BY
_____ TOUR MANAGER.

I HAVE READ THE TERMS OF THIS RIDER AND UNDERSTAND
THAT THEY ARE AN INTEGRAL PART OF THE ATTACHED
CONTRACT. I AGREE TO THE TERMS OF THE CONTRACT
AND THIS ACCOMPANYING RIDER.

ACCEPTED AND AGREED   ACCEPTED AND AGREED
TO: TO:

By: _____   _____
PURCHASER   ARTIST

APPENDIX F

REQUEST FOR PROPOSAL FOR A CITY "X"
CITY FESTIVAL

OBJECTIVE

The City of "X" is seeking to contract with a qualified, creative, and experienced business organization to organize, promote, plan, manage, direct, and conduct a festival in 19__ or 19__, at a central location within the City. The festival must be family-oriented, with quality programming, foods, and entertainment reflective of the rich diversity of peoples and traditions in the City of "X." Programming and presentations should be mixed in such a manner as to showcase the "legitimate" art forms as well as general audience entertainment acts. The goal is to attract attendance by people of varied ethnic backgrounds and interests, in an environment of mutual goodwill and celebration.

BACKGROUND

The City of "X", using municipal employees and independent contractors, has for several years planned, organized, promoted, managed, and conducted a weekend-long event called "Street Scene," in the public streets and on other public property in the Civic Center portion of downtown City "X." The last Street Scene event attracted approximately 750,000 people.

The City of "X" has decided that it will no longer present festivals and celebrations using municipal employees. Instead, the City has decided to contract with private business concerns to present such events. The City believes that the private sector is capable of presenting creative public events that will highlight the great cultural and ethnic diversity of the people of City "X," including, but not limited to their foods, music, art, drama, and entertainment as well as the various businesses and industries representative of the City.

The City expects that a private contractor will generate sufficient sponsors, income, and community participation, so that any extraordinary municipal expenses associated with the event will be reimbursed.

ELEMENTS OF RESPONSE

Proposals submitted in response to this request must contain the following elements for presentation of a single annual event as noted above.

1. A theme for the festival, including a creative conceptual plan for the development of an annual event, the type and tone of the event, the image it would present, and how it compares with the past Street Scene festivals.

2. A description of the type and quality of music, food and any cultural activities such as music, art, drama, and entertainment that will be included.

3. A specific location, including whether it will be held in the same Civic Center location as previously, in a park, or at another location.

4. The physical design of the festival in the designated location, including size of the area, the number of people it will accommodate, and factors such as sufficient signs to assure safety and preservation of the image of the festival.

5. Provisions that the organizer will make for public health, safety, and security, including but not limited to logistics, facilities, type of personnel to be used, and fencing.

6. Availability (or non-availability) of beer, wine, and other alcoholic beverages, including a description of where those beverages will be sold and consumed, and any other appropriate limitations to control consumption of such beverages.

7. The planned date(s) of the event, and the duration of the event, including opening and closing time each day. Also state whether it will be tried to another event such as Labor Day, Columbus Day, the City "X" Arts Festival, etc.

8. A description of how local and City-wide community groups, as well as major businesses and industries in the City, will be involved in the event, and what sectors of the community will be involved.

9. A description of the publicity campaign for the event, including a timetable for disseminating information to the public.

10. The proposed structure and staffing of the organization or portion of the organization that will present the event.

11. A detailed budget for the first year of the contract, including a realistic breakdown of revenue commitments necessary to finance costs incurred in organizing and holding the festival.

12. A financial plan: (a) to reimburse the City for the cost of all extraordinary municipal services (i.e., services above and beyond those normally provided during the applicable time period for the area where the event will be held); and (b) for providing revenue to the City as a result of the festival. If the proposer does not intend to provide revenue to the City, the reasons should be given.

13. A statement of whether or not the organization putting on the event is a nonprofit organization, and an explanation of how the organizer will make profits (accept sponsorships and endorsements, charge admission, sell coupon books, etc.) and account for revenues.

14. Experience.

    The proposer must demonstrate the capability to organize and operate a large, successful festival of the type desired by the City.

    a. *Previous events*
       List and describe the events staged by the firm and its key employees, including location, duration, size, attendees, and number of sponsors.

    b. *Work effort*
       Describe in detail the work performed by the firm in general, and specifically related to the events described in 14(a).

    c. *References*
       List the name of the governmental agency or private organization that contracted for your firm's services, names of responsible parties in these agencies, and nature of your contractual relationship. Include names, addresses, and telephone numbers.

    d. *Sponsors*
       List and describe the sponsors secured for the events, including duration of sponsor's support, and what the support consisted of (cash, in-kind contributions).

    e. *Results*
       List the extent of success of the events including revenues generated, costs, public participation, and profits.

    f. *Financial Condition*
       Provide financial statements, copies of annual reports, and any additional information to indicate the current financial condition of the firm.

g. *Other*

Include any other relevant information that would be helpful to the City in evaluating your firm's qualifications.

TERM

The term of the contract will be one year with two, one year options to be exercised at the City's sole discretion.

DEADLINE

Statements must be responsive and to the point. Responses must be received by the City Clerk's Office by 4:00 p.m., on June __, 19__.

CITY REVIEW

A special panel will review the information provided in each response received prior to the designated time deadline, will interview the finalists for verbal presentations, and will then present a recommendation to the City Council for approval.

PROPOSERS CONFERENCE

A public meeting will be held on May __, 19__ at 10:00 A.M. in Room 238, City Hall. This will be an information question and answer session. No transcripts will be prepared from this session.

Inquiries may be directed to the Office of the Chief Legislative Analyst at (000) 000-0000.

SOUTH AFRICA STATEMENT

All proposers are subject to the City's anti-apartheid policy, Section 10.31 et seq., Article 5, Chapter 1, Division 10 of the City "X" Administrative Code. The policy restricts the City from contracting for goods and services with persons or entities doing business in or with South Africa and requires contracting parties to submit a statement under penalty of perjury regarding their South Africa business connections. Under the provision of Section 10.31.5 of the City "X" Administrative Code, the City shall have the authority to terminate a contract, and to refuse any payment that might be owed to the contractor for services performed, if the City determines that such contractor was ineligible under said Article at the time of entering into the Agreement or became ineligible thereafter.

Attached is the City's form regarding doing business in South Africa. It must be completely filled out and returned as part of the proposal before the City will consider the proposal. Failure to do so will result in any proposal being deemed to be non-responsive.

EQUAL OPPORTUNITY AND NONDISCRIMINATION

The successful proposer must comply with the applicable nondiscrimination and affirmative action provisions of the laws of the United States of America, the State of Z, and the City. In performing the Agreement with the City, the contractor shall not discriminate in its employment practices against any employee or applicant for employment because of such person's race, religion, national origin, ancestry, sex, age, or physical handicap. The proposer shall comply with the provisions of the City "X" Administrative Code Sections 10.8 through 10.13, to the extent applicable. A successful proposer must also comply with all rules, regulations, and policies of the City's Office of Contract Compliance relating to nondiscrimination and affirmative action, including the filing of all forms required by said Office. Any subcontract entered into by the successful proposer relating to the contract with the City is also subject to these provisions.

MINORITY BUSINESS ENTERPRISE AND WOMEN'S BUSINESS ENTERPRISE GOALS (MBE/WBE)

It is the policy of the City to utilize minority- and women-owned business enterprises (MBE's and WBE's) in all aspects of contracting relating to procurement, construction, and personal services. The City also welcomes and encourages joint ventures between minority- and women-owned and non-minority- and non-women-owned firms. This policy is explicitly intended to increase minority- and women-owned business participation in City contracts. The City's goals for MBE/WBE participation in performance of the contract are 18% for minority business enterprises and 4% for women business enterprises. Proposers are required to meet the goals of the City by making a good faith effort in the utilization of MBE/WBE's in the performance of their contract, which may include subcontracting, joint venture arrangements, and/or the purveying of goods and services from MBE/WBE suppliers.

The information listed below must be completed on a separate sheet and submitted with the proposal.

1. Whether the proposer is an MBE or WBE.

2. Name of each MBE/WBE joint venture partner.

3. Name of each proposed MBE/WBE subcontractor.

4. Name of each MBE/WBE supplier.

5. Description of work to be performed by each MBE/WBE.

6. Estimated dollar value or percentage of work performed by each MBE/WBE.

7. If the information indicates that the MBE/WBE participation goals may not be met, a detailed statement of the good faith efforts taken to meet the said goals shall be required and submitted with the proposal.

EVALUATION AND AWARD

Evaluation for all qualified responsive proposals will be conducted by a panel of City staff and presented to the City Council for selection based on: (1) the experience related ability of the organization to organize, promote, plan, manage, direct, and conduct an annual country music festival within the City; (2) the proposal for the event itself; and (3) various City standards and requirements. Since the proposals could be widely varied in terms of what is offered, criteria for the evaluation of this aspect of the proposals cannot be prestructured and will depend on the City's staff's professional evaluation. Fifty percent of the weight of the evaluation will be for the first factor, and 35 percent will be for the second factor, and the remaining fifteen percent will serve to evaluate such factors as equal opportunity, affirmative action, nondiscrimination, and MBE/WBE participation.

After review of the responses, the City may negotiate a contract to carry out the objectives of this Request with one or more proposers. If the City should so act, it retains the right, in its discretion, to award subsequent contracts to such proposer(s). The City may in its discretion decide not to pursue of the proposals submitted pursuant to this Request, and is under no obligation to negotiate a contract with any party who submits such proposals.

If the City does award one or more contracts pursuant to this Request, the contract(s) shall contain various provisions including but not limited to a required audit, indemnification of the City, and reimbursement of City costs.

A P P E N D I X   G

REQUEST FOR PROPOSAL FOR A CITY "Y" MARATHON

OBJECTIVE

The City of "Y" seeks an experienced organization to plan and execute an annual marathon race in the City of "Y." The plan must provide for a marathon which is properly financed, sponsored, and publicized; which will draw top name runners; and which involves a maximum number of the City's communities including ethnic groups and geographic regions. Since the City's experience in sponsoring a marathon is minimal, the City is relying upon the expertise of the proposers in explaining in detail how they would conduct a successful marathon if awarded a contract.

BACKGROUND

Other major cities in the United States have successful and popular annual marathon races—the most notable being the New York Marathon and the Boston Marathon. The City has found that it would be beneficial to establish an annual marathon within the City, involving as much of the City's communities as possible.

Although several marathons have been organized and run in City "Y" in prior years, none of these has had nearly the amount of runner and spectator participation as the well established marathons in cities such as New York or Boston.

REQUIREMENTS

1. The marathon entity must demonstrate the capability to organize and operate a large, successful marathon.

2. The proposal must contain the following elements:

   a. A proposed budget for the first two years of the marathon.

   b. An indication of the level and extent of commitments for sufficient funding to finance costs incurred in organizing and holding the marathon with no cost to the City.

c. The proposed structure and staffing of the marathon organization.

d. A plan for recruiting and securing top name runners as well as average runners for the marathon.

e. A plan for designing the marathon course in accordance with the above mentioned objectives, and for certification of the course by TAC as well as any other necessary organization.

f. A plan for securing volunteer assistants.

g. A plan for obtaining community involvement.

h. A plan for the publicizing of the event such that support from runners, local communities, sponsors, and the local and national media is obtained.

i. The entity's experience in organizing races, i.e., marathons, 10 K runs, etc., detailing what sponsors they obtained for such races, when and where the races were conducted, and other information the proposer would believe to be helpful to the City in making its evaluation.

DEADLINE

Proposals should be received by the City Clerk's Office by 5:00 p.m., December __, 19__.

PROPOSER'S CONFERENCE

There will be a pre-proposal submission conference of prospective proposers in room 252 of City Hall on November __, 19__, for the purpose of answering any questions regarding this RFP.

FURTHER NEGOTIATIONS

The City reserves the right to request and obtain additional information from any proposer and to negotiate any additional terms and conditions.

NON-DISCRIMINATION AND AFFIRMATIVE ACTION

The successful proposer shall comply with the provisions of Section 10.8 of the City "Y" Administrative Code relating to non-discrimination and affirmative action.

AWARD

Upon the selection of a successful proposer, and the award of a contract, if the City should so act, the City retains the right, in its discretion, to award subsequent contracts to such proposer. The City is under no obligation to award a contract to any party who submits a proposal pursuant to this request.

John Smith, President
Anyname, Inc.
Main Street
Anytown, USA 00000

Dear Mr. Smith:

This letter is a follow-up to scheduling your oral interview set for the week of January __, 19__, regarding your City "Y" Marathon proposal.

The panel of interviewers requests that you give a brief presentation on your group's technical expertise in organizing and managing large marathons, as well as on your funding for the proposed City "Y" marathon. It would be very helpful if as many of your principals as possible would be at the interview, and if your sponsors could also be there so that they would be available to answer questions the panel may have. Some of the general areas the interviewers are interested in exploring are that the prospective proposer:

1. Has the capability to put together a sound financial package (i.e., that the sponsors are firm).

2. Be able to secure the support of local and Southern California running clubs.

3. Be able to provide adequate medical assistance.

4. Have experience in putting on all aspects of marathons.

5. Give a firm commitment that the marathon will not cost the City any money.

6. Have the ability to bring out the spectators and general community support, and to effectively use volunteers.

7. Have the ability to efficiently and effectively manage the revenues and expenses generated by the proposed marathon.

8. Comply with non-discrimination and affirmative action provisions of the law in its employment and other practices.

More specific questions may also be asked.

We appreciate your patience in this process and look forward to meeting with you.

Very Truly Yours,

PROPOSAL EVALUATION FORM FOR
(   )

(   ) Representatives present: _____

_____

_____

I.   TECHNICAL CAPABILITY TO ORGANIZE AND
     OPERATE LARGE MARATHON

   Score: Weighted ___[35]___ Assigned _____

Suggested Evaluation Criteria

Race director's marathon experience and staff's general marathon experience in:

- meeting runners' needs
- course set up
- registration and information management
- start and finish lines

Also, organization's structure, whether they previously worked together as a team and whether the organization structure is adequate.

Suggested General Questions

1. How many course marshals and aid stations (and station personnel) will you have? What functions will they perform? Is that a realistic number? How does that compare to other major marathons?

2. Are your principals held together by contract? What happens if one or several drop out?

3. How will runners return to the start area or the area where their cars are? Will it be free or at cost, or will it be the runner's responsibility?

4. Do you have the ability to provide adequate medical assistance? What will that assistance be?

5. What provisions will you make to handle runners' questions or any last minute problems the day of the race?

II. EVALUATION OF PROPOSER'S SPONSORSHIP OR
     FINANCING, THEIR PROPOSED BUDGET, AND
     WHETHER THE CITY COSTS WILL BE COVERED

   Score: Weighted ___[30]___ Assigned _____

Suggested Evaluation Criteria

- firm sponsorship commitment
- sufficient budget to cover City's costs
- willingness to put up cash deposit or performance bond, and insurance
- fiscal safeguards
- relationships with previous sponsors

Suggested General Questions

1. Would you be willing to provide a cash deposit or bond as security to perform?

2. What steps will you take to provide a "hold harmless" guarantee to the City, and would you obtain insurance?

3. Do you envision turning a profit? If so, when? What will be done with the profit (if any)?

4. Describe the procedures you will use to ensure proper use of sponsor funds and how you will effectively manage the revenues and expenses generated by the proposed marathon.

COMMENTS:

III.   RECRUITING AND SECURING ELITE AND AVERAGE RUNNERS

   Score: Weighted __[10]__ Assigned _____

Suggested Evaluation Criteria

- elite athlete enticements
- plans and experience regarding elite athlete contacts
- general ability to secure elite runners
- ties to existing runners' organizations
- promotion through other than running clubs (i.e., advertising, etc.)
- general ability to enroll non-elite runners

Suggested General Questions

1. Do you envision a race for all runners? Do you want to place a limitation of any kind on the number of runners?

2. How does your prize money compare with that of existing top marathons? What is the top prize money being offered for 19__?

3. What will happen if the "name" runners don't appear or want to race? Will the race continue?

4. Are you able to secure the support of local and county running clubs?

COMMENTS:

IV.   THE NATURE OF THE MARATHON COURSE, COURSE CERTIFICATION AND EVENT SANCTIONING BY TAC

   Score: Weighted __[5]__ Assigned _____

Suggested Evaluation Criteria

   ▪ satisfaction of Council's objectives
   ▪ ability to obtain TAC sanction and TAC certification of course

Suggested General Questions

1. Is there a fee set by TAC to obtain the TAC sanction or TAC's certification of the course? If so, how much is it?

2. Describe the procedures for obtaining the TAC sanction and their certification of the course, and what that means to the race.

COMMENTS:

V.   COMMUNITY INVOLVEMENT OTHER THAN SECURING VOLUNTEERS

   Score: Weighted __[5]__ Assigned _____

Suggested Evaluation Criteria

   ▪ geographic diversity
   ▪ ethnic diversity
   ▪ planned degree of community involvement and past experience

- feasibility of plans
- originality of plans

Suggested General Questions

1. Is your proposed community involvement similar to New York, Boston, or Chicago?

2. What is your experience in turning out large numbers of people for an event and how did you do it?

COMMENTS:

VI.   PLAN TO SECURE VOLUNTEERS

Score: Weighted __[5]__ Assigned _____

Suggested Evaluation Criteria

- diversity of sources
- number of volunteers
- support of Southern California running clubs
- feasibility of plan

Suggested General Questions

1. What is your past experience in recruiting and effectively using a large number of volunteers?

COMMENTS:

VII.   PUBLICITY PLAN

Score: Weighted __[5]__ Assigned _____

Suggested Evaluation Criteria

- experience of public relations staff
- quality and quantity of information flow
- sufficient staffing, and experience

Suggested General Questions

1. Do your public relations people have any specific experience at promoting marathons?

2. Will the marathon itself be the featured activity, or will it have equal weight to marketing, media, hype, concerts, dinners, parties, etc. connected with the marathon?

3. How do you feel about quality vs. quantity of information flow?

COMMENTS:

VIII.   AFFIRMATIVE ACTION COMPLIANCE

Score: Weighted __[5]__ Assigned _____

Suggested Evaluation Criteria

- staffing
- ownership
- equality of prize money and inducements to run

Suggested General Questions

1. How will you comply with non-discrimination and affirmative action provisions of law? Will the prize money structure be equal in number and amount for men and women?

COMMENTS:

_____

(Reviewer)

A P P E N D I X   H *

International Federations and National Governing Bodies

The Role of IFs and NGBs

An International Federation is an autonomous organization and is responsible for the governance of its sport on the international level. The IFs conduct the events in their respective sports at the Olympic Games, as well as in other international competitions, working in conjunction with the NOCs and the IOC.

Each IF establishes its own eligibility rules for its sport. An IF can have one set of eligibility rules for the Olympic Games, which must be approved by the International Olympic Committee, and another set of rules for all other international competitions (i.e., world championships).

As a general rule, there is a single federation governing each Olympic sport, except one IF governs both speedskating and figure skating, and another federation governs the sports of biathlon and modern pentathlon.

In order for a sport to be added to the Olympic Games program, the respective IF must first gain recognition from the International Olympic Committee as a federation organized under the principles of the IOC's charter.

Second, the federation must prove that the men's or mixed (open) sports are being "widely practiced" (national championships, world championships, international competitions) in at least 75 countries and four continents. For women's sports, the requirement is at least 40 countries and three continents.

Only sports widely practiced by men and/or women in at least 25 countries and three continents may be included in the program of the Olympic Games.

Even then, a sport might not join the Olympic lineup. There are currently 15 international federations recognized by the IOC whose sports are not on

*Permission from the United States Olympic Committee.

alai), racquetball, roller skating, softball, sports acrobatics, squash, tackwondo, underwater swimming and water skiing.

Sports are admitted to the Olympic program six years before the next Olympic Games and no changes are permitted thereafter. The IOC also reviews the Olympic programs after each Olympic Games and reserves the right to update standards for the admission or deletion of sports, disciplines or events.

An IF can make proposals to the IOC concerning the revision and development of the events in its own sport, and recommend the addition or deletion of an event on the program of the Olympic Games. International Federations also select judges, referees and other technical officials for international competitions, including the Olympic Games. The IF is responsible for resolving all technical issues, such as officiating disputes.

Each International Federation recognizes a single National Governing Body (NGB) in each country participating in the sport. An NGB must be an organization which has membership open to all athletes in its country. It must also have membership open to all national organizations concerned with promoting the sport.

National Governing Bodies are responsible for approving or sanctioning competitions open to all athletes in its country. Approved or sanctioned competitions are conducted under the rules of the NGB.

In the measurable sports (archery, athletics, shooting, swimming, speedskating and weightlifting), national or world records set in a competition sanctioned by the NGB will be properly certified upon preparation and presentation of the proper papers.

The only "national championship" that an IF recognizes in a sport is that which is conducted by the sport's respective National Governing Body. Other championship competitions are merely those of the sponsoring organization.

U.S. OLYMPIC COMMITTEE DIRECTORY
(As of October 1, 1991)

**UNITED STATES
OLYMPIC COMMITTEE**

**William J. Hybl
President**

**Olympic House
(USOC Headquarters)**

1750 East Boulder Street
Colorado Springs, CO 80909
(719) 632-5551
Dr. Harvey Schiller, Executive
Director

**Public Information and
Media Relations**

Mike Moran, Director
Bob Condron, Assistant Director
Gayle Plant, Senior Coordinator
Jeff Cravens, Coordinator,
Programs
Tawna Miller, Manager –
Graphics
(719) 578-4529
FAX: (719) 578-4677

**U.S. Olympic
Training Centers**

1776 East Boulder Street
Colorado Springs, CO 80909
(719) 578-4500
Charles Davis, Director

421 Old Military Road
Lake Placid, NY 12946
(518) 523-2600
FAX: (518) 523-1570
Gloria Chadwick, Director

U.S. Olympic Education Center
c/o Northern Michigan
University
Marquette, MI 49855

INTERNATIONAL OLYMPIC COMMITTEE
Chateau de Vidy
CH-1007 Lausanne
Switzerland
(41.21) 25 3271/3272
FAX: (41.21) 241 552
Juan Antonio Samaranch,
President
Francois Carrard, Director
General
Michele Verdier, Public Relations
Officer

ARCHERY
National Archery Association
(NAA)
1750 E. Boulder St.
Colorado Springs, CO 80909
(719) 578-4576
FAX (719) 632-4733
Harold Kremer, President
Christine McCartney, Executive
Director
International Federation:
Federation Internationale de
Tir a l'Arc (F.I.T.A.)
Via Cerva 30
20122 Milan, Italy
Telephone: (39.2) 79 6038
FAX: (1.818) 994 3889

MAJOR COMPETITIONS (1991)
March 1-3—North, East, West,
South
National Regional Indoor,
various sites
May 24-26—North, East, West,
South
1991 USOF Trials, various
sites.
June 6-9—Pan American Games
Trials, Long Beach, Calif.
July 28-Aug. 2—National Target
Championships, Oxford, Ohio
Aug. 20-24—World Target
Championships, Crakow, POL

ATHLETICS

The Athletics Congress (TAC)
P.O. Box 120
Indianapolis, IN 46206
(317) 261-0500
FAX: (317) 261-0481
Frank Greenberg, President
Ollan Cassell, Executive Director
Pete Cava, Press Information
Director
International Federation:
International Amateur Athletic
Foundation (I.A.A.F)
3, Hans Crescent, Knightsbridge
London SWIX OLN
Great Britain
Telephone: (44.71) 581 8771
FAX: (44.71) 589 7373

MAJOR COMPETITIONS
(1991)

Feb. 22—USA/Mobil Indoor
Track and Field Championships,
New York, N.Y.
March 8-10—IAAF World Indoor
Track and Field Championships,
Saville, ESP
March 24—IAAF World Cross
Country Championships,
Antwerp, BEL
June 11-15—USA/Mobil Outdoor
Track and Field Championships,
New York, N.Y.
Aug. 24-Sept. 1—IAAF World
Track and Field Championships,
Toyko, JPN

BADMINTON

U.S. Badminton Association
(USBA)
920 "O" Street
Lincoln, NE 68508
(402) 438-2473
FAX: (402) 438-2474
Martin French, President
Len Williams, Executive Director
International Federation:
The International Badminton
Federation (I.B.F.)
Unit 4, Manor Park
Mackenzie Way
Cheltenham, Gloucestershire
GL51 9TX, Great Britain
Telephone: (44.242) 234904
FAX: (44.242) 517157

MAJOR COMPETITIONS
(1991)

Jan. 16-20—U.S. Senior
International Championships,
Miami, Fla.
Mar. 14-17— U.S. Senior
Nationals, TBA
April 29-May 12—7th World
Championships, Copenhagen,
DEN

BASEBALL

U.S. Baseball Federation (USBF)
2160 Greenwood Avenue
Trenton, NJ 08609
(609) 586-2381
FAX: (609) 587-1818
Mark Marquess, President
Richard Case, Executive Director/
CEO
Bob Bensch, Communications
Director
International Federation:
International Baseball Association
(I.B.A.)
Suite 490, Pan American Plaza
201 S. Capitol Avenue
Indianapolis, IN 46225
Telephone: (317) 237 5757

BASKETBALL

USA Basketball
1750 East Boulder Street
Colorado Springs, CO 80909
(719) 632-7687
FAX: (719) 632-3277
David Gavitt, President
William Wall, Executive Director
Craig Miller, Asst. Executive
Director for Public Relations
International Federation:
Federation Internationale de
Basketball
(F.I.B.A.)
P.O. Box 7006 07
Kistlerhofstr. 168
8000 Munich 70
Germany
Telephone (49.89) 78 3036/37/38
FAX: (49.89) 78 53 596

MAJOR COMPETITIONS (1991)

June 20-28—20th USA Japan
College Baseball
Championships, JPN
July 5-14—USA-Cuba Series (six
games), Millington, Tenn. and
Santiago, CUB
July 17-22—USA-Korea series
(three games), Millington, Tenn.
July 24-26—USA-Canada Series
(three games), Windsor, CAN,
and Battle Creek, Mich.

MAJOR COMPETITIONS (1991)

April 25-28—USA Basketball
Invitational Tournament,
Colorado Springs, Colo.
TBA—R. Williams Jones Cup (M/
W), Taipei, Taiwan
July 26-Aug. 4—FIBA Junior
World Championships (M),
Edmonton, Alberta, CAN

BIATHLON

U.S. Biathlon Association (USBA)
P.O. Box 5515
Essex Junction, VT 05453
(802) 655-4524
FAX: (802) 655-4592
Howard Buxton, President
Jed Williamson, Program Director
International Federation:
Union Internationale de Pentathlon
Moderne et Biathlon
(U.I.P.M.B.)
Douglasstr. 11, 1000 Berlin 33
Germany
Telephone: (49) 30 826 4858
FAX: (49) 30 826 6308

MAJOR COMPETITIONS (1991)

Jan. 2-6—National
Championships, Lake Placid,
N.Y.
Jan. 2-6—World Championships,
Lake Placid, N.Y.
Feb. 18-24—World
Championships, Lahti, FIN
March 17-31—Rocky Mountain
Cup Series, Alberta, British
Columbia, CAN

BOBSLED

U.S. Bobsled and Skeleton
Federation
P.O. Box 828
Lake Placid, NY 12946
(518) 523-1842
FAX: (518) 523-9491
William Napier, President
International Federation:
Federation Internationale de
Bobsleigh et de Tobagganing
(F.I.B.T.)
Via Piranesi 44/b
20137 Milan, Italy
Telephone: (39.2) 757 3319/719751
FAX: (39.2) 738 0624/738 8443

MAJOR COMPETITIONS (1991)

Jan. 26-27—Pre-Olympic Trials
Two-man Lake Placid, N.Y.
Feb. 2-3—Pre-Olympic Trials
Four-man, Lake Placid, N.Y.
Feb. 9-10—Pre-Olympic Trials
Two-man, Lake Placid, N.Y.
Feb. 16-17—Pre-Olympic Trials
Four-men, Lake Placid, N.Y.
Feb. 23-24—USA vs. USSR
Challenge Two-man, Lake
Placid, N.Y.
March 9-17—Olympic Trials, Lake
Placid, N.Y.

BOWLING

U.S. Tenpin Bowling Federation
5301 South 76th Street
Greendale, WI 53129
(414) 421-9008
FAX: (414) 421-1194
Joyce Dietch, President
Gerald Koenig, Executive Director
Dave DeLorenzo, Public Relations
Manager (Men)
Jerry Topczewski, Public Relations
Manager (Women)
International Federation:
Federation Internationale des
Quilleurs (FIQ)
Linnustajanti 61 49
SF-02940 Espoo 94, Finland
(3580) 594541

MAJOR COMPETITIONS (1991)

April 27-May 4—FIQ American
Zone Juvenile Championships,
Guadalajara, MEX
July 21-27—Team USA National
Finals, Atlanta, Ga.
Aug. 20-21—FIQ World
Championships, SIN
Nov. 2-12—World Cup, Beijing,
CHN

BOXING

USA Amateur Boxing Federation
(USA/ABF)
1750 East Boulder Street
Colorado Springs, CO 80909
(719) 578-4506
FAX: (719) 632-3426
Billy Dove, President
Jim Fox, Executive Director
TBA, Director of
Communications
International Federation:
Association Internationale de Boxe
Amateur
(A.I.B.A.)
Postamt Volkradstrasse
Postlagemd
1137 Berlin, Germany
Telephone: (37.2) 229 3414
FAX: (37.2) 229 3413

MAJOR COMPETITIONS (1991)

Feb. 25—U.S. Championships,
Colorado Springs, Colo.
March 9-10—World Chapionships'
Challenge, Bangkok, THA
May 25—USA-Cuba Dual Meet,
TBA, USA
Nov. 13-25—World
Championships, Sydney, AUS

CANOE/KAYAK

For information on Olympic programs:

U.S. Canoe and Kayak Team
Pan American Plaza, Suite 470
201 South Capitol Avenue
Indianapolis, IN 46225
(317) 237-5690
FAX: (317) 237-5694
Steve Parsons, Chairman
Chuck Wielgus, Executive Director
Craig Bohnert, Communications Director

For information on recreational programs:

American Canoe Association (ACA) 8580
Cinderbed Road, Suite 1900
P.O. Box 1190
Newington, VA 22122-1190
(703) 550-7523
Don Sorenson, Commodore

International Federation:
International Canoe Federation
G. Massaia 59
50134 Firenza, Italy
(39.55) 484052

MAJOR COMPETITIONS (1991)

Whitewater Slalom

May 6-7—U.S. National Team Trials, Duckdown, Tenn.

May 26-27—Champion International Race #1, Vail, Colo.

June 1—Champion International Race #2, Durango, Colo.

June 13-23—World Championships, Taoen, YUG

July 27-28—Pre-Olympics, Seu d'Urgell, ESP

Aug. 3—Champion International Race #3, Wausau, Wis.

Aug. 10—Champion International Race #4, Carlton, Minn.

Aug. 17—Champion International Race #5, South Bend, Ind.

Sprint

June 1-2—Jr. & Sr. World Championships & Pan American Team Trials, Lake Placid, N.Y.

Aug. 21-25—World Championships, Paris, FRA

Aug. 31-Sept. 1—Pre-Olympic Regatta, Barcelona, ESP

CYCLING

U.S. Cycling Federation (USCF)
1750 East Boulder Street
Colorado Springs, CO 80909
(719) 578-4581
FAX: (719) 578-4628
Richard DeGarmo, President
Jerry Lace, Executive Director
Steve Penny Media and
Public Relations Director
International Federation:
Federal International Amateur de
Cyclisme (F.I.A.C.)
Via Cassia, N.490
00198 Rome, Italy
Telephone: (39.6) 336 8827/366
8584
FAX: (39.6) 366 8584

MAJOR COMPETITIONS
(1991)

July 3-10—USCF Senior Road
Championships, Park City,
Utah
July 9-13—USCF Senior Track
Championships, Redmond,
Wash.
July 10-20—Jr. World
Championships, Allentown, Pa.
Aug. 13-24—Senior World
Championships, Stuttgart, FRG

DIVING

United States Diving, Inc. (USD)
Pan American Plaza
Suite 430
301 South Capitol Avenue
Indianapolis, IN 46225
(317) 237-5252
FAX: (317) 237-5257
Modd King Hogue, President
Todd Smith, Executive Director
Dave Shatkowski, Director of
Communications
International Federation:
Federation Internationale de
Natation Amateur (F.I.N.A.)
Averida Diagonal 615-21-1
Barcelona 08028, Spain
Telephone (34.3) 419 2682
FAX: (34.3) 419 1322

MAJOR COMPETITIONS
(1991)

March 15-17—Four Nations Meet/
Alamo Challenge, Moscow,
URS
April 17-21—Phillips 66 Indoor
Championships, Minneapolis,
Minn.
May 8-12—Almo International,
TBA
June 12-16—HTH Classic, Pan
Am Trials, Princeton, N.J.
Aug. 14-18—Phillips 66 Outdoor
Championships, Bartlesville,
Okla.

EQUESTRIAN

American Horse Shows
Association (AHSA)
220 East 42nd Street, Suite 409
New York, NY 10017-5806
(212) 972-2472
FAX: (212) 983-7286
James C. Wofford, President
Chrystine Jones Tauber, Executive
Director
Kathleen Fallon, Director of Public
Relations
For information on Olympic
programs:
U.S. Equestrian Team (USET)
Gladstone, N.J. 07934
(201) 234-1251
FAX: (201) 234-9417
Finn Casperson, President
Bob Standish, Executive Director
Marty Bauman, Director of Public
Relations
International Federation:
Federation Equestre Internationale
(F.E.I.)
Bolligenstrasse 54
P.O. Box 3000
Berne 32, Switzerland
Telephone: (41.31) 42 9342
FAX: (41.31) 42 8927

MAJOR COMPETITIONS (1991)

April 10-14—Volvo Show
  Jumping World Cup Finals,
  Gothenberg, SWE
April 26-28—Rolex/Kentucky
  Three-Day Event, Lexington,
  Ky.
June 14-16—Miller's-USET
  Dressage Championships,
  Gladstone, N.J.
June 20-22—USET Show Jumping
  Championships, Gladstone, N.J.
Oct. 25-27—USET Fall Three-
  Day Championships, Fair Hill,
  Md.

FENCING

U.S. Fencing Association (USFA)
1750 East Boulder Street
Colorado Springs, CO 80909
(719) 578-4511
FAX: (719) 632-5737
Michael Mamlouk, President
Carla-Mae Richards, Executive
Director
Colleen Walker, Media Relations
International Federation:
Federation International d'Escrime
(F.I.E.)
32, rue de la Boetie
75008 Paris, France
Telephone: (33.1) 45 611472/45
611484
FAX: (33.1) 45634685

MAJOR COMPETITIONS
(1991)

Jan. 11-13—NAC Open #2-5
  Weapons, Ventura, Calif.
Feb. 15-18—J.O. Championships,
  Little Rock, Ark.
March 16-17—World Cup Sabre,
  Herndon, Va.
March 28-April 1—World U-20
  Championships, Istanbul, TUR
April 19-21—NAC Open #3,
  Hagerstown, Md.
May 8-12—World Cadet
  Championships, Foggia, ITA
June 13-23—World
  Championships, Budapest,
  HUN
June 29-July 7—National
  Championships, St. Charles, Ill.

FIELD HOCKEY

Field Hockey Association of
America (FHAA) (Men)
U.S. Field Hockey Association
(USFHA) (Women)
1750 East Boulder Street
Colorado Springs, CO 80909
(719) 578-4587 (FHAA)
(719) 578-4567 (USFHA)
FAX: (719) 632-0979 (Both)
Allan Woods, President (FHAA)
Edwin R. Cliatt, Executive
Director (FHAA)
Ann M. Cuka, Project
Administrator (FHAA)
Dr. Judith Davidson, President
(USFHA)
Carolyn Moody, Executive
Director (USFHA)
Noreen Landis-Tyson, Director of
Public Relations (USFHA)
International Federation:
Federation Internationale de
Hockey (F.I.H.)
Avenues des Arts 1 (bte 5)
1040 Brussels, Belgium
Telephone (32.2) 219 4537

MAJOR COMPETITIONS (1991)

March 15-17—Men's National
Team Trials, Colorado Springs,
Colo.
March 22-24—Women's National
Indoor Championships,
Northampton, Mass.
March 30-April 10—Men's
Caribbean Tour, JAM and CUB
April 20-May 1—Men's
International Tour, TBA
June 21-23—Women's National
Futures Tournament, Trenton,
N.J.
June 26-30—Women's Bud Light/
USA Field Hockey Classic,
Trenton, N.J.
July 14-25—World University
Games (Men), Sheffield, GBR
Oct. 12-27—Women's Olympic
Qualifying Tournament,
Auckland, NZL
Nov. 28-Dec. 1—Women's
Hockey Festival, TBA

FIGURE SKATING

U.S. Figure Skating Association
(USFSA)
20 First Street
Colorado Springs, CO 80906
(719) 635-5200
FAX: (719) 635-9548
Franklin S. Nelson, President
Ian Anderson, Executive Director
Kristin Matta, Public Relations/
Media Manager
International Federation:
International Skating Union
(I.S.U.)
Promenade 73
7270 Davos-Platz, Switzerland
Telephone: (41.83) 37577
FAX: (41.83) 36 671

GYMNASTICS

(Artistic and Rhythmic)
U.S. Gymnastics Federation
(USGF)
Pan American Plaza, Suite 300
201 South Capitol Avenue
Indianapolis, IN 46225
(317) 237-5050
FAX: (317) 237-5069
Mike Donahue, President
Mike Jacki, Executive Director
Patti Auer, Media/Public Relations
Coordinator
International Federation:
Federation Internationale de
Gymnastique (F.I.G.)
Juraweg 12
3250 Lyss, Switzerland
Telephone: (41.32) 84 1960
FAX: (41.32) 84 2955

MAJOR COMPETITIONS
(1991)

Jan. 3-5—International Precisions,
Helsinki, FIN
Jan. 22-27—European Figure
Skating Championships, Sofia,
BUL
Feb. 8-10—Basler Cup, Basle, SUI
Feb. 10-17—U.S. Championships,
Minneapolis, Minn.
March 11-17—World Figure
Skating Championships,
Munich, FRG

MAJOR COMPETITIONS
(1991)

Feb. 22-23—McDonald's America
Cup (M/W), Orlando, Fla.
Feb. 26—McDonald's International
Mixed Pairs (M/W), Atlanta,
Ga.
March 15-17—U.S. Challenge (M/
W), Allentown, Pa.
June 7-9—U.S. Championships,
Cincinnati, Ohio
Sept. 6-15—Artistic World
Championships, Indianapolis,
Ind.

ICE HOCKEY
USA Hockey
2997 Broadmoor Valley Road
Colorado Springs, CO 80906
(719) 576-4990
FAX: (719) 576-4975
Walter Bush, President
Baaron Pittenger, Executive
Director
Tom Douglis, Public Relations
Coordinator
International Federation:
International Ice Hockey
Federation (I.I.H.F.)
Bellevuestrasse 8
A-1190 Vienna, Austria
Telephone: (43.1) 32 5252
FAX: (43.1) 32 6772

MAJOR COMPETITIONS (1991)
Dec. 26-Jan.4—IIHF World Junior
Championships, Saskatchewan,
CAN
April 19-May 5—IIHF World
Championships, Helsinki/
Tempere, FIN
Sept.-Feb. 1992—Olympic Tour,
various sites

JUDO
United States Judo, Inc. (USJ)
P. O. Box 10013
El Paso, TX 79991
(915) 565-8754
FAX: (915) 545-2697
Frank Fullerton, President/Media
Contact
International Federation:
International Judo Federation
(I.J.F.)
Avenida del Trabajo 2666
C.P. 1406
Buenos Aires, Argentina
Telephone: (54.1) 632 5002

MAJOR COMPETITIONS (1991)
Feb.8-10—Paris International
Tournament, Paris, FRA
April 19-20—USJI Senior National
Championships, Honolulu,
Hawaii
July 24-28—National Jr. Olympic
Judo Championships, Lorain,
Ohio
July 25-28—World Judo
Championships, Barcelona, ESP
Nov. 1-2—U.S. International
Invitational Judo
Championships, Colorado
Springs, Colo.

LUGE

U.S. Luge Association (USLA)
P.O. Box 651
Lake Placid, NY 12946
(518) 523-2071
FAX: (518) 523-4106
Dwight Bell, President
Ron Rossi, Executive Director
Christina Compeau, Public
Relations and Media Coordinator
International Federation:
Federation Internationale de Luge
de Course (F.I.L.)
Olympiadestrasse 168
8786 Rottermann, Austria
Telephone: (43.3614) 22 66

MAJOR COMPETITIONS (1991)

Jan. 16-20—Junior World
    Championships, Konigssee,
    GER
Jan. 23-27—Senior World
    Championships, Sigulda, URS
Feb. 13-17—Senior World Cup,
    Igls, AUS
Feb. 23—NYNEX Luge
    Invitational, Lake Placid, N.Y.
March 2-3—3M National Luge
    Championships (three heats),
    Lake Placid, N.Y.

MODERN PENTATHLON

U.S. Modern Pentathlon
Association (USMPA)
P.O. Box 8178
San Antonio, TX 78208
(512) 246-3000
FAX: (512) 246-2646
Guy Troy, President
William Hanson, Executive
Director
International Federation:
Union Internationale de Pentathlon
Moderne et Biathlon (U.I.P.M.B.)
Douglasstr. 11
1000 Berlin 33, Germany
Telephone: (49) 30 826 4858
FAX: (49) 30 826 6308

MAJOR COMPETITIONS (1991)

March 18-21—San Antonio World
    Cup, San Antonio, Texas
May 24-26—U.S. Nationals, TBA
Aug. 21-25—Senior World
    Championships, Spokane, Wash.
Sept. 11-14—Jr. World
    Championships, Barcelona, ESP
Oct. 20-Nov. 4—Women's World
    Championships, Sydney, AUS

RACQUETBALL

American Amateur Racquetball
Association (AARA)
815 North Weber
Colorado Springs, CO 80903
(719) 635-5396
FAX: (719) 635-0685
Van Dubolsky, President
Luke St. Onge, Executive Director
Linda Mojer, Public Relations
Director
International Federation:
International Racquetball
Federation (I.R.F.)
815 North Weber, Suite 101
Colorado Springs, CO 80903-2947
Telephone: (719) 635 5396
FAX: (719) 635 0685

ROLLER SKATING

U.S. Amateur Confederation of
Roller Skating (USAC/RS)
P.O. Box 6579
Lincoln, NE 68506
(402) 483-7551
FAX: (402) 483-1465
Charles Wahlig, President
George H. Pickard, Executive
Director
Dwain Hebda, Sports Information
Director
International Federation:
Federation Internationale de
Roller-Skating (F.I.R.S.)
P.O. Box 6579
1550 South 70th Street
Lincoln, NE 68506
Telephone: (402) 483 7551/489
6802
FAX: (402) 483 1465

MAJOR COMPETITIONS (1991)

March 22-30—PARC Tournament
of the Americas, Santiago, CHI
April 4-7—IRF World
Intercollegiate Championships,
Tucson, Ariz.
May 22-27—Ektelon U.S.
National Singles
Championships, Houston, Texas
June 22-26—Ektelon U.S. Junior
Olympic Racquetball
Championships, Burnsville,
Minn.
Oct. 23-27—Ektelon U.S.
National Doubles
Championships, Phoenix, Ariz.

MAJOR COMPETITIONS (1991)

May 24-27—7th U.S. Outdoor
Speed Championships, Colorado
Springs, Colo
July 5-13—30th World Roller
Hockey Group A
Championship, Oporto, POR
Aug. 2-15—55th U.S. Artistic and
Indoor Speed Championships,
Philadelphia, Pa.
Aug. 19th—World Speed Track,
Ostende, BEL
Aug. 29-Sept. 2—5th U.S. Jr.
Olympic Championships, Tulsa,
Okla.
Oct. 5-12—36th World Artistic
Championships, Sydney, AUS

ROWING

U.S. Rowing Association (USRA)
Pan American Plaza, Suite 400
201 South Capitol Avenue
Indianapolis, IN 46225
(317) 237-5656
FAX: (317) 237-5646
Peter Zandbergen, President
Paula Oyer, Executive Director
Maureen Merhoff, Director of
Communications
International Federation:
Federation Internationale des
Societes d'Aviron (F.I.S.A.)
Case postal 352
2001 Neuchatel
Switzerland
Telephone (41.38) 257222
FAX: (41.38) 259118

MAJOR COMPETITIONS (1991)

April 6-7—San Diego Crew
Classic/FISA World Cup
June 20-23—USRowing National
Championship, Indianapolis,
Ind.
July 25-28—American Rowing
Championships, Camden, N.J.
Aug. 18-25—Senior World
Championships, Vienna, AUS
Sept. 26-29—USRowing Masters
National Championships,
Austin, Texas

SHOOTING

National Rifle Association (NRA)
1600 Rhode Island Avenue, N.W.
Washington, DC 20036
(202) 828-6000
FAX: (202) 223-2691
Richard Riley, President
Gary Anderson, Executive
Director, General Operations
Lones Wigger, U.S. Team
Director
1776 East Boulder Street
Colorado Springs, CO 80909
(719) 578-4559
International Federation:
Union International de Tir
(U.I.T.)
Bavariaring 21
8000 Munich 2, Germany
Telephone: (49.89) 53 4293/53
1012
FAX: (49.89) 530 9481

MAJOR COMPETITIONS (1991)

Feb. 20-March 2—UIT World
Cup, Cairo, EGY
March 8-13—UIT World Cup,
Guatemala City, GUA
March 10-17—UIT World Cup,
Mexico City, MEX
March 17-23—UIT World Cup,
Chino, Calif.
April 8-15—UIT World Cup,
Lonato, ITA
April 17-22—UIT World Air Gun
Championships, Stavanger,
NOR
April 28-May 5—UIT World Cup,
Seoul, KOR
May 21-27—UIT World Cup,
Zagreb, YUG
May 27-June 2—UIT World Cup,
Munich, GER
June 2-6—UIT World Cup, Suhl,
GER
June 2-8—UIT World Cup,
Zurich, SUI
June 16-28—U.S. International
Shooting Championships,
Chino, Calif.
Oct. 30-Nov. 3—National 300
meter Rifle Championships, Ft.
Benning, Ga.
Nov. 5-14—UIT Trap and Skeet
World Championships, Perth,
AUS

SKIING

U.S. Ski Association (USSA)
U.S. Ski Team (USST)
P.O. Box 100
Park City, UT 84060
(801) 649-9090
FAX: (801) 649-3613
Serge Lussi, President
Howard Peterson, Chief Executive
Officer
Tom Kelly, Director of
Communications
Ron Goch, News Bureau
Coordinator
Jolene Aubel, Press Officer
Maggie Dyer, Media Assistant
International Federation:
Federation Internationale de Ski
(F.I.S.)
CH-3652 Oberhoffen Thunersee
Switzerland
Telephone: (41.33) 44 6161
FAX: (41.33) 43 5353

MAJOR COMPETITIONS (1991)

Jan. 9-18—Subaru U.S. Cross
Country Championships, Lake
Placid, N.Y.
Jan. 18-20—Freestyle World Cup,
Breckenridge, Colo.
Jan. 22-Feb. 2—World Alpine
Skiing Championships,
Saalbach, AUT
Jan. 25-27—Subaru U.S. Jumping
Championships, Steamboat
Springs, Colo.
Jan. 26-27—Subaru U.S. Nordic
Combined Championships,
Steamboat Springs, Colo.
Feb. 7-17—World Nordic
Championships, Valdi Fiemme,
ITA
Feb. 10-17—World Freestyle
Championships, Lake Placid,
N.Y.
Feb. 11-17—Subaru U.S. Alpine
Championships, Crested Butte,
Colo.
March 8-10—Men's Alpine World
Cup, Aspen, Colo.
March 16-17—Women's Alpine
World Cup, Vail, Colo.
March 20-24—Alpine World Cup
Finals, Waterville Valley, N.H.
March 30—U.S. Inverted Aerial
Championships, Lake Placid,
N.Y.
April 4-7—Subaru U.S. freestyle
Championships, Winter Park,
Colo.

SOCCER
U.S. Soccer Federation (USSF)
1750 East Boulder Street
Colorado Springs, CO 80909
(719) 578-4678
FAX: (719) 578-4636
Alan Rothenberg, President
Hank Steinbrecher, Secretary
General
Kevin Payne, National
Administrator
John Polis, Director of Public
Relations
International Federation:
Federation Internationale de
Football Association (F.I.F.A.)
Case postale 85
8000 Zurich, Switzerland
Telephone: (41.1) 55 5400
FAX: (41.1) 56 6239

MAJOR COMPETITIONS
(1991)
May 18-Aug. 8—Open Cup,
various sites
June 22-July 4—Women's
Amateur, Over-30 Cups,
various sites
June 29-July 17—Men's Amateur,
Over-30 Cups, various sites
April—CONCACAF Under-17
Tournament, CRC
April—CONCACAF Women's
Tournament, HAI

SOFTBALL
Amateur Softball Association
(ASA)
2801 N.E. 50th Street
Oklahoma City, OK 73111
(405) 424-5266
FAX: (405) 424-3855
O.W. "Bill" Smith, President
Don Porter, Executive Director
Bill Plummer, Director of
Communications
International Federation:
Federation Internationale de
Softball (I.S.F.)
P.O. Box 11437
2801 N.E. 50th Street
Oklahoma City, OK 73111
Telephone: (405) 424 3855

MAJOR COMPETITIONS
(1991)
Aug. 16—Women's Major Fast
Pitch, Midland, Mich.
Aug. 30-Sept. 2—Men's Major
Slow Pitch
Aug. 30-Sept. 2—Women's Major
Slow Pitch
Sept. 6-14—Men's Major Fast
Pitch

SPEEDSKATING
U.S. International Speedskating
Asociation (USISA)
c/o U.S. Ski Association
P.O. Box 100
Park City, UT
(801) 649-0903/0920
FAX: (801) 649-3613
Bill Cushman, President
Katie Class, Program Director
Sean Callahan, Director of Public
Relations and Publicity
(414) 475-7465/5489
Interantional Federation:
International Skating Union
(I.S.U.)
Promenade 73
7270 Davos-Platz, Switzerland
Telephone: (41.83) 37577
FAX: (41.83) 36 671

MAJOR COMPETITIONS (1991)
Feb. 2-3—Women's World
Championships, Hamar, NOR
Feb. 9-10—Men's World
Championships, Heerenve, HOL
Feb. 23-24—World Sprint
Championships, Inzell, FRA
March 2-3—Women's World Cup
Series Finals, HOL
March 2-12—World Winter
University Games-Short Track,
Sapporo, JPN
March 8-9—Men's World Cup
Series Final, Inzell, FRG

SWIMMING
U.S. Swimming, Inc. (USS)
1750 East Boulder Street
Colorado Springs, CO 80909
(719) 578-4578
FAX: (719) 578-4669
Bill Maxson, President
Ray Essick, Executive Director
Jeff Dimond, Director of
Information Services
International Federation:
Federation Internationale de
Natation Amateur (F.I.N.A.)
Avenida Diagonal 615-21-1
Barcelona 08028, Spain
Telephone: (34.3) 419 2682
FAX: (34.3) 419 1322

MAJOR COMPETITIONS (1991)
Jan. 3-13—FINA World
Chapionships, Perth, AUS
April 3-7—Phillips 66/USS Sprint
Nationals, Seattle, Wash.
Aug. 12-16—Phillips 66/USS
Summer Nationals, Boca Raton,
Fla.
Aug. 22-25—Pan Pacific
Swimming Championships,
Edmonton, Alberta, CAN
Nov. 29-Dec. 1—U.S. Open,
TBA

SYNCHRONIZED SWIMMING

U.S. Synchronized Swimming, Inc. (USSS)
Pan American Plaza, Suite 510
201 South Capitol Avenue
Indianapolis, IN 46225
(317) 237-5700
FAX: (317) 237-5705
Barbara McNamee, President
Betty Watanabe, Executive Director
Laura La Marca, Membership Communications
International Federation:
Federation Internationale de Natation Amateur (F.I.N.A.)
Avenida Diagonal 615-21-1
Barcelona 08028, Spain
Telephone: (34.3) 419 2682
FAX: (34.3) 419 1322

MAJOR COMPETITIONS (1991)

Feb. 20-25—U.S. Jr. Championships, Federal, Wash.
March 21-23—U.S. Collegiate Championships, Berkeley, Calif.
April 17-21—U.S. National Championships, Tonawanda, N.Y.
June 22-30—U.S. Age Group Championships, Fairfax, Va.
July 24-28—U.S. Open Championships, Oklahoma City, Okla.
July—II FINA Jr. World Championships, TBA
Sept.—V FINA Woorld Cup

TABLE TENNIS

U.S. Table Tennis Association (USTTA)
1750 East Boulder Street
Colorado Springs, CO 80909
(719) 578-4583
FAX: (719) 632-6071
Dan Seemiller, President
Linda Gleeson, Office Manager
International Federation:
International Table Tennis Federation (I.T.T.F.)
53, London Road
St. Leonards-on Sea
East Sussex TN37 6AY
Great Britain
Telephone: (44.424) 72 1414
FAX: (44.424) 43 1871

MAJOR COMPETITIONS (1991)

March 1-3—Hall of Fame Championships, Augusta, Ga.
April 24-May 6—41st World Championships, Chiba City, JPN
June 19-23—U.S. Open, Midland, Mich.
Nov. 29-Dec. 1—U.S. Open Team Championships, Detroit, Mich.
Dec.—U.S. National Championships, TBA

TAEKWONDO

U.S. Taekwondo Union (USTU)
1750 East Boulder Street
Colorado Springs, CO 80909
(719) 578-4632
FAX: (719) 578-4642
Kyongwon Ahn, President
Sang Lee, Secretary General
International Federation:
The World Taekwondo Federation
(W.T.F.)
635 Yuksam-DongKangnam-Ku
Seoul, Korea
Telephone: (82.2) 556 2505/557
5446
FAX: (82.2) 553 4728

MAJOR COMPETITIONS (1991)

May 16-18—National
  Championships, Portland, Ore.
May 16-18—World Cup, YUG
June 13-16—Team Trials,
  Colorado Springs, Colo.
Oct. 23-31—World
  Championships, Athens, GRE

TEAM HANDBALL

U.S. Team Handball Federation
(USTHF)
1750 East Boulder Street
Colorado Springs, CO 80909
(719) 578-4582
FAX: (719) 578-4654
Dr. Peter Buehning, President
Michael D. Cavanaugh, Executive
Director
Evelyn Anderson, Asst. Executive
Director/Media Contact
International Federation:
Federation Internationale de
Handball (I.H.F.)
Boite postale 312
CH-4020 Bale, Switzerland
Telephone: (41.61) 331 5015
FAX: (41.61) 23 1344

MAJOR COMPETITIONS (1991)

April 26-28—USTHF National
  Championships, Oklahoma City
  Okla.
May 1-June 30—Regional Jr.
  National Championships, TBA
Aug. 3-18—Jr. National
  Championships, TBA
Aug. 30-Sept. 8—Jr. Women's
  World Championships, FRA
Sept. 4-14—Jr. Men's World
  Championships, GRE

TENNIS
U.S. Tennis Association
1212 Avenue of the Americas
12th Floor
New York, NY 10036
(212) 302-3322
FAX: (212) 764-1838
David Markin, President
M. Marshall Happer III, Executive
Director
Ed Fabricius, Director of
Communications
International Federation:
Federation Internationale de Tennis
(I.T.F.)
Palliser Road, Barons Court
London W14 9EN, Great Britain
Telephone: (44.1) 381 8060
FAX: (44.1) 381 3989

MAJOR COMPETITIONS
(1991)
Dec. 31-Jan. 1—Australian Men's
  Hardcourt Championships,
  North Adelaide, AUS
March 27-June 9—French Open,
  Paris, FRA
June 24-July 7—Wimbledon,
  London, GBR
Aug. 26-Sept. 8—U.S. Open,
  New York, N.Y.

VOLLEYBALL
U.S. Volleyball Association
(USVBA)
359 E. Fountain Blvd. Suite I-2
Colorado Springs, CO 80910-1740
(719) 637-8300
FAX: (719) 597-6307
William Baird, President
Cliff McPeak, Executive Director
International Federation:
Federation Internationale de
Volleyball (F.I.V.B.)
Avenue de la Gare 12
1003 Lausanne, Switzerland
Telephone: (41.21) 20 8932/33/34
FAX: (41.21) 20 8865

MAJOR COMPETITIONS
(1991)
May 17-July 28—World League
  (M), various sites
July 14-25—World University
  Games (M&W), Sheffield, GBR
Aug. 25-Sept. 3—NORCECA
  Zone Championships (M&W),
  Regina, Saskatchewan, CAN
Nov. 8-17—World Cup (W), JPN
Nov. 22-Dec. 1—World Cup (M),
  JPN

WATER POLO

United States Water Polo (USWP)
Pan American Plaza, Suite 520
201 South Capitol Avenue
Indianapolis, IN 46225
(317) 237-5599
FAX: (317) 237-5590
Richard Foster, President
John Duir, Executive Director
Eileen Sexton, Director of Media
and Public Relations
International Federation:
Federation Internationale de
Natation Amateur (F.I.N.A.)
Avenida Diagonal 615-21-1
Barcelona 08028, Spain
Telephone: (34.3) 419 2682
FAX: (34.3) 419 1322

WEIGHTLIFTING

U.S. Weightlifting Federation
(USWF)
1750 East Boulder Street
Colorado Springs, CO 80909
(719) 578-4508
FAX: (719) 578-4654
Jim Schmitz, President
George Greenway, Executive
Director
Mary Ann Rinehart,
Communications Director
International Federation:
International Weightlifting
Federation (I.W.F.)
Rosenberg Hp. U.1
1374 Budapest P.F. 614, Hungary
Telephone: (36.1) 311 162/318 153
FAX: (36.1) 311162

MAJOR COMPETITIONS (1991)

Jan. 3-13—VI FINA World
Championships, Perth, AUS
Jan. 25-27—Women's Indoor
Nationals, Berkeley, Calif.
June 20-23—Jr. Women's
International Tournament,
Annapolis, Md.
June 26-30—VII Women's Water
Polo World Cup, TBA
July 15-22—Men's VII FINA Cup,
Barcelona, ESP
Aug. 31-Sept. 8—VI Junior Water
Polo World Championships,
TBA
TBA—Senior Men's Outdoor
Nationals, TBA

MAJOR COMPETITIONS (1991)

Feb. 16—National Collegiate
Championships, Shreveport, La.
April 5-7—National Junior
Championships (17-19), Peoria,
Ill.
April 19-21—National Masters
Championships, Washington,
D.C.
May 4-13—Junior World
Championships, Wolmirstedt,
GER
June 29-30—National Junior
Championships (14-16), Blaine,
Minn.
Sept. 27-Oct. 3—World
Championships,
Dunaueschingen, GER
Sept. 28-29—American Open,
Blaine, Minn.

WRESTLING

USA Wrestling
225 South Academy Boulevard
Colorado Springs, CO 80910
(719) 597-8333
FAX: (719) 597-3195
Terry McCann, President
Jim Scherr, Acting Executive
Director
Gary Abbott, Director of
Communications
International Federation:
Federation Internationale de Lutte
Amateur (F.I.L.A.)
Avenue Ruchonnet 3
1003 Lausanne, Switzerland
Telephone: (41.21) 312 8426
FAX: (41.21) 23 6073

MAJOR COMPETITIONS (1991)

April 6-7—World Cup of Freestyle
Wrestling, Toledo, Ohio
May 8-11—John E. dePont
Freestyle U.S. National
Championships, Las Vegas,
Nev.
May 8-11—Everlast Filtration
Systems Greco-Roman U.S.
National Championships, Las
Vegas, Nev.
May 24-26—Concord Cup (Greco-
Roman), Concord, Ga.
May 28-June 1—Freestyles World
Team Trials, TBA
June 19-21—U.S. Open
International (Freestyle), Tampa,
Fla.
June 30-July 4—Greco-Roman
World Team Trials,
Warrensburg, Mo.
Sept. 26-29—Greco-Roman World
Championships, Varna, BUL
Oct. 2-5—Freestyle World
Championships, Varna, BUL
Nov.—World Cup of Greco-
Roman Wrestling, Athens, GRE
Dec. 27—Grand Masters of
Olympic Wrestling, Pittsburgh,
Pa.

YACHTING
U.S. Yacht Racing Union
(USYRU)
P.O. Box 209
Newport, RI 02840
(401) 849-5200
FAX: (401) 849-5208
William Martin, President
John B. Bonds, Executive Director
Deirdre Wilde, Acting
Communications Director
Jonathan R. Harley, Olympic
Yachting Director
International Federation:
International Yacht Racing Union
(I.Y.R.U.)
60, Knightsbridge
Westminster, London SW1X 7JX
Great Britain
Telephone: (44.1) 235 6221/2
FAX: (44.1) 245 9861

MAJOR COMPETITIONS
(1991)
March 28-April 3—U.S. Women's
Singlehanded, Doublehanded
and Boardsailing
Championships, San Diego,
Calif.
Aug. 22-24—U.S. Independence,
Newport, R.I.
Sept. 5-8—Hinman Trophy (U.S.
Team Race Championships)
Sept. 9-14—Mallory Cup (U.S.
Men's Sailing Championships),
Cleveland, Ohio
Sept. 24-28—Adams Cup (U.S.
Women's Sailing
Championships), San Francisco,
Calif.

AFFILIATED SPORTS ORGANIZATIONS

CURLING
U.S. Curling Association (USCA)
1100 Center Point Drive
Box 971
Stevens Point, WI 54481
(715) 344-1199
FAX: (715) 344-6885
Thomas L. Satrom, President
David Garber, Executive Director
International Federation:
International Curling Federation
(I.C.F.)
2 Coates Crescent
Edinburgh EH3 7AN, Great
Britain
Telephone: (44.31) 225 7083
FAX: (44.31) 220 1351

KARATE
The USA Karate Federation
1300 Kenmore Blvd.
Akron, OH 44314
(216) 753-3114
FAX: (216) 753-6967
George Anderson, President
Internatinal Federation:
World Union of Karatedo
Organizations
(W.U.K.O.)
Senpaku Shinko Bldg.
1-15-16 Toranomon, Minato-Ku
Tokyo 105, Japan
Telephone: (813) 502 2371

ORIENTEERING

U.S. Orienteering Federation
P.O. Box 1444
Forest Park, GA 30051
(404) 363-2110
Sam Burd Jr., President
Robin Shannonhouse, Executive
Director
John Nash, Media/Publicity
Contact
(914) 941-0896
International Federation:
International Orienteering
Federation (I.O.F.)
P.O. Box 76
19121 Sollentuna, Sweden
Telephone: (46) 8353455
FAX: (46) 8357168

SQUASH RACQUETS

U.S. Squash Racquets Association
23 Cynwyd Red.
P.O. Box 1216
Bala Cynwyd, PA, 19004
(215) 667-4006
FAX: (215) 667-6539
George A. Haggarty, President
Darwin Kingsley III, Executive
Director
International Federation:
International Squash Rackets
Federation (I.S.R.F.)
82, Cathedral Road
Cardiff, Wales CF1 9 CN
Great Britain
Telephone: (44.222) 374 771/388
446
FAX: (44.222) 37 4409

SPORTS ACROBATICS

U.S. Sports Acrobatics Federation
3595 East Fountain Blvd, Suite K-1
Colorado Springs, CO 80910
(719) 596-5222
FAX: (719) 596-5568
Thomas Blalock, President
Dr. Jed Friend, Executive Director
Tracey Jo Mancini, Marketing
Director
International Federation:
International Federation of Sports
Acrobatics (I.F.S.A.)
18, Tolbouhin Boulevard
1000 Sofia, Bulgaria
Telephone: (359.2) 66 1556/66
8651

TRAMPOLINE AND TUMBLING

American Trampoline and
Tumbling Association
1610 East Cardwell
Brownfield, TX 79316
(806) 637-8670
FAX: (806) 637-9046
Connie Mara, President
Ann Sims, Executive Director
Kathy Wells, Public Relations
Director
FAX: (806) 797-8367
FAX: (806) 797-8424
International Federation:
International Trampoline
Federation (F.I.T.)
Otzbergstrasse 106000
Frankfurt-am-Main 71
Germany
Telephone: (46.69) 675 818

TRIATHLON
Triathlon Federation USA
3595 East Fountain Blvd., Suite F-1
Colorado Springs, CO 80910
(719) 597-9090
FAX: (719) 597-2121
Michael Gilmore, President
Mark Sisson, Executive Director
Gary Scott, Deputy Director/
Media Contact

WATER SKIING
American Water Ski Association
799 Overlook Drive S.E.
Winter Haven, FL 33884
(813) 324-8259
Tony Baggiano, President
Duke Cullimore, Executive
Director
Don Cullimore, Public Relations
Director
International Federation:
International Water Ski Federation
(I.W.S.)
Via Augusta 18
08006 Barcelona, Spain
Telephone: (34.3) 217 4434
FAX: (34.3) 217 7635

UNDERWATER SWIMMING
Underwater Society of America
849 West Orange Ave.
No. 1002
South San Francisco, CA 94080
(415) 583-8492
George Rose, President
International Federation:
Confederation Mondiale des
Activities
Subaquatiques (C.M.A.S.)
47, rue du Commerce
75015 Paris, France
Telephone: (33.1) 45 754275

Community-Based Multisport Organizations (10)

Amateur Athletic Union (AAU)
3400 West 86th Street
P.O. Box 68207
Indianapolis, IN 46268
(317) 872-2900
FAX: (317) 875-0548
Gussie Crawford, President
Stan Hooley, Executive Director

American Alliance for Health, Physical Education, Recreation and Dance (AAHPERD)
1900 Association Drive
Reston, VA 22091
(703) 476-3461
FAX: (703) 476-9527
Doris Corbett, President
Dianne Murphy, Media Contact

Catholic Youth Organization (CYO)
1011 First Avenue
New York, NY 10022
(212) 371-1000
J. Peter Grace, President
Rev. Edward Barry, Executive Director

Jewish Community Centers Association
15 East 26th Street
New York, NY 10010
(212) 532-4949
FAX: (212) 481-4174
Lester Pollack, President
Arthur Rotman, Executive Vice President
Henry Hecker, Media Contact

National Exploring Division, Boy Scouts of America
1325 Walnut Hill Lane
P.O. Box 152079 (S210)
Irving, TX 75015-2079
(214) 580-2423
FAX: (214) 580-2502
William "Bill" Rogers, Director, Program Development

National Association of Police Athletic Leagues
200 Castlewood Drive
North Palm Beach, FL 33408
(407) 844-1823
FAX: (407) 863-8984
Michael J. Marella, President
Det. Joseph Johnson, Executive Director

National Congres of State Games
P.O. Box 2318
Billings, MT 59103
(406) 245-8106
FAX: (406) 248-7414
Tom Osborne, President/Media Contact

U.S. National Senior Sport Organization
14323 S. Outer 40 Road, Suite N-300
Chesterfield, MO 63017
(314) 878-4900
FAX: (314) 878-9957
Ellen Conant, President
Douglas Cordeman, Executive Director
Cathy Cassoltt, Media Contact
(314) 421-6460

YMCA of the USA
101 North Wacker Drive
Chicago, IL
60606
(312) 977-0031
FAX: (312) 977-9063
Harold Davis, Chairman
David Mercer, National Executive
Director
Jan McCormick, Director of
Marketing/Communications

YWCA of the USA
726 Broadway, 5th Floor
New York, NY 10003
(212) 614-2700
FAX: (212) 677-9716
Glendora Putnam, President
Gwendolyn Calvert Baker,
Executive Director
Jane Tinkerton, Communications
Director

Education-based Multisport Organizations (4)

National Association of Intercollegiate Athletics (NAIA)
1221 Baltimore
Kansas City, MO 64105
(816) 842-5050
FAX: (816) 421-4471
Wayne Dannehl, President
James Chasteen, Executive
Director
Jim Offner, Communications
Specialist

National Collegiate Athletic Association (NCAA)
6201 College Blvd.
Overland Park, KS 66211-2422
(913) 339-1906
FAX: (913) 339-1950
Albert Witte, President
Richard Schultz, Executive
Director
Jim Marchiony, Director of
Communications

National Federation of State High School Associations (NFSHSA)
P.O. Box 20626
Kansas City, MO 64195
(816) 464-5400
FAX: (816) 464-5571
Bernie Saggau, President
Brice Durbin, Executive Director
Bruce Howard, Publications/
Communications Director

National Junior College Athletic Association (NJCAA)
P.O. Box 7305
Colorado Springs, CO 80933-7305
(719) 590-9788
FAX: (719) 590-7324
Lea Plarski, President
George Killian, Executive Director

Armed Forces (1)

U.S. Armed Forces Sports
Hoffman Building # 1
Room 1416
2461 Eisenhower Avenue
Alexandria, VA 22331-0522
(202) 325-8871
FAX: (202) 325-2511
Charles P. Bennett, Executive
Director
Thomas Hlavacek, Director of
Communications
Jim Joy, U.S. Marine Corps
representative
John Mojer, U.S. Air Force
representative
George Schaefer, U.S. Navy
representative
Philip Cota, U.S. Army
representative

Disabled In Sports (8)

American Athletic Association for the Deaf
1134 Davenport Drive
Burton, MI 48529
(313) 239-3962
Martin Belsky, President
Cole Zulauf, Publicity Director
(606) 223-3999

Dwarf Athletic Association
3725 W. Holmes Road
Lansing, MI 58911
(517) 393-3116
Len Sawisch, President

United States Cerebral Palsy Athletic Association
34518 Warren Road
Suite 264
Westland, MI
48185
(313) 425-8961
FAX: (313) 425-8961
Grant Peacock III, President
Michael Mushett, Executive
Director
Duncan Wyeth, Media Contact
(517) 373-8193
FAX: (517) 373-0565

National Handicapped Sports
1145 19th St., N.W.
Suite 717
Washington, DC 20036
(301) 652-7505
FAX: (301) 632-0790
Doug Sato, President
Kirk Bauer, Executive Director

National Wheelchair Athletic Association
3595 East Fountain Blvd., Suite L-10
Colorado Springs, CO 80910
(719) 574-1150
FAX: (719) 578-4654
Paul DePace, Chairman
Patricia Long, Office Manager

Special Olympics International
1350 New York Avenue, N.W.
Suite 500
Washington, DC 20005
(202) 628-3630
FAX: (202) 737-1937
Doug Single, President & CEO
Jule M. Sugarman, Executive
Director
Sargent Shriver, Chairman of the
Board

U.S. Association for Blind Athletes

33 North Institute
Brown Hall #015
Colorado Springs, CO 80903
(719) 630-0422
Oral Miller, President
Roger Neppl, Executive Director

USOC State and Regional Fund Raising Chairs

Northeast Region

Chair: Walter E. Bartlett, Vice
President-Marketing/Technology,
New England Telephone &
Telegraph Company, Boston,
Mass.

Connecticut

Sandra J. Bender, Executive Vice
President, Connecticut Bank &
Trust, NA, Hartford, Conn.

Maine

Mark Fasold, Vice President, L.L.
Bean, Inc., Freeport, Maine

New Hampshire

Carroll Winch, Vice Chair,
BankEast Trust Co., Manchester,
N.H.

Massachusetts

Paul C. O'Brien, Chairman &
CEO, New England Telephone &
Telegraph Company, Boston,
Mass.

Northern New York

John M. Barr, Director-World
Wide
Communications, Eastman-Kodak,
Rochester, N.Y.

Rhode Island

William Gilbane Jr., Gilbane
Building Co., Providence, R.I.

Metro New York Region

Chair: Emery Westfall, Vice
President, Business Affairs, Major
League Baseball Partnership, New,
N.Y.

New York Board of Governors

Ken Aretsky, Chairman, 21 Club,
New York, N.Y.

Michael Clendenin, Assistant Vice
President, New York Telephone
Co., New York, N.Y.

John J. Conefry, Senior Vice
President, Merrill Lynch Pierce
Fenner & Smith Plainsboro, N.J.

Peter Kriendler, Chairman
Emeritus, "21" Club, New York,
N.Y.

John L. Steffens, President, Merrill
Lynch Consumer Markets, Merrill
Lynch & Company, Inc.,
Plainsboro, N.J.

Hon. Kenneth Taylor, New York,
N.Y.

Mid-Atlantic Region

Chair: H.L. Yoh Jr., Chairman &
CEO, Day & Zimmermann, Inc.,
Philadelphia, Pa.

Delaware

Dorothy Baker, USOC State
Council, Wilmington, Del.

Eastern Pennsylvania
Michael Joseph Joyce, Managing
Partner, Deloitte & Touche,
Philadelphia, Pa.

Kentucky
John R. Hall, Chairman & CEO,
Ashland Oil, Inc., Ashland, Ky.

Maryland
Phyllis B. Brotman, President &
CEO, Image Dynamics, Inc.,
Baltimore, Md.

Virginia
Thomas Allen, Chairman, East
Coast Oil Corporation,
Richmond, Va.

Washington, D.C.
Oliver T. Carr Jr., Chairman, The
Oliver Carr Co., Washington,
D.C.

West Virginia
John Mork, President, Eastern
American Energy Corp,
Charleston, W.Va.

Western Pennsylvania
Eugene Barone, President & CEO,
Blue Cross of Western
Pennsylvania, Pittsburgh, Pa.

Southern Region—
Southeast Division
Chair: H.C. "Buddy" Henry, Jr.
Executive Vice President, Bell
South Enterprises, Atlanta, Ga.

Alabama
Larry D. Striplin Jr, Chairman of
the Board, Circle S Industries,
Inc., Selma, Ala.

Florida
W.C. "Court" Lantaff, Assistant
Vice President, Corporate/
Community Affairs, Southern-Bell
- Florida, Miami, Fla.

Georgia
William Porter Payne, President
Atlanta Organizing Committee,
Atlanta, Ga.

Mississippi
Ben Puckett Sr., President/General
Manager, Puckett Machinery Co.,
Jackson, Miss.
Earl F. Jones, Co.-Chairman of
the Board, MMI Hotel Group,
Jackson, Miss.

North Carolina
Irwin Belk, Officer & Director,
The Belk Group of Stores, Inc.,
Charlotte, N.C.

South Carolina
Robert Onorato, President, RCO
Inc., Hilton Head Island, S.C.

Tennessee
James L. Barksdale, Executive
Vice President and Chief
Operating Officer, Federal Express
Corporation, Memphis, Tenn.

Southern Region—
Southwest Division
Chair: C.J. Silas, Chairman &
CEO, Phillips Petroleum Co.,
Bartlesville, Okla.

Arkansas
James House, Executive Vice
President Marketing, Arkansas
Blue Cross and Blue Shield, Little
Rock, Arkansas

Bill Phillips Vice President/Special
Business, Arkansas Blue Cross and
Blue Shield, Little Rock, Arkansas

Colorado
George Gillett, Jr.,
Chairman Vail Allociates
Vail, Colo.
Robert Hawk, President
Carrier Information Provider
Division
US West Communications,
Denver, Colo.

Louisiana
Robert L. Pettit Jr. Kidder,
Peabody & Co., New Orleans, La.

New Mexico
Jack Rust, President, Rust Tractor
Company, Albuquerque, N.M.

Oklahoma
C.J. Silas, Chairman & CEO,
Phillips Petroleum Co.,
Bartlesville, Okla.

Texas
Ernest Deal, Senior Chairman of
the Board, First City Bank, Texas
- Dallas, Dallas, Texas

Mid-America Region
Chairman: Barry Burkholder,
Division Executive, Citicorp
Consumer Bank, Chicago, Ill.

Illinois
K. Dane Brooksher, Vice
Chairman - Midwest Region,
KPMG Peat Marwick, Chicago,
Ill.

Indiana
Richard C. Notebaert, President &
CEO Indiana Bell, Indianapolis,
Ind.

Iowa
Willaiam F. Vernon Jr., Chairman
& CEO, Vernon Company,
Newton, Iowa

Michigan
Joseph E. Cappy, Group Vice-
President, International
Operations, Chrysler Corporation,
Highland Park, Mich.

Minnesota
Bob Bjorklund, The Principal
Financial Group, Minneapolis,
Minn.

Phil McElroy, The Principal
Financial Group, Minneapolis,
Minn.

Nebraska
E.A. Conley, Chairman,
Guarantee Mutual Life Insurance,
Omaha, Neb.

Donald D. Adams, Consultant,
First Tier, Inc, Lincoln, Neb.

North Dakota
C.W. Andrews, General Manager,
Distribution Services,
Northwestern Bell Telephone,
Fargo, N.D.

G.E. Steinkopf, Northwestern Bell
Telephone, Fargo, N.D.

South Dakota
Donald Skaro, President, Instant
Sign Center, Sioux Falls, S.D.

Western Region
Arizona
Jay C. Stuckey Jr., Chief Executive Officer, Republic Companies, Phoenix, Ariz.

Hawaii
Michael A. Wood, Senior Vice President, Marketing Manager, First Interstate Bank of Hawaii, Honolulu, Hawaii

Montana
Dan Walker, Director, Public Affairs, U.S. West Communications, Billings, Mont.

Washington
Hon. Albert Rosellini, Governor of Washington

Index